GLOBAL ACCOUNTING PERSPECTIVES

Jagdish N. Sh
Brooker Prof
Graduate Sc
University of

Abdolreza Es
Assistant Pro
Bentley Colle

GN64
PUBLISH
SOU
CINCINNAT

ISBN: 0-538-80338-X

Library of Congress Catalog Card Number: 88-60621

1 2 3 4 5 6 7 8 M 3 2 1 0 9 8

Printed in the United States of America

PREFACE

Directly or indirectly, the accounting practices of a company are affected by the international context of business. For example, as a company begins to depend on foreign sources for its procurement of products, components, or raw materials, its cost accounting practices become directly affected by the prices set or dependence on foreign currencies. Similarly, as a company's sales depend more and more on offshore markets, either directly or indirectly, its revenue accounting practices will depend more on currency fluctuations and foreign exchange practices.

The complexity of accounting practices increases even more significantly when a company engages in private investment in foreign markets. It becomes subject to accounting practices and government regulations of the foreign country in its depreciation policy, asset valuation, profit calculations, and repatriation of dividends and capital.

Indeed, as the government tax policy, trade policy, and national economic policy become more and more driven by the global economy, it becomes essential even for a domestic market-oriented company to understand the principles of international accounting.

This volume is designed as a supplement to the textbooks on managerial accounting for the MBA program, as well as the advanced undergraduate programs in business. It is intended to fulfill the accreditation requirements for internationalizing the required courses in business schools.

The volume is prepared to serve the following educational needs in managerial accounting:

- It details the complexity of the international environment, especially as it relates to cultural traditions and governmental rules and regulations related to accounting practices.

Accounting is the financial language of business. Its syntax, semantics, and practices vary in different countries.

- It examines whether and when to extend or adjust the public accounting and the managerial accounting practices across international markets.
- It provides an annotated bibliography that will facilitate self-study or special projects related to international accounting.

A number of criteria were utilized in selecting the articles for this volume:

- The articles must be managerial in orientation and relevant to accounting practices.
- They must be written by authors who are well recognized for their contributions to the field.
- They must represent a worldwide perspective rather than just the U.S. perspective.

Although this volume is designed as a supplement to the required managerial accounting courses in the MBA and the undergraduate programs, it is equally useful in the executive MBA programs and corporate executive seminars on international accounting practices.

CONTENTS

INTRODUCTION

WHY INTERNATIONAL ACCOUNTING IS GROWING

International accounting practices are growing at a fast pace for a number of reasons. First, international trade (both imports and exports) is growing. Second, private foreign investment is also growing very rapidly, especially from Europe and Japan into the United States. Third, there is a strong economic interdependence between the advanced countries and the less-developed countries. This is encouraging both trade and private foreign investment in both directions. For example, there is a spectacular rise in the growth of multinationals from the less-developed countries such as Korea, Taiwan, India, and Brazil. Finally, the formation of a number of economic alliances such as the EEC, the ASEAN block, the North African block, the Pan American block, and the Arab block, in recent years has increased the frequency of international transactions and, therefore, international accounting practices.

THE ENVIRONMENTAL FACTORS INFLUENCING INTERNATIONAL ACCOUNTING

On one hand, international accounting is growing, and on the other hand, it is experiencing a number of compatibility issues. Accounting is the financial language of business, and as it crosses national boundaries, it is encountering the problems of linguistic differences among countries and cultures. We need to understand the global environment of accounting practices and begin to identify the issues of compatibility, transferability, and protocol conversions. The following conceptual framework attempts to broadly classify the major forces that are likely to shape the future of international accounting practices.

Accounting practices are likely to vary significantly by the business culture of a country or a region. It is the silent languages of business which determine the accounting practices more than the spoken languages. For example, the role of

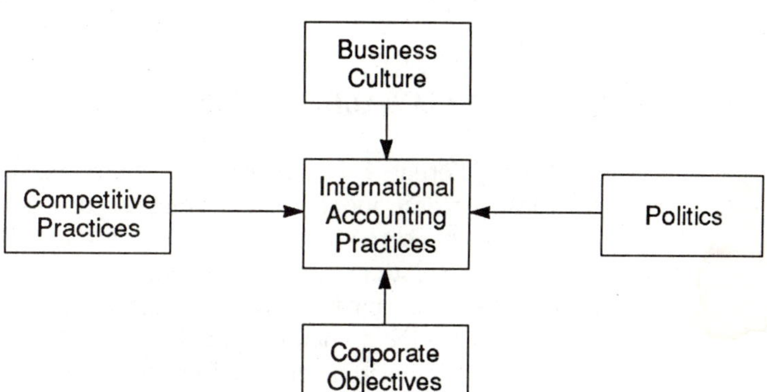

friendship in business transactions, the nature of agreements (formal vs. informal), the value of material possessions, as well as perceptions of time and space, determine the business culture. As some countries engage in business transactions and physically transfer products based on informal non-written communication, the nature of accounting procedures and practices must be significantly different as compared to countries which use more formal and written contractual communications. Similarly, if friendship is key to a business culture, loan repayments or accounts receivable and accounts payable are differently.

In addition to business culture, the politics of accounting standards also vary from country to country. In some countries, the standards of accounting practice are set by the government; in others, they are left to the professional private organizations. In still others, accounting standards are set by a mixed public-private approach and in others it is a multi-shareholder plebiscite in which both the government and the industry take into account the desire of labor unions, industry and trade associations, as well as public opinion. This makes international accounting much more complex. The incompatibility of technical standards resembles the incompatibility of engineering standards in telecommunications, and computers across national borders.

A third major factor effecting international accounting practice relates to corporate objectives of profits and growth. Companies tend to set different corporate objectives in various countries for strategic reasons. For example, many U.S. companies are willing to sacrifice the profit objective for a considerably longer period of time in China than they would in the U.S. The accounting practices are likely to be adjusted for the Chinese investment to ensure that the strategic objectives of the corporation are properly accounted for. Similarly, a corporation diversifying into other countries through acquisitions and mergers is likely to utilize different accounting practices than a comparable diversification program undertaken with in a country.

Finally, the international accounting practice is likely to be influenced by the competitive practices of the world. Many competitive practices such as cross subsidization, cartel arrangements, dumping and even payoffs are prevalent in the global economy. It is very likely that a company engaged in international business will respond to these competitive practices in a manner that may or may not be appropriate from the standpoint of standard domestic accounting practices. Therefore, it is likely to set different accounting practices, hopefully within the legal and ethical boundaries, for competitive purposes.

UNIVERSAL ACCOUNTING OR LOCALIZED ACCOUNTING?

In light of the different and more complex international environment, whether a company must globalize its accounting practices or customize for each country is constantly debated. There are trade-offs on both sides. A universal accounting procedure will be more efficient, streamlined, and easy to communicate for both internal managerial and external public accounting purposes. On the other hand, it may be necessary to localize the accounting practice partly because of managerial needs in different competitive environments and partly because local government rules and regulations may mandate such localization.

The following managerial framework may be used to determine to what extent a company is likely to lean toward universal accounting practices in a global business environment.

If industry practices and governmental procedures for disclosure are the same in a foreign country, it is possible to extend accounting practices on an universal basis. On the other hand, if both industry practices and government procedures are different in a foreign country, it will be necessary to localize the accounting practices. This is very true, for example, when a U.S. company does business with the East European countries.

Although the industry practices may be the same, it is possible that governmental rules and regulations including the tax policy of a country may require a different accounting practice. In that case, the company needs to adjust its external reporting systems. This is very common among the industrial nations, especially between Europe and the United States.

Similarly, if the government rules and regulations are the same in a foreign country but the industry practice related to cost accounting, income statements, and balance sheet preparations vary due to differentiated industry practice, it will be desirable to adjust the internal managerial accounting procedures. This is, for example, very true in project management businesses such as defense, construction, or the government. In fact, this also seems to be very prevalent in professional services such as legal, accounting and medical practices.

		Government Procedures: Same	Government Procedures: Different
Industry Practices	Same	Universal Accounting Practice	Adjust External Accounting
Industry Practices	Different	Adjust Managerial Accounting	Localized Accounting Practice

SUMMARY

This volume consists of four parts. Part I discusses the environmental forces which operate on international accounting practices. Several articles emphasize the cultural and political dimensions of internation accounting.

Part II focuses on managerial accounting practices and policies. It includes articles that discuss similarities and differences in the accounting practices of most advanced countries as indicated by the annual report of corporations. Also, issues of managing currency exchange risks and translating financial statements from foreign operations are discussed in this part.

Part III focuses on the audit and cost accounting practices across nations. For example, selection of an auditor in foreign countries is often based on the number of worldwide offices an audit firm has. It also discusses the accounting practices of divisionalized companies and how they vary depending o organizational design variables.

Part IV is a special topic devoted to translation of foreign currency operations. In particular, it discusses the impact of adopting the SFAS No. 52 standard set by the Federation of Accounting Society. As the foreign currency is allowed to fluctuate in the world markets, it requires specific agreed upon procedures to translate financial statments from one currency to another.

I THE ENVIRONMENT OF INTERNATIONAL ACCOUNTING

1. PRAGMATIC AND ACADEMIC BASES OF INTERNATIONAL ACCOUNTING[1]

M. A. Qureshi
Dr. Mahmood A. Qureshi holds a Senior Post at the School of Business, San Francisco State University, San Francisco, California, U.S.A.

The purpose of this article is to explore the international dimensions of accounting. Its focus is on financial accounting or external financial reporting by publicly held companies. The discussion is organized around three basic questions, which are:

What is international accounting?
Why should we study it?
How should we study it?

A conceptual approach has been adopted to analyze the above questions. Any reference to a certain country or to a specific accounting practice has been deliberately avoided.

What is International Accounting?

Arguments thrive when terms are undefined or ill-defined. Therefore the merit of a good workable definition is obvious. It helps eliminate semantics, clarify terms, and facilitates orderly discussion. Yet, the term international accounting seems to lack precise meaning or definition, even though it is being increasingly referred to in the literature of accounting. This defect however, should not surprise us since there does not exist a generally accepted definition of the term accounting either.[2] Nor should we be amazed over the growing list of the unresolved issues in accounting. There may be a causal relationship between these observations. On the basis of this relationship one could predict that international accounting (whatever it means) is inevitably headed then *toward even more confusion.*

Perhaps we should lower our definitional expectations and settle for something less precise. A search through the literature devoted to the international aspects of accounting leads to the identification of three major concepts.[3] These concepts are:

1. Parent-Foreign Subsidiary Accounting
2. Comparative Accounting
3. Universal Accounting

M. A. Qureshi, "Pragmatic and Academic Bases of International Accounting," *Management International Review* 19.2 (1979): 61–67. Reprinted by permission.

1. Parent-Foreign Subsidiary Accounting

This concept of international accounting is the oldest in content and the most narrow in scope. Financial accounting texts have traditionally devoted a chapter or so to foreign branch or subsidiary accounting and the problems of currency translation. The term international accounting under this concept is reduced to consolidating the accounts of the parent company and the foreign subsidiary, and handling the ensuing problems of translating foreign currency into local denominations. The framework of this concept presents an extremely limited viewpoint—narrow in scope, and shallow in content. It could simply kill the growth and development of the international area of accounting.

2. Comparative Accounting

Under this concept the term international accounting seems to involve: (a) awareness of the international diversity in corporate accounting and reporting practices, (b) understanding of the accounting principles and practices of individual countries, and (c) ability to assess the impact of the diverse accounting practices on financial reporting. The framework of this concept does not envisage a grand universal accounting system. It recognizes though the environmental factors, political philosophies, economic structures, legal systems, etc., that shape the varying practices between nations and accepts these practices. This approach seems more realistic and may well be a stepping stone to the ultimate goal of developing a universal accounting system.

3. Universal Accounting

This concept refers to a world accounting system—a universally accepted set of accounting principles. The ambition of this concept is to develop principals and practices of accounting which would be accepted and adhered to by the world community. Although highly idealistic, this may well be the ultimate goal of accounting. If achieved, it would eliminate the disparity between domestic accounting and accounting abroad.

Reviewing the current literature and discerning the trends we might conclude that presently the term international accounting refers to comparative accounting practices.[4] We should also note though that efforts are being made to achieve harmonization of divergent accounting practices. It should be emphasized nevertheless, that complete harmonization may never be achieved. This is because complete harmonization is synonymous with uniformity which can hardly be achieved at the national level much less at the international level.

The graphical presentation on the next page summarizes our discussion thus far: We now turn to the second question.

Why Should We Study International Accounting?

In philosophical terms accounting is basically a pragmatic discipline. In simple English it means that accounting is a highly practical subject. It is referred to as the language

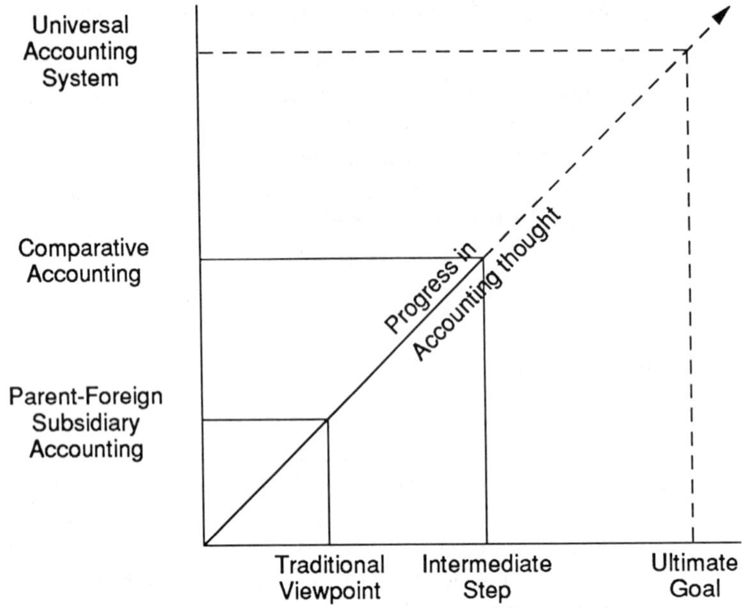

of business. It emerged in response to societal needs. It therefore derives its justification from its usefulness to business and society.

The pragmatism of accounting carries through to international accounting as well. The emergence of the multinational enterprise on the world economic scene was a "big bang" that shook up accountants. Their financial reports lacked international comprehensibility and acceptance. The massive growth of the multinational enterprise has been followed by an increasing demand for financial information by the world community of stockholders, investors, creditors, etc. The leading stock exchanges of the world impose listing requirements that put additional pressures on accounting and reporting for the multinational enterprises. More and more we are becoming aware of the national accent of accounting. Each country follows a set of principles, rules, or conventions that have evolved in the political, legal, economic, and cultural environments of that country. Resultantly, a multinational enterprise operating in several countries is exposed to diverse accounting viewpoints. The need and desirability for the harmonization of divergent accounting practices should be sufficiently evident.

International accounting thus has evolved to cope with the challenge posed by the multinational form of business organization. Indications are that this form of organization is quite likely to be the major business thrust during the remainder of this century. Undoubtedly it will be paralleled by a growing need for international accounting expertise. The professional accountant of the future will have to possess international accounting knowledge. As a result, his mobility will greatly increase internationally. This phenomenon can be observed in the European Economic Community already.

Let us pause at this juncture and reflect on the pragmatic justification of international accounting. It makes a lot of sense in the context of multinational business.

What would happen though, hypothetically speaking, if the international business operations cease? A promulgation by the United Nations stops the formation and operation of multinational enterprise. Would there still be justification for the study of international accounting? A pragmatic answer would be, No! However, international accounting may have academic bases. Its study may be justified on academic grounds alone. Let us explore this proposition.

A profession attains a distinct status in society because it fulfills a social need in a distinct way. Its members possess certain expertise which they acquire though prolonged education, training, and experience. Their expertise represents a differentiated knowledge which the non-members do not possess. They need, nevertheless, the benefit of this knowledge in coping with their problems and obligations. As long as a profession fulfills societal needs satisfactorily it will continue to enjoy social acceptance and distinct status. It should be emphasized however, that the nature of societal need does not remain unchanged, but grows in complexity, variety, and sophistication with time. It is therefore necessary that professional expertise should be constantly updated, expanded, and refined to keep apace with the march of time. But professional expertise itself is based on a theoretical structure, consisting of abstractly defined postulates, principles, and assumptions. It therefore naturally follows that this theoretical structure be constantly subjected to question, inquiry, and research. A responsible profession would derive ideas from whatever source, wherever they may be for its enlightment, improvement, and strength.

That accounting is a profession is generally accepted and widely acknowledged. Its members possess a differentiated knowledge and a specialized expertise that are deemed essential for monitoring the proper functioning of private enterprise. Private enterprise operates in a market economy that is constantly influenced by changes in social, political, economic, and legal environments. A static accounting profession would soon become obsolete in a dynamic environment. For its survival and growth it must spot its weaknesses, search for new knowledge, expand its base, and improve its performance. This ought to be a continuous process and not a sporadic one. Furthermore, the profession should derive knowledge from whatever source, wherever it may be. This means that developments in other professions and disciplines within national boundaries, and those elsewhere in the world are equally relevant and useful.

Unfortunately, professional accountants are most resistant to new knowledge, especially if it is developed outside of their own domain. Thus a bright idea from another discipline or from another country is most likely to be bypassed. In this regard accounting as a discipline or as a profession runs counter to other professions and disciplines. The development of streptomycin,[5] an antibiotic effective in treating tuberculosis, becomes a part of the common body of knowledge of the medical profession all over the world. An engineering marvel attained in one country would enrich the engineering profession in other parts of the world. Einstein's improvement on the Newtonian concept of gravity[6] found its way into the books on physics wherever they were published. Keynes' *General Theory of Employment, Interest and Money* must be studied by a student of economics regardless of his nationality. But the accounting profession in one country stays unaffected, happily and proudly, of the related developments in other countries. Resultantly, the profession deliberately deprives itself of the benefits of research in another field of study or country. It is no suprise that accounting professionals remain so provincial in their thinking and so narrow in their outlook. Perhaps effective transmigration of accounting knowledge between countries could enlighten them. Let us therefore dwell on the process of transmigrating international accounting knowledge.

How Should We Study International Accounting?

Conferences organized at the international level are believed to provide an effective forum for exchange of knowledge on unresolved issues. Accountants are second to none in using this medium. The following conferences are devoted to the international exchange of accounting thought:

1. International Congress of Accountants
2. Inter-American Accounting Conference
3. Asian and Pacific Accounting Convention
4. U.E.C. Congress
5. European Congress of Accountants

The International Congress of Accountants is the oldest and considered to be the most prestigious. Its first conference was held in 1904. The subsequent conferences were held intermittently until 1928. Since 1952, the Congress has held its conferences regularly every five years, the last one having taken place in Munich, Germany in 1977. The effectiveness of these conferences however, has been limited because of a variety of reasons. First, the purpose of the Congress apparently is to unify efforts and expand knowledge, and to bring about some harmony in diverse accounting practices. But in effect, the conference may lend legitimacy to individual viewpoints, such as—"This is how we do it." Secondly, the papers presented at the conference, often of high intellectual quality, scarcely have any impact on the thinking of the participants, or on the accounting practices of the countries which they represent. These papers are carefully edited, efficiently printed, and neatly bound in a volume. The copies of this volume are received by the participants and libraries, and are quietly shelved. Occasionally, a doctoral student's inquisitiveness may lead him to this source of knowledge. Thirdly, each conference is independent and stands on its own, resulting in lack of continuity between conferences. Thus, whatever headway is achieved in furthering an argument in one conference withers away by the time the next conference is held.

Of the remaining congresses as listed above, the U.E.C. Congress needs special mention. This Congress has several standing committees, which work on various accounting issues and present reports or resolutions at each conference. Their focus is on the accounting problems of the member countries of the European Common Market.

Perhaps one of the most significant developments related to international accounting has been the formation of the International Accounting Standards Committee (IASC) in 1973. The express objective of this Committee is "to formulate and publish in the public interest, basic standards to be observed in the presentation of audited accounts and financial statements, and to promote their world wide acceptance and observance."[7] The IASC is headquartered in London, and its members represent accounting bodies of 53 countries. It has a continuous program of professional activities and has already issued several standards of accounting practice that hopefully shall be adopted by the member countries. According to a pronouncement, some of the standards shall soon be adopted in the United Kingdom.[8]

Does this mean we have developed a system to deal with the diverse international accounting practices? Has the process of harmonization begun? Before answering these questions, let me bring to your notice the formation of the International Federation of Accountants (IFAC). The idea of a Federation was conceived at the 10th International Congress of Accountants held in Sydney, Australia, in 1972. It was formally established at the 11th International Congress of Accountants held in Munich, Germany, in 1977. The IFAC is headquartered in New York City, U.S.A., and may have a membership of 100 accounting bodies from 70 countries eventually. Its aims and objectives parallel those of IASC.

What is the purpose of this proliferation? Wouldn't the standards recommended by IFAC conflict with those of the IASC? But, wastage of resources, duplication of effort, and conflicting standards may not be the only problem. Deep down there may be something even more serious.

It is conceivable that the IFAC or the IASC would submit to the reasoning of the members advocating the accounting philosophies of economically dominant nations. Resultantly, the whole process may become a convenient mechanism for imposing the accounting practices of dominant nations upon others under the garb of official pronouncements.

Are joint efforts, one may ask, really more fruitful than individual endeavor in achieving scholarly progress? Seldom has an association, society, or federation been credited with an intellectual breakthrough. The Diesel engine was developed by Rudolph Diesel.[9] It was not an achievement of some association of Mechanical Engineers. The Lockheed Corporation of the U.S.A. is planning on investing in an idea called Ocean Thermal Energy Conversion. The idea was first formulated by a French physicist.[10] Whoever heard of a committee being awarded a Nobel Prize for its scholarly work? The list of the individuals winning the Nobel Prize is long. And last, but not least, the idea of double entry bookkeeping did not occur to an institute, association, or Congress; it owes its origin to the genius of an Italian monk named Pacioli.[11]

The point is, that joint efforts tend to seek consensus, agreement, and harmony. These apparently desirable objectives are directly opposed to intellectual freedom and unbiased thinking. It would therefore be a big mistake if committee work replaced individual endeavours, and official recommendations substituted for individual ingenuity. A committee may evaluate the suitability of an idea for adoption. The creation of the idea, however, should be the responsibility of individuals with intellect, genius, and imagination. We are not building a case against international conferences and committees, but we are certainly questioning their role. A comparison of divergent accounting practices may have merit in that it points to differing viewpoints. Nevertheless, it is a static approach to improving the standards of professional practice. It simply states, "what is." It cannot argue, "what ought to be." Any recommendation, in order to be preferred, must rest on a stronger logical base. Naturally, therefore, a debate on the soundness of the underlying concepts would be more useful than the comparison of practices that these concepts support. Besides, an agreement is more likely to be achieved when discussion concentrates on concepts, and logic prevails; it is less likely to be achieved when practices are compared and national pride is at stake.

Summary

International Accounting is a loose term. By and large it refers to comparative accounting practices. The accountants interest in international accounting seems predominantly pragmatic. The advent and growth of multinational enterprise prompted them to study its accounting implications. But the study of international accounting may be justified on academic grounds alone. It may be an effective force for exchange of professional thinking and intellectual advancement in accounting between countries. Such an exchange of accounting knowledge is essential for the enlightenment of the accounting professionals and for improvement of the accounting professions in every country. Therefore, international accounting should neither be considered independent of, nor a supplement to accountant's common body of knowledge. On the other hand it should be viewed as an expression of concern and exchange of dialogue by the accountants focussing on accounting issues at the international level. Traditionally, international conferences have provided a mechanism for the flow of ideas between professionals of different countries. In the case of accounting, the international mechanism has tended to emphasize dialogue around techniques and procedures. This mechanism, it is contended should provide a forum for debating the underlying reasoning and concepts.

Research in accounting is the responsibility of accountants in every nation. This responsibility should *not* be delegated to *any* international accounting body. This would curb freedom of thought and deter intellectual advancement. Qualities such as intelligence, foresight and rational thinking are not the monopoly of any one nation. These qualities are widely distributed over the citizens of the world. Let them contribute to the development of a better, more responsible accounting profession, and help them make these contributions available internationally.

Notes and References

1. This article is a revised version of a paper presented under the same title at the First Congress of European Accounting Association which was held in Paris during March 13–15, 1978.
2. Consider for example, the following definitions of accounting, each of which represents a radically different viewpoint:

   Accounting is:

   "The art of recording, classifying, and summarizing in a significant manner and in terms of money, transactions and events which are, in part at least, of a financial character, and interpreting the results thereof."

   The American Institute of Certified Public Accountants.

"Identifying, measuring and communicating economic information to permit users to form judgments and make decisions."

American Accounting Association.

"A method of retrospective and contemporary monetary calculation designed to provide a continuous source of financial information as a guide to future actions in markets."

Raymond J. Chambers.

"The quantitative description and projection of income flows and wealth aggregates based on (certain) basic assumptions."

Richard Mattessich

3. Werich, Thomas R., *et. al.*, "International Accounting: Varying Definitions," *The International Journal of Accounting Education and Research,* Fall, 1971, pp. 79–87.
4. This observation is based on a survey of papers presented at the International Congress of Accountants held in Munich, Germany in 1977, and those presented at the First Congress of the European Accounting Association. The articles published in the *International Journal of Accounting Education and Research* also point to the comparative nature of international accounting.
5. *Encyclopaedia Britannica,* Micropaedia, 15th Edition, Vol. 9, p. 612, Chicago: Encyclopaedia Britannica, Inc., 1975.
6. *Encyclopaedia Britannica,* Macropaedia, 15th Edition, Vol. 6, p. 512, Chicago: Encyclopaedia Britannica, Inc., 1975.
7. Quoted from Harvey Iain, "International Standards—Why We Need Them," *Accountancy,* March, 1977, p. 98.
8. *Ibid.*, p. 96.
9. *Encyclopaedia Britannica,* Macropaedia, Vol. 5, p. 725, Chicago: Encyclopaedia Britannica, Inc., 1975.
10. *The Guardian,* March 7, 1978, London and Manchester.
11. An alternative viewpoint is that the system of double entry bookkeeping had become operational long before Pacioli published his *Summa* in 1494. See Richard Brown, ed., *A History of Accounting and Accountants,* Edinburgh: Jack, 1905; Reprinted by B. Franklin, New York, 1966, p. 107.

Income. – Extraordinary → Sell F.A and don't reflect.
– when you recognise.

Stock → Freight warehousing handling
cash discounts
increase profits

Liabilities → . Timing recognition of liabilities
Delaying or advance credits.
. Off balance sheet.
. Hidden subsidiary

2. THE DEVELOPMENT OF INTERNATIONAL ACCOUNTING STANDARDS: AN ANTHROPOLOGICAL PERSPECTIVE

WILLIAM J. VIOLET

William J. Violet is Assistant Professor of Accounting at Moorhead State University.

Introduction

In the past few decades, the international business community has become increasingly aware of the importance of accounting in reporting financial data.[1] Multinational transactions have precipitated the evolution of truly international corporations. Demands of owners, creditors, and many other users of financial reports have encouraged the development of International Accounting Standards (IAS). The official body established for promulgating IAS has been the International Accounting Standards Committee (IASC). The necessity for IAS results from the needs of users for financial data that are relevant, meaningful, understandable, comparable, verifiable, timely, neutral, and adequate for making economic decisions.[2] IAS form the "standardized" basis for comparing and contrasting financial activities of multinationals at the international level.

The preceding summary merely suggests the ambitious efforts by the IASC to instill some accounting uniformity into the reporting of the complex business transactions of multinational concerns.[3] Standards promulgated by the IASC have come under criticism, however, from some of the countries which earlier vociferously advocated their establishment.[4] The author suggests that the success of the IASC has been limited by cultural variables and attempts to delineate several cultural determinants which influence the promulgation and acceptance of international accounting theories and standards. Hopefully, some of the cultural constraints limiting the establishment and development of both IAS and the IASC in their current context will be clarified.

In the past, several accounting authors have considered determinants of international accounting standards from political, economic, and social contexts.[5] This paper considers international accounting from a systems concept of culture in the hope that an anthropological viewpoint will stimulate further cultural research toward the establishment of a truly international accounting system and will enable accountants of various countries to visualize their particular accounting systems from the perspective of a cultural relativist.

William J. Violet, "The Development of International Accounting Standards: An Anthropological Perspective," *International Journal of Accounting, Education, and Research* 18.2 (Spring 1983): 1–12. Reprinted by permission.

Cultural Determinants

Herbert Feigl, in his introductory lecture on the philosophy of science, categorized the sciences with a simple analogy. All disciplines, hence the knowledge of man, are comparable to a glass of ice water. Philosophy is the glass, anthropology the water on which all the ice cubes of knowledge float and into which they melt. Each ice cube represents a particular science such as physics, chemistry, biology, history, and logic. From this example, anthropology is clearly an important "fluid" in the flow of knowledge between peoples.

Anthropology may be defined simply as the study of mankind and his relationships to the universe.

> *Depending on the methods and goals of the anthropologists, anthropology may be a biological science, a social science—or humanity. Because man is a part of nature, anthropology is a natural science with two major subdivisions: physical anthropology (or human biology) and cultural anthropology.*[6]

Anthropology studies mankind in its entirety; it is a synergistic analysis of man's being and his relationships to the external world.

Since no discipline is independent of philosophy and anthropology, the author will be concerned with the role of anthropological thought as it relates to the establishment and enforcement of international accounting standards and examines accounting as a social function, that is, a product of its culture.

Sociocultural theories of anthropology attempt to explain social phenomena. Social phenomena occur between individuals and the institutions created by their society. These institutions may be intangible but are symbolized or represented by various types of tangible matter. For example, the religion of a society incorporates the philosophical beliefs and very often the legal statutes of the society. Physical representations consist of printed matter, symbols, and other tangible forms of animal and plant life.

Social phenomena are products of a given culture. Culture may still be described by the classical definition—it is learned behavior.[7] Culture and the social institutions of a culture must be learned in contrast to instinctive reactions to environmental factors. While instinctive reactions are determined through genetic codes, culture is an

> . . . *integrated system of learned behavior patterns that are characteristic of the members of a society and that are not the result of biological inheritance.* . . . *Culture is therefore acquired behavior. But it is as much a part of the natural universe as the stars in the heavens, for it is a natural product of man's activities, and man is part of nature.*[8]

Culture is a product of mankind, invented to cope with the natural environment as well as social phenomena. Mankind has, in turn, become a product of that culture. Culture and mankind are in a constant state of evolution, creating and refining one another.[9] Mankind's basic needs—described by Maslow as food, shelter, sex, social relationships, and self-actualization—have driven mankind to formulate a culture to satisfy them.[10] Maslow's list of needs may be expanded, however, to include needs beyond the basic ones.

Claude Levi-Strauss was an early pioneer in French structuralism which searched for basic or universal structures underlying cultural behavioral patterns.[11] (The search for accounting postulates by Moonitz[12] would be characteristic of employing structuralism as defined by Levi-Strauss.) Levi-Strauss employed structuralism to search for relationships between social institutions and social behavior. He expanded Maslow's classification of basic social needs to include a need for order.[13] For this, consider the importance of accounting, not accounting as currently practiced, but rudimentary accounting for order, that is, classification, control, and safeguarding of assets. In a primitive hunting society, for example, hunters will need to classify, control, and safeguard their resources to ensure their continuance and that of their society. Since their essentials may include spears, each hunter may be responsible for producing and ensuring availability of an appropriate number of weapons. The hunters are responsible for controlling and safeguarding their spears. In effect, the rudiments of accounting for resources exist in even the most basic societies. As such, the accounting for scarce resources is a function utilized by most individuals. In this instance, accounting is informal and relies on an individual's memory and oral communication. A need for order, as advocated by Levi-Strauss, fosters a need for accounting for resources.

Anthropologists have long since noticed a great diversity of cultures and cultural developments in various civilizations. A culture grows and develops in response to environmental stimuli. An imperative selection exists for each culture. Ruth Benedict explains imperative selection as follows:

> *Our only scientific course is to consider our own culture, as far as we are able, as one example among innumerable others of the variant configuration of human culture.*
>
> *The cultural pattern of any civilization makes use of certain segments of the great arc of potential human purposes and motivations . . . any culture makes use of certain selected material techniques or cultural traits. The great arc along which all the possible human behaviors are distributed is far too immense and too full of contradictions for any culture to utilize even any considerable portion of it. Selection is the first requirement. Without selection no culture could even achieve intelligibility, and the intentions it selects and makes its own are a much more important matter than the particular detail of technology or the marriage formality that it also selects in similar fashion.*[14]

Culture is selected, then, through a process of determining what needs and wants are to be satisfied and, also, what needs have priority and how mankind interacts with the environment and other people. The diversity of cultural development proceeds from a foundation of satisfying wants and needs. To satisfy these insatiable wants, mankind and society evolve a culture which defines and establishes an economic system to allocate scarce resources efficiently for the satisfaction of human wants. Culture is the system which encompasses and determines the evolution of social institutions, social phenomena and mankind itself. In turn, these elements formulate culture. A constant evolutionary state exists. On a broader scale, it can be argued that cultures evolve from hunting to agriculture to industrialization. Cultural evolution involves the development of a culture through the acceptance of customs. Customs entail employing tangible or intangible elements by a society in a particular manner.

Various customs are employed throughout a culture. When observing and analyzing a culture, the ethnographer must be familiar with the concept of synergy as it relates to a cultural system. Each element of a culture cannot be understood by itself. Culture is more than the sum of each of the elements attributed to it. The definition of synergy is applicable: "The whole is greater than the sum of its parts." Customs and their interrelationships form a culture which is in a constant stage of evolution as external and internal influences alter its functioning. Customs are selected by a culture through reference to basic assumptions.

> *The selection of the customs that go to make up a culture is never wholly random and haphazard. Selection is made with reference to a set of deeplying assumptions, or postulates, about the nature of the external world and the nature of man himself. These assumptions as to the nature of existence are called existential postulates . . . about whether things or acts are good and to be sought after or bad and to be rejected. These are called normative postulates or values. . . .*
>
> *Both existential and normative postulates are the reference points which color a people's view of things, giving them their orientation toward the world around them and toward one another.*[15]

Culture enables mankind to interpret the environment and explain the immediate, surrounding social phenomena. Mankind has developed and assimilated customs to cope with social phenomena.

Postulates of a culture determine a systematic choice by a society for explaining and rationalizing social phenomena. Based on these postulates, customs are created and adopted. Customs develop into or exist as social institutions. Further, social institutions envelop various customs which enable a culture to adapt to a causal environment within the parameters and constraints of the postulates it has established.

As a social institution, an accounting system must reflect the postulates of its culture. By examining and studying the normative and existential postulates of a culture, society's accounting system and its use in communicating financial data to various users may be defined and understood. It is essential to understand a given culture's postulates before an analysis or judgment concerning a particular system can be formulated. An accounting system represents its postulates and as a language reflects those postulates.

Accounting As A Language

Language is the most pervasive of the cultural variables. A language facilitates flexibility of thought and at the same time restricts thought development. Each language is as unique as its cultural setting which creates it. In turn, a language contributes to its culture's evolution.

Accounting, as a communication process, is a symbolic language which researchers have recently analyzed.[16]

What Is Language?

Language is the foundation for establishing culture and, like culture, it is learned behavior.[17] Languages are created, developed, and evolved within the framework of cultural postulates established by a particular society. Therefore, language reflects the postulates established by the society which employs it. Cultural postulates define the boundaries within which a language operates. Culture, through language, enables mankind to interpret the environment and explain the social phenomena occurring around it within the context of its postulates. Obviously, then, postulates directly determine language evolution. A diversity of languages represents a broad spectrum of postulates and cultures. In fact, "without language, culture . . . would be wholly impossible."[18]

As a subpart of a culture, language is influenced continually by all other elements or subparts of its culture. Language can only be understood from within the framework where it operates and is maintained. Our perceptions of reality and phenomena are established through language. The importance of language in shaping perceptions and personality was introduced in the Sapir-Whorf Hypothesis: "language and our thought grooves are inextricably interwoven, are, in a sense, one and the same."[19] Language and accounting, as a symbolic written system, are determinants of behavior, personality, and thought process. Edward Sapir comments:

> *Human beings do not live in the objective world alone, nor alone in the world of social activity as ordinarily understood, but are very much at the mercy of the particular language which has become the medium of expression for their society. It is quite an illusion to imagine that one adjust to reality essentially without the use of language and that language is merely an incidental means of solving specific problems of communication or reflection. The fact of the matter is that the "real" world is to a large extent unconsciously built up on the language habits of the group. No two languages are ever sufficiently similar to be considered as representing the same social reality. The worlds in which different societies live are distinct worlds, not merely the same world with different labels attached.*[20]

The impact of language on our culture and its importance in formulating perceptions and interpretations of causal events is great.

Specifically, Belkaoui in his sociolinguistic research examines accounting as a language:

> *Accounting can be viewed as a language, which embodies both lexical and grammatical characteristics (Belkaoui [1978]). Within the linguistic relativity school, the role of language is emphasized as a mediator and shaper of the*

> *environment; this would imply that accounting language may predispose "users" to a given mode of perception and behavior. This explanation is congruent with the "Sapir-Whorf Hypothesis" . . . .*
> *. . . accounting may be defined as a set of lexical or symbolic representations, such as debit, credit, etc., assigned a meaning through translation rules known as accounting terminologies and used as parameters for a set of grammatical or manipulative rules known as accounting techniques.*[21]

His definition classifies accounting as a language. Interacting with other cultural phenomena, accounting shapes and is shaped by its culture, postulates, and native language.

Defining and employing accounting as a language enables accountants to obtain a new perspective for understanding the role of accounting in society. Accountants refer to accounting as the language of business. It is a product and a symbolic expression of the existing culture. Though largely symbolic, accounting possesses the necessary attributes of a language. It is a language between the entities and individuals of a culture. Linguistically, accounting may appear to lack the classical oral elements of a specific language. It is a specialized symbolic communication. Because accounting is integrated into a cultural system, its growth and evolution within a society are strongly influenced by a particular society's language.

Earlier, cultural postulates were defined as normative and existential. Normative postulates are developed by a society to evaluate human behavior and goals, that is, values and direction. Existential postulates determine a people's view on how causal relationships are interpreted. A cultural's language is created according to its cultural postulates and subsequently reflects those postulates. Further, these postulates contribute to the evolution of the language which defines them. In turn, individual behavior perceptions and responses arise from language constraints. Accounting as a symbolic language is formulated and evolved on the cultural postulates of a society. The postulates of a particular culture are the postulates of its accounting language.

Evidence demonstrating the individuality of accounting languages and their particular normative-existential postulate structures can be derived from Frederick Choi's recent cross-cultural comparison of a Japanese firm and a U.S. firm.[22] The financial statements of the Japanese firm were translated through generally accepted accounting principles to facilitate comparability of the firms. Mr. Choi's results are most interesting:

> *In our preceding analysis, translating the primary financial statements of a Japanese company to secondary reports consistent with U.S. accounting norms proved potentially misleading. . . . secondary financial statements, as presently construed, fail to recognize that a foreign reader's investment risks and rewards are highly dependent on the socioeconomic environment of the reporting company's country of domicile.*[23]

The individuality of the two diverse accounting languages, U.S. and Japanese, inhibits comparability. The accounting languages of the two firms are different. These languages were created within the postulate framework found in their respective countries. Comparability is inhibited because the underlying cultural postulates are different. "Something is lost in the translation," so to speak.

IAS and Cultural Relativism

Accounting is a social institution established by most cultures to report and explain certain social phenomena occurring in economic transactions. As a social institution, accounting has integrated certain cultural customs and elements within the constraints of cultural postulates. Accounting cannot be isolated and analyzed as an independent component of a culture. It is, like mankind and other social institutions, a product of culture and contributes to the evolution of the culture which employs it. Since accounting is culturally determined, other cultural customs, beliefs, and institutions influence it.

Consider the accounting system employed in the United States. Early accounting practices and concepts were assimilated and adopted through acculturation from the British.[24] The British practices were a product of British culture. Since American culture has significantly paralleled British culture, the acculturation process was adaptive rather than revolutionary, and early British accounting practices were adapted to the American culture.

As domestic business expanded beyond the national borders, American culture was and is being presented to neighboring countries. American business transactions are, in effect, an ambassador to the American way of life. The U.S. accounting system reflects the country's culture. Being pragmatically developed and applied to various social phenomena, American accounting has been developed to cope with specific American business problems. With the rapid increase in international business operations, several accounting organizations have attempted to adapt this domestic system to the international environment. Considering cultural theory, one may question this attempt. Consider the adaption of generally accepted accounting principles to the translation of foreign currencies. Certain foreign currencies may be translated, but in reality the originating country may not even be able to substantiate the value of its currency because of internal or external circumstances.

Does the American accounting system provide a rational system of accounting for other nations? This system has been highly praised for its efficiency and reliability in portraying financial data for economic decisions. In a highly industrialized and technological society, generally accepted accounting principles may be sufficient to resolve most issues concerning the practical and the conceptual. Accounting as a cultural product has evolved in the United States to resolve certain business-related issues. The complexity of this accounting system has grown in response to the complexity of the technology, the sociopolitical system, and financial transactions.

Cultures parallel to the American industrialized techno-structure exist throughout the world in Britain, Canada, West Germany, Japan, and, to a lesser extent, several other countries. If cultural differences concerning political structures, beliefs, traditions, philosophies, and social phenomena are mentioned, however, an infinite variety of cultural variables could be illustrated. Each unique culture produces a unique accounting structure shaped by a multitude of cultural constraints and variables. Visualize an accounting structure for two societies which are both industrialized but diametrically opposed philosophically. The systems may be parallel industrially, yet conventions and cultural variables may contribute to substantial differences of accounting procedures. One nation's culture may well have been determined largely by geographical and physical barriers.

One can expect accounting principles to vary depending on cultural variances. Can an accounting system of one culture be compared or contrasted with an accounting system of another culture? Comparisons are essential for practicability and perspective, but arbitrary contrasts offer little relevance. Since accounting is the product of a culture, similarities and differences will be present between cultures. Contrasting two cultural products becomes very subjective. Ethnocentrism is highly probable. Cross-cultural comparisons suffer from variables beyond the observer's control. Cultural impressions cannot be totally alienated from an observer formulating observations and conclusions. Franz Boas was extremely critical of cross-cultural comparisons and the evolutionary theories comparing cultural similarities.[25]

Even though cross-cultural comparisons have been facilitated through the gathering of statistical data,[26] cultural comparisons must be viewed with skepticism. Many cultural variables can be compared with respect to the concept of synergy. In this regard, the theory of cultural relativism is explained by Hoebel:

> *The concept of cultural relativity states that standards of rightness and wrongness (values) and of usage and effectiveness (customs) are relative to the given culture of which they are a part. In its most extreme form, it holds that every custom is valid in terms of its own cultural setting. In practical terms, it means that anthropologists learn to suspend judgment, to strive to understand what goes on from the point of view of the people being studied, that is, to achieve empathy, for the sake of humanistic perceptions and scientific accuracy . . . . [He] who lacks this trait—who cannot put aside all chauvinist ethnocentrism, that is, the habit of uncritically judging other people's behavior according to the standards set in his own culture—can never become a . . . cultural anthropologist.*[27]

Cultural relativity does not refute cultural comparison but qualifies the comparisons which can be made. In the areas of economics and finance, even comparisons of different industries are subject to qualifications. Often comparisons between companies of different industries are extremely limited. An individual company's financial data are relative to other companies operating in the same or in essentially a similar industrial setting. Therefore, comparisons made between two companies of different industries are often irrelevant. Adding the dimension of internationalism further complicates defining an individual company's industry.[28] Cultural variables further dissipate a definable industry.

Cultural products, like the cultures which produce them, can be compared, but only if certain assumptions and qualifications are made by the researcher. All too often, accounting systems of various countries are compared without reference to the unique cultures or cultural variables which produce them. Such cross-cultural comparisons are limited in relevance.[29] Ethnographic field work for considering an accounting system may yield a better result. In this view, the concept of cultural relativism becomes a determining variable. Judgments concerning a particular country's accounting concepts and practices should be made in light of its cultural system and environment.[30] It is because of the infinite diversity of cultural systems that a diversity of accounting methods may continue to exist in the world. A country which does not recognize a parent-subsidiary relationship cannot be expected to condone consolidation practices. At an Arthur Young Professors' Roundtable, Mr. Sy Cip introduced the concept of cultural relativism:

> *Accounting principles, standards, and practices are usually a direct product of the circumstances and influences of their environment and are most meaningful if viewed against such factors. Accordingly, accounting methods and applications originating in one country have probably the greatest utility in that country or in one with similar environment. They could be quite inappropriate or may work undue hardships in countries of dissimilar environments.*
>
> *In the development of international accounting standards it is therefore essential that the diverse and differing environments where such standards are intended to be applied are first understood and appreciated. Failure to consider environmental differences or circumstances will likely deter the acceptance of any established international standards.*[31]

The evolution of an accounting system is a complex process, and comparisons between such systems should be qualified. Comparisons between economies and technologies must also be qualified. An accounting system, in some stage of development, exists in all societies. As technology develops and complexities of economic transactions arise, an accounting system must evolve to interpret and report economic transactions to its society. Eventually, multinationals develop in some societies requiring an accounting system which reports to various cultures under the constraints of legalistic statutes and ownership. An accounting system is a culture's response for supplying owners and society with essential financial data for making economic decisions. Cultural determinants may limit the growth of this system. To critique or compare accounting systems is difficult because a particular accounting methodology may be the best accounting practice employable in a particular culture. The concept of cultural relativism inhibits value judgments. If a given culture or society is satisfied with the accounting information generated by its system, a criticism may not be relevant. An inference may be drawn that a particular accounting system may be "the best possible system" for a society because it reflects that society's cultural variables and technology.

IAS will someday be established and enforced for the majority of nations. Their acceptance and enforcement must be done by individual nations on a voluntary basis. Understanding cultural variances will lend credibility to these standards and hasten their establishment, not by a few industrialized nations, but by the world accounting community.

The ethnographic studies performed by cultural anthropologists, if considered, will assist in the establishment of IAS. At least an ethnographic perspective will provide an awareness of cultural differences. Such an awareness will contribute to an overall flexibility in establishing and enforcing IAS within the cultural parameters characteristic of every society.

Notes

1. Norlin G. Rueschhoff, *International Accounting and Financial Reporting* (New York, London: Praeger Publishers, 1976), p. 3.
2. American Institute of Certified Public Accountants, *Professional Standards,* vol. 3 (New York: Commerce Clearing House, 1981), pp. 7225–27.
3. Joseph Cummings, "The International Accounting Standards Committee: Current and Future Developments," *International Journal of Accounting* (Fall 1975): 31–37.
4. For a more complete discussion, see Gerhard Mueller, *International Accounting* (New York: Macmillan, 1967), pp. 1–26.
5. For in-depth discussion, see Mueller, *International Accounting,* pp. 205–37; and Rueschhoff, *International Accounting and Financial Reporting,* pp. 108–12.
6. E. Adamson Hoebel, *Anthropology: The Study of Man,* 4th ed. (New York: McGraw-Hill, 1972), p. 18.
7. For an in-depth introduction to culture, see Hoebel, *Anthropology,* pp. 21–54, 541–59. A more technical analysis beyond the introductory level is discussed by Bronislaw Malinowski's functional theory of culture, *A Scientific Theory of Culture and Other Essays,* 8th printing (Chapel Hill: University of North Carolina, 1977).
8. Hoebel, *Anthropology,* p. 22.
9. Ibid., pp. 21–53.
10. Ernest Hilgard, Richard Atkinson, and Rita Atkinson, *Introduction to Psychology,* 6th ed. (New York: Harcourt, Brace, Jovanovich, 1975), pp. 334–35.
11. For a further detailed discussion on French structuralism, see James A. Boon, *From Symbolism to Structuralism* (New York: Harper & Row, 1972).
12. Maurice Moonitz, "Why Do We Need 'Postulates' and 'Principles'?" *The Journal of Accountancy* (December 1963): 42–46.
13. For a complete discussion of structuralism and the relationship of classification as a universality, see Claude Levi-Strauss, *Structural Anthropology* (New York: Basic Books, 1963).
14. Ruth Benedict, *Patterns of Culture,* preface by Margaret Mead (Boston: Houghton Mifflin, 1934), p. 237.
15. Hoebel, *Anthropology,* p. 26.
16. Current linguistical analysis of accounting has been carried out by A. Belkaoui, "The Interprofessional Linguistic Communication of Accounting Concepts: An Experiment in Sociolinguistics," *Journal of Accounting Research* (Autumn 1980): 362–73; E. Flamholtz and E. Cook, "Cognitive Meaning and Its Role in Accounting Change: A Field Study," *Accounting Organizations and Society* (October 1978): 115–40; and R. Libby, "Bankers' and Auditors' Perceptions of the Message Communicated by the Audit Report," *Journal of Accounting Research* (Spring 1979): 99–122.
17. Hoebel, *Anthropology,* pp. 610–11.

18. Ibid., p. 594.
19. Edward Sapir, *Language* (New York: Harcourt, 1921), p. 232.
20. David G. Mandelbaum, ed., *Selected Writings of Edward Sapir* (Berkeley: University of California Press, 1949), p. 162.
21. Belkaoui, "Linguistic Communication of Accounting Concepts," pp. 362–63.
22. For a complete discussion of this cross-cultural comparison and its resulting implications, see Choi, "Primary-Secondary Reporting: A Cross-Cultural Analysis," *International Journal of Accounting* (Fall 1980): 83–104.
23. Ibid., pp. 96–97.
24. William Kanaga, "International Accounting: The Challenge and the Changes," *Journal of Accountancy* (November 1980): 55–56.
25. For an in-depth discussion of Franz Boas and his interpretation of cultural relativism, see *Social Evolution* (Cleveland: Meridan, 1963).
26. A coded data retrieval system created by George Murdock and implemented by John Whiting and Irvin Child was employed for hypothesis testing in contrast to Boasian anthropology. See John Whiting and Irvin Child, *Child Training and Personality: A Cross-Cultural Study* (New Haven: Yale University Press, 1953).
27. Hoebel, *Anthropology*, pp. 27–28.
28. See Choi, "Primary-Secondary Reporting: A Cross-Cultural Analysis."
29. Ibid.
30. See the American Accounting Association, *A Statement of Basic Accounting Theory* (Evanston, Ill.: AAA, 1966), for a discussion on considering environmental information as a financial data.
31. Sy Cip, "Establishing and Applying Standards in Diverse Economic and Social Environments," *International World Accounting Challenges and Opportunities*, ed. John Burton (New York: Arthur Young, 1981), pp. 85–96.

3. ACCOUNTING IN THE ARENA OF WORLD POLITICS

CROSSCURRENTS OF INTERNATIONAL STANDARD-SETTING ACTIVITIES.

LANE A. DALEY

Ph.D., is assistant professor of accounting at the University of Minneapolis, Minnesota. Dr. Daley is a member of the American Accounting Association.

GERHARD G. MUELLER

CPA. Ph.D., is professor of accounting and director of the Graduate Professional Accounting Program at the University of Washington, Seattle. Dr. Mueller is a member of the AAA, the American Institute of CPAs, the Washington Society of CPAs and the Financial Executive Institute.

It is no longer any secret that the affairs of accounting are inextricably intertwined with politics.[1] Within the profession, relatively mundane items like publication of a membership directory for firms belonging to the SEC practice section of the AICPA division for CPA firms, and the broader big GAAP versus small GAAP issue have become charged with political emotions. Their respective resolutions—like those of similar earlier issues—will be influenced heavily by political processes.

In the external environment of the profession, politicization of issues and resultant approaches to their solutions is even more of a factor. Professional governance, professional licensing and reciprocity in individual jurisdictions and disclosure of peer review results are standout examples.

Unparalleled in intensity of politicization, however, is the matter of accounting standard setting.[2] Who should set standards and by what authority? Who should enforce standards and by what means? Should standard setting be broad and philosophical or narrow and procedural? Must standard setters "find" consensus in the community and then set their standards accordingly, or should they build consensus after they have already arrived at judgmental positions? Is one standard-setting body enough, or should there be several? One could easily fill an entire article with questions of this type.

The fact that political dimensions attach to professional accounting affairs is no longer very interesting, but the question of how political dimensions manifest themselves and how they affect accounting-related outcomes is of interest.

Our article focuses on the international consequences of accounting standard setting. Worldwide, there are at least twenty national standard-setting organizations or boards, with precious little synchronization of activities between them.

From a political perspective, national financial accounting standard setting the world over occurs from four different baselines:

1. The purely political approach, as found predominantly in France and West Germany. Here national legislative action decrees accounting standards.
2. The private, professional approach, exemplified by Australia, Canada and the United Kingdom. In these cases, financial accounting standards are set and enforced by private professional actions only.
3. The public/private mixed approach, for which the U.S. is the leading example and which countries like Japan appear to be emulating. Here standards are basically set by private sector bodies which behave as though they were public agencies and whose standards are enforced through governmental actions.
4. The broadly mixed system, like that in the Netherlands, where not only accounting professionals and governmental agencies but also labor unions, industry and trade associations take an active direct hand in setting and enforcing accounting standards.

No wonder, then, that the results of these various national standard-setting activities are heterogeneous and often contradictory. Moreover, this is a major reason why international political attention is being visited on accounting. In support of this assertion, consider the following:

- Philips Industries of the Netherlands received highest marks for its annual report in the *Financial Times* (London) 1980 survey of annual reports of major companies worldwide. Yet currently Philips is considering a major change in its financial reporting based largely on replacement cost measurements. Its board of directors believes that the company's earnings are understated by world standards.
- Just two years ago, the Royal Dutch Petroleum Company was unable to receive an unqualified report from its independent accountants, because British and U.S. standards for income tax allocation were contradictory. Whatever the company did in this respect caused a qualification by one of its joint auditors (Dutch/U.K./U.S.).
- Swiss multinational companies are regularly publishing financial reports that materially exceed national requirements. Allegedly, this is done to secure better international financial credit, open the possibility of listing shares on stock exchanges outside of Switzerland and improve general market and product images.
- In the competition for market shares, U.S./U.K.-based multinational accounting service firms claim to be better acquainted with world standards of financial accounting, to have more reliable transnational service networks and in general to be able to serve multinational companies more effectively.
- Certain U.S. accounting standards, especially those relating to foreign exchange translations and the equity method of accounting for certain intercorporate investments, are said to have circumscribed the ability of U.S. enterprises to bid competitively in multinational merger negotiations.[3] The advent of the Foreign Corrupt Practices Act of 1977, together with comparatively conservative U.S. income tax laws as they affect multinational operations, have assertedly weakened the multinational competitive position of U.S.-based enterprises (e.g., in multinational corporate mergers and/or takeovers).

- Third World countries clamor for accounting standards and rules that could be used to control the operations of multinational corporations within their borders. Broadly speaking, representatives of Third World countries often claim that today's financial accounting has a pervasive British-American bias and is tailored strongly to the needs of the highly industrialized countries.
- U.S. corporate managements often claim that excessive "fine tuning" has given U.S. financial accounting an unwarranted emphasis on short-term profitability measurements. By contrast, Japanese financial accounting standards are thought to be more long-term oriented. Again, this is asserted to limit the multinational competitiveness of U.S.-based enterprises.
- In many technical aspects (inflation accounting, financial statement consolidation, Lifo inventory pricing, lease accounting, pension accounting, research and development accounting, foreign exchange translation and other similar items), national accounting standards require different treatments of similar transactions and circumstances.[4] This is seen by many as a failure of underlying technical processes and full justification for political intervention.

Individually and in combination, reasons like those just enumerated have politicized accounting internationally. Next, we explore who the international accounting players are and what their game is.

Who Is Involved?

Accounting standard-setting efforts are taking place in three major international arenas. Both global and regional bodies are at work in each arena. Moreover, several groups best described as "lobbyists" are active throughout the entire international environment as they seek to represent the best interests of the constituencies.

The first international accounting arena is composed of international political bodies such as the United Nations (UN), the Organization for Economic Cooperation and Development (OECD), the European Economic Community (EEC) and the African Accounting Council (AAC). These agencies seek to formulate various financial and nonfinancial reporting requirements in a purely political manner. Representation on their accounting committees or working groups is by treaty, and the selection process to choose an individual to represent a country is not based on accounting expertise but, rather, on political considerations. For instance, the U.S. Department of State (with assistance from a national advisory committee) represents U.S. accounting interests at the UN and the OECD.

The second sphere of influence consists of the private standard-setting boards whose representation is from national professional accounting groups. Their predominant purpose is setting international financial reporting standards. The International Accounting Standards Committee (IASC) and the Association of Southeast Asian Nations Federation of Accountants (AFA) are in this group.

The third grouping consists of international professional accounting organizations that deal with various professional issues such as auditing standards, educational requirements and ethical standards for the profession in the international setting.

This arena includes the International Federation of Accountants (IFAC), the Union Européenne des Experts Comptables Economiques et Financiers (UEC) and the Asociación Interamericana de Contabilidad (AIC).

The "lobbyists" are widespread, representing many interested parties. National standard-setting bodies have obvious interests in the actions of the international bodies and thus may at times become lobbyists. One illustration of such "interface" is the June 1981 attendance of Donald J. Kirk, chairman of the Financial Accounting Standards Board, at a regular IASC meeting. Academic organizations sometimes act as lobbyists when topical research is undertaken and results are used as inputs to standard-setting processes. Other parties such as the International Chamber of Commerce, the National Foreign Trade Council, the International Confederation of Free Trade Unions, the Business and Industry Advisory Committee and the Trade Union Advisory Committee act as lobbyists to promote goals that are in their best interests.

In the preceding paragraphs only about one-half the groups and organizations active in the international accounting arena are identified by name. The large number of bodies directly involved provides one measure of the size and scope of what we are talking about. Hence, to keep the issue manageable and reasonably focused, we will concentrate on the international political and private standard-setting bodies. Interrelationships among these bodies are highlighted in exhibits 1, 2 and 3, pages 25 and 26, respectively.

Exhibit 1 lists the countries most often represented in international bodies ranked by the incidence of international representation. Of the 37 countries listed (a country had to be represented on at least three bodies to be included) the "most represented" 7 are all Western, developed nations. Only 1 of the 37 is an African nation. None are from the Middle East.

Exhibit 2 examines the geographical distribution of the membership of the major international groups. Here we see an interesting pattern of fairly independent regional groups and highly interrelated global bodies. The developing world appears to be more highly represented in the global groups than exhibit 1 suggests. Although such additional representation is present, it is not made up of single countries represented in many bodies as is common for the Western nations. The Western countries may have comparatively greater access to international accounting standard-setting groups and agencies.

Exhibit 3 examines the cross representation among some major international accounting bodies. The results are very similar to those in exhibit 1, but the data in exhibit 3 point out much more clearly the high degree of correlation in the representation on the global bodies. The IASC is formed from a subset of the IFAC representation. Almost every OECD country is represented in both IASC and IFAC. Similarly the UEC is almost completely represented in the OECD, IASC and IFAC.

These are the participants in the international accounting standards efforts. Their activities are indicative of a large concern over issues of accounting and reporting practices worldwide. Both political and private professional groups are concerned enough to expend much time and money to influence the ongoing process of internationalization of accounting.

Exhibit 1*

SELECTED REPRESENTATION ON INTERNATIONAL STANDARD-SETTING BODIES BY INDIVIDUAL COUNTRY

Country	AAC	AFA	CAPA	EEC	UEC	AIC	IASC	IFAC	OECD	UN**	
Canada	—	—	X	—	—	X	X	X	X	X	6 Group Representation
France	—	—	—	X	X	—	X	X	X	X	
Germany	—	—	—	X	X	—	X	X	X	X	
Italy	—	—	—	X	X	—	X	X	X	X	
Netherlands	—	—	—	X	X	—	X	X	X	X	
Great Britain	—	—	—	X	X	—	X	X	X	X	
United States	—	—	X	—	—	X	X	X	X	X	
Belgium	—	—	—	X	X	—	X	X	X	—	5 Group Representation
Denmark	—	—	—	X	X	—	X	X	X	—	
Ireland	—	—	—	X	X	—	X	X	X	—	
Japan	—	—	X	—	—	—	X	X	X	X	
Luxembourg	—	—	—	X	X	—	X	X	X	—	
Norway	—	—	—	—	X	—	X	X	X	X	
Philippines	—	X	X	—	—	—	X	X	—	X	
Australia	—	—	X	—	—	—	X	X	X	—	4 Group Representation
Brazil	—	—	—	—	—	X	X	X	—	X	
Finland	—	—	—	—	X	—	X	X	X	—	
Greece	—	—	—	—	X	—	X	X	X	—	
India	—	X	X	—	—	—	—	X	—	X	
Malaysia	—	X	X	—	—	—	X	X	—	—	
Mexico	—	—	—	—	—	X	X	X	—	X	
New Zealand	—	—	X	—	—	—	X	X	X	—	
Nigeria	X	—	—	—	—	—	X	X	—	X	
Panama	—	—	—	—	—	X	X	X	—	X	
Pakistan	—	—	X	—	—	—	X	X	—	X	
Portugal	—	—	—	—	X	—	X	X	X	—	
Singapore	—	X	X	—	—	—	X	X	—	—	
Spain	—	—	—	—	X	—	X	X	X	—	
Sweden	—	—	—	—	X	—	X	X	X	—	
Argentina	—	—	—	—	—	X	—	X	—	X	3 Group Representation
Bangladesh	—	—	X	—	—	—	X	X	—	—	
Cyprus	—	—	—	—	—	—	X	X	—	X	
Dominican Republic	—	—	—	—	—	X	—	X	—	X	
Fiji	—	—	X	—	—	—	X	X	—	—	
Iceland	—	—	—	—	X	—	—	X	X	—	
Sri Lanka	—	—	X	—	—	—	X	X	—	—	
Thailand	—	X	X	—	—	—	—	X	—	—	
Representatives	1	5	14	9	16	7	32	37	21	19	
Total Number of Representations in Body	23	5	18	9	18	21	42	53	23	30	

*Adapted from United Nations Report E/C.10/AC.3/7 of September 9, 1980. Second session of the Ad Hoc Intergovernmental Working Group on International Standards of Accounting and Reporting-Commission on Transnational Corporations-UN Economic and Social Council.

**Member of the UN intergovernmental working group.

Exhibit 2*

REPRESENTATION ON INTERNATIONAL STANDARD-SETTING BODIES BY CONTINENT

Body	Africa	Asia	Middle East	Europe	North America	Latin America	Australia/ New Zealand	Total
AAC	23	—	—	—	—	—	—	23
AFA	—	5	—	—	—	—	—	5
CAPA	—	13	1	—	2	—	2	18
EEC	—	—	—	9	—	—	—	9
UEC	—	—	—	18	—	—	—	18
AIC	—	—	—	—	2	19	—	21
IASC	5	9	1	16	2	7	2	42
IFAC	4	11	3	18	2	13	2	53
OECD	2	1	—	15	2	2	1	23
UN**	8	4	1	9	2	6	—	30

*Adapted from United Nations Report E/C.10/AC.3/7 of September 9, 1980. Second session of the Ad Hoc Intergovernmental Working Group on International Standards of Accounting and Reporting-Commission on Transnational Corporations-UN Economic and Social Council.

**Member of the UN intergovernmental working group.

Exhibit 3*

INTERREPRESENTATION AMONG MAJOR INTERNATIONAL STANDARD-SETTING BODIES

Body	AAC	AFA	CAPA	EEC	UEC	AIC	IASC	IFAC	OECD	UN**
AAC	23	—	—	—	—	—	1	1	—	3
AFA	—	5	5	—	—	—	3	5	—	1
CAPA	—	5	18	—	—	2	13	16	5	5
EEC	—	—	—	9	9	—	9	9	9	5
UEC	—	—	—	9	18	—	16	16	17	5
AIC	—	—	2	—	—	21	5	11	2	7
IASC	1	3	13	9	16	5	42	39	20	17
IFAC	1	5	16	9	16	11	39	53	22	21
OECD	—	—	5	9	17	2	20	22	23	8
UN**	3	1	5	5	5	7	17	21	8	30

*Adapted from United Nations Report E/C.10/AC.3/7 of September 9, 1980. Second session of the Ad Hoc Intergovernmental Working Group on International Standards of Accounting and Reporting-Commission on Transnational Corporations-UN Economic and Social Council.

**Member of the UN intergovernmental working group.

The following sections of this article take a brief look at the activities of international political and private accounting standard setters, discuss the goals of these international bodies and anticipate what evolutionary processes might be set into motion.

What is Happening?

In the political arena, three organizations are of primary interest—the UN, OECD and EEC. The UN has been at work since 1977 promulgating accounting standards at the committee level. Technical papers were developed to form the basis for the work of the Intergovernmental Working Group of Experts on International Standards of Accounting and Reporting. These technical papers contain many specific accounting standards regarding the substance of corporate annual reports as well as rules for such issues as consolidation.

The most notable portion of the papers is the extension of requirements to include data that heretofore were excluded from annual reports. These data are primarily oriented toward employment information and technology transfers. This focus appears to be a response to the desires of the developing nations to extract data from the multinational enterprises (MNEs) which they do not feel powerful enough to extract via national controls. Economic development and assisting and "protecting" employees of MNEs are other goals of the UN effort.

For the time being the UN accounting standards efforts focus on the MNEs. Eventually application to all companies the world over is envisioned. Should international accounting standards ever be adopted as a resolution by the UN, enforcement will require actions of either national standard-setting bodies or national governments to carry the force of law. Adoption by the UN certainly would change the political standing of the standards proposed (at a minimum, legitimize them), but it would not mean direct or immediate implementation.

The OECD began its international accounting standards efforts with its June 21, 1976, declaration by the governments of OECD member countries on international investment and multinational enterprises. Since the OECD is made up of developed countries, it represents a different view toward the MNE than does the developing world. This is evident in the reporting standards recommended by the OECD. These standards ignore the recommendations of the UN to expand the data set contained in corporate annual reports. They tend to be distillations of national standards already used in the countries represented. Unlike the UN, the OECD has not really broken any new ground with any of its recommendations. Like the UN, the OECD is powerless to enforce its recommendations aside from national adoption. The treaty creating the OECD does not extend police powers to the organization.

The EEC is unlike the UN and the OECD in a very important way. This body has been granted police powers via the Treaty of Rome. Thus it is setting accounting standards by fiat (not uncommon in Europe on the national level), and these standards must be adopted by the member countries in due course. Relevant activity so far is reflected in the Fourth Directive and the Seventh Directive (in draft form), which specify many measurement methods and reporting requirements to be used by companies in the EEC. Technical issues like consolidation rules are included. The noteworthy facet of this process is that the standards are actually being set by treaty—a mechanism we have not discussed. In fact, all accounting activity in the international political sector is premised on treaty agreements. The only difference is in the powers of enforcement that the underlying treaties specify.

At the private professional level, the IASC has been most active. At present, there are 16 difinitive IASC standards. Forty-two countries are represented on the IASC and, as we have seen, Western countries dominate the organization. The IASC is setting standards in a manner very similar to that used by the American Institute of CPAs committee on accounting procedure in the 1950s. It has not broken any new ground; rather, the IASC attempts to review the procedures currently in use in countries around the world and distill or "harmonize" these by recommending a limited set of acceptable alternatives. The IASC has been beneficial to some countries as a source of information input to regional or national standard-setting processes. Frederick Choi notes that the AFA has used many of the IASC recommendations in preparing its own reporting standards.[5] As with the UN and the OECD, the IASC has no legitimate legal or political power. It acts as an adviser, and its recommendations must be adopted at the national level before any real implementation is possible. In addition, given its Western bias, many of the developing nations criticize the IASC for being insensitive to their situations and needs.

In summary, only one international organization presently promulgating accounting standards has the ability to enforce its recommendations. In addition, little is being done that might be described as new in character. The OECD and the IASC have not ventured into any new issues, and the EEC is still laying the groundwork for such an adventure. Only the UN has really extended itself. However, its work is still ongoing so that it is impossible to predict the nature of the final outcome.

What Goals Have Been Set?

With the plethora of parties involved in international accounting standard-setting activity, what can be said about the overall goal associated with this effort? Many accountants view the goal of this process as the "standardization" of worldwide financial reporting requirements for profit-oriented enterprises. In fact, the very term "accounting standard" underscores this fact. It is reinforced by the work of groups such as the UN that desire to develop requirements for the entire private sector the world over. Other groups like the OECD focus only on the MNEs but seem to desire ultimately the same uniformity (i.e., they don't want to "discriminate" unduly against MNEs).

Given that complete standardization has not been possible in many countries even at the national level, the likelihood for such development at the international level is small indeed. This has prompted groups like the EEC to adopt a position that does not seek uniformity but, rather, harmonization. The latter, as nearly as can be discerned, means that there will be acceptable alternatives but these alternatives must be such that they will not contradict each other (i.e., be fair and reasonable). This method of operations is typical of the British-American mode of standard-setting.

As yet no one has suggested that synchronization (or a method of providing means to resolve differences when the various national standards contradict one another as in the Royal Dutch Petroleum example cited earlier) might be the most appropriate mechanism—at least in the short run. Synchronization would recognize that standards are only appropriate when enforceable by the legitimate powers of the state. Hence it is a problem of international politics as well as international economics when national accounting standards create barriers to economic activity. Contradictory national accounting standards may best be resolved at the political level with treaties binding the respective parties. This would not require the establishment of new standards; it would simply give recognition to the fact that situations occur in which it is in the best interests of national societies (as a whole) to allow some special "pardon" in selected matters of accounting and financial reporting.

The promise for the future of international standard setting in accounting lies in some form of a flexible interactive relationship, in which international standards are either interwoven directly into national standards or some mechanism for international resolution of specific conflicts evolves. At present the former is apparently farther along the road of development than the latter.

What Does the Future Hold?

It is inappropriate for anyone to project a single set of future outcomes. Therefore, we intend to provide three possible scenarios given the information currently available. The importance of these scenarios does not lie in their accuracy but, rather, in conjecturing the roles of involved international groups and their interaction(s) with national standard-setting bodies. It is this interaction that is of critical importance to the local practitioner as well as the national government.

Our first scenario focuses on the MNEs, since they are the companies most likely to be affected by international accounting standards developments. The second examines likely developments in the international political sector and the third assesses the ability of organizations like the IASC to develop into a leadership position in international standard-setting processes.

The MNEs are the parties bearing much of the cost of the lack of international agreement on accounting standards. Multiple sets of records and reports are needed for meeting each country's requirements. If published statements do not meet local requirements, the companies bear the cost of qualified audit opinions (as in the case of Royal Dutch Petroleum). To the extent that this imposes additional capital costs, the lack of accounting agreement translates into real economic cost. Thus there is a possible incentive for the MNEs to impose accounting and financial reporting mechanisms in which they, either as a group or individually, choose a set of reporting standards and use their economic clout to encourage governmental units to adopt the mechanisms selected. Such a strategy could be particularly successful in countries where the national government is in a weak bargaining position relative to the MNE.

Since such behavior will not necessarily resolve the problem of the qualified audit opinion in all countries, managements of MNEs must either believe that in the long run their actions will result in resolution of the problem or that they will be able to convince capital contributors that the effects of opinion qualifications are trivial.

Actions of this type must be weighed carefully, however, against possible political costs. MNEs are already under scrutiny for assorted disproportionate effects on the local political economy. MNEs' actions are bounded by the potential loss of profitable industry due to political decisions by national governments. It is for this reason that MNEs are unlikely to find it in their best interests to attempt to dictate public policy directly as it relates to accounting standards. If the MNEs were to become the primary force in accounting standard-setting processes, local professional accounting groups would lose power and influence regarding the process.

For purposes of the second scenario, international political processes provide the impetus for setting international accounting standards. This would require several major changes in the current environment but has the advantage of being a mechanism embraced at present by many societies for deciding public policy issues. It allows both general preference and intensity of preference to influence the decision process, and it would be done outside private professional organizations that might seek to work mainly in their own best interests. For such a scenario to develop, a much stronger set of international treaties must become available. Enforcement powers must be given to international political bodies or agreements consummated that stipulate binding national support for any standards set. This scenario also would require formal ties between national and international standard-setting processes. Either national bodies such as the FASB would become obsolete or they would be relegated to (1) dealing with issues left uncovered by the international bodies and (2) lobbying for the interests of their local constituencies at the international level.

The second scenario seems plausible. First there is the actual activity of the EEC. Many regions of the world are attempting to use the EEC model to develop regional integration. Should they be successful (along EEC lines), several regionally oriented international groups could emerge that might be capable of setting regionally enforceable accounting standards. The question then would be whether these regional groups can find a mechanism to resolve interregional differences. At present, only the UN provides a theater for such activity, an there is no evidence that it can successfully deal with a situation as postulated.

The last scenario is a continuation or minor modification of the British-American model as used by the IASC. In this scenario the IASC would work with national standard-setting bodies to develop integrated accounting standards, which then would be adopted by the national groups as "accepted" alternatives. Several factors would have to be altered if the IASC were to accomplish this. First, the IASC would have to obtain a wider base of representation to become a truly global body. There are some indications that this is under way, but much more must be done.[6] Second, the IASC would have to begin to develop the types of formal working relationships with national bodies necessary for the conjectured development to take place. Third, the IASC would have to become a leader in dealing with accounting issues. This last step has huge costs, since the IASC would run the risk of exposing itself to disenchantment by members and may possibly lose support. Furthermore, IASC operations would have to be expanded significantly, including adequate research. Again, this would be very costly. If the IASC does not become the world leader in setting standards, it will never be a truly significant force except in providing information to areas of the world that are in the process of developing their own standards.

If the IASC becomes the dominant force in the international sphere, the national professions will serve a most important role in selecting representatives and in providing input to the entire process. It is in this scenario where the greatest amount of responsibility would rest with the national professions. Indeed, in almost any scenario one clear implication exists for the national professions. Decisions made on national accounting standards (which for a long time have been viewed as issues of national public policy) are in fact dynamically interrelated with issues of international public policy.[7] It is not sufficient that CPAs in the U.S., as a national profession, attend only to issues that are relevant to their own interests. American CPAs must increasingly recognize the international effects of local decisions.

Summary

This article began with an examination of the activities in the international sector as they relate to the setting of accounting standards. We discovered a great deal of involvement in the international sphere of many different interest groups. There is a flavor of Western dominance in much of the representation on international accounting bodies and much interpollination in that representation. We suggested three views of what the goals of the international accounting standard-setting process might be and then examined three scenarios of possible future developments.

In all cases there is a long way to go. Formal ties between international groups and national governments are necessary if international standard setters are to develop police powers to enforce their own recommendations. Alternatively, private sector standard setting as constituted at present (i.e., no direct enforcement powers accruing to standard setters) must become more internationally oriented if it is to survive. Greater accounting "internationalization" is crucial to obtaining any kind of harmonization or synchronization of reporting requirements between nations.

Finally, we asserted that accounting professionals must cultivate an international orientation to understand the multidimensional effects of developing national standards. If nothing else, this will prepare them for a time when the promulgation of international standards may directly affect the CPA with a domestic practice because of the formal arrangements for national-international standard-setting interactions. The pressure for these interactions, we submit, is not coming from the political organizations (UN, OECD, EEC), the international professional bodies (IASC, IFAC, UEC) or the national standard setters (FASB, ASC in the U.K.). It is coming from the users of the products of accounting—MNEs, regulators, financial analysts, bankers, labor unions and all the other interested parties CPAs purport to serve.

Notes

1. S. J. Gray, J. C. Shaw and L. B. McSweeney, "Accounting Standards and Multinational Corporations," *Journal of International Business Studies,* Spring/Summer 1981, pp. 121–136; David Solomons, "The Politicization of Accounting," JofA, Nov. 78, pp. 65–72.

2. Canadian Institute of Chartered Accountants, "The Report of the Special Committee on Standard Setting (SCOSS), *CA Magazine,* June 1981, pp. 35–49; Donald J. Kirk, "Concepts, Consensus, Compromise and Consequences: Their Roles in Standard Setting," JofA, Apr. 81, pp. 83–86; Thomas A. Murphy, "Setting Accounting Standards—A Suggestion from a Businessman," *Financial Executive,* August 1979, pp. 52–57; Joshua Ronen and Michael Schiff, "The Setting of Financial Accounting Standards—Private or Public?" JofA, Mar. 78, pp. 66–73.
3. Frederick D. S. Choi and Gerhard G. Mueller, *Introduction to Multinational Accounting* (Englewood Cliffs, N.J.: Prentice-Hall, Inc., 1978), p. 152–153. The Financial Accounting Standards Board issued FASB Statement no. 52, *Foreign Currency Translation* (see Official Releases, page 125), last December. See "FASB Replaces Standard on Foreign Currency Translation," JofA. Jan. 82, p. 9.
4. R. D. Nair and Werner G. Frank, "The Impact of Disclosure and Measurement Practices in International Accounting Classifications," *Accounting Review,* July 1980, pp. 426–450; R. D. Fitzgerald, A. D. Stickler, and T. R. Watts, eds., *International Survey of Accounting Principles and Reporting Practices* (London: Price Waterhouse International, 1979).
5. Frederick D. S. Choi, "ASEAN Federation of Accountants: A New International Accounting Force," *International Journal of Accounting Education and Research,* Fall 1979, pp. 53–66.
6. The IASC Consultative Group, formed late in 1981, consists of participants nominated by the International Federation of Stock Exchanges, the International Association of Financial Executives Institutes, the International Chamber of Commerce, the International Confederation of Free Trade Unions, the International Coordinating Committee of Financial Analyst's Associations and the World Bank.
7. See *World Accounting Report* (London: Financial Times, July 1981), pp. iv–v, for public policy implications over standard setting within the EEC.

II ——— MANAGERIAL ACCOUNTING: GLOBAL POLICIES AND STRATEGIES

4. FINANCIAL ACCOUNTING STANDARDS: A MULTINATIONAL SYNTHESIS AND POLICY FRAMEWORK

FREDERICK D. S. CHOI and VINOD B. BAVISHI*

Frederick D. S. Choi is professor of accounting and international business at New York University. Vinod B. Bavishi is assistant professor of accounting at the University of Connecticut (Storrs). *The study was sponsored in part by Business International Corporation, which holds the copyright to the survey data included. The authors express their appreciation to Business International for allowing them to share the results of this research with their academic colleagues.*

When corporate financial statements were issued and used solely within the confines of a single country, a uninational (ethnocentric) approach to the formulation of accounting standards seemed justified and desirable. In the context of expanded international trade and investment flows, however, ethnocentric approaches to accounting policy formulation are becoming less appropriate.[1]

A private-sector response to the need for an international standard-setting mechanism was the creation in 1973 of the International Accounting Standards Committee (IASC). Headquartered in London, this forty-six–nation member body has issued a steady stream of standards attempting to narrow international accounting differences. Despite an impressive publication record, IASC has not had a high degree of national support for its pronouncements.[2] A recent survey of the annual reports of 200 companies based in twenty IASC member countries reveals that few disclose conformity with or identify deviations from IASC standards.[3]

Today, the IASC faces a credibility problem not unlike that which confronted the U.S. Accounting Principles Board prior to its demise. This credibility problem is attributed, in part, to an operating procedure that is inappropriate for a harmonization effort no longer in its infancy. Specifically, this paper argues that the IASC can and should assert more of a leadership role in the international standards-setting process lest the initiative fall to intergovernmental agencies which may prove less than desirable. This may be accomplished to some extent by adopting a working procedure which systematically isolates and deals with key international accounting differences rather than rationalizing commonalities in terms of a limited set of acceptable alternatives. An appropriate policy framework is derived via a content analysis of the annual reports of the world's leading industrial companies.

Frederick D. S. Choi and Vinod B. Bavishi, "Financial Accounting Standards: A Multinational Synthesis and Policy Framework," *International Journal of Accounting, Education, and Research* 18.1 (Fall 1982):159–84. Reprinted by permission.

The International Standards Dilemma

Analysis of financial statements within the confines of a single nation is facilitated by common language, currency, and, above all, financial reporting formats. This situation is significantly altered when financial analysis is conducted across national boundaries. When reading foreign financial statements, initial disorientation often stems from differences in language, accounting terminology, currency denomination, and format. Problems of a more serious nature relate to differences in the extent of financial disclosure and accounting measurement standards.[4] Message distortions caused by international accounting and reporting differences can, in the extreme, lead to suboptimal business and investment decisions, thereby reducing the allocational efficiency of capital markets and, ultimately, societal welfare.[5]

While international accounting uniformity is posited as a remedy to the foregoing scenario, accountants face a dilemma. If we accept the proposition that the environments in which accounting operates are not the same in different countries, it stands to reason that accounting must necessarily differ if it is to remain socially useful. Evidence in support of environmentally stimulated and justified differences in accounting runs directly counter to efforts at worldwide harmonization of accounting.[6]

Closer investigation, however, suggests that the international accounting standards emerging at the present time are not aimed at all companies irrespective of size; rather, they are actually directed at the large multinational enterprises whose investment and financing activities and, therefore, accounting products, transcend national boundaries.[7] The size distinction promises to resolve the international standards dilemma.

Evolution of International Accounting Standards

In an insightful essay, Alister Mason provides historical perspective on the international standards movement.[8] Selected excerpts from his historical account are summarized in the following paragraphs.

Perhaps the earliest proponent of international accounting standards was Jacob Kraayenhof, who, as president of the Seventh International Congress of Accountants (Amsterdam 1957), keynoted the urgency of international cooperation and standardization. Not until a decade later (1966) would his words give way to action with the formation of the Accountant's International Study Group (AISG), a three-nation undertaking whose terms of reference were

> *to institute comparative studies as to accounting thought and practice in participating countries (Canada, the United Kingdom, and the United States), to make reports from time to time which, subject to the prior approval of the sponsoring Institutes, would be issued to members of those Institutes.*[9]

During its eleven-year life, the AISG issued twenty studies on accounting and auditing topics. While few of these studies had an impact on standards subsequently issued in the three-member countries, they demonstrated the feasibility and benefits of international cooperation.

A real breakthrough was acieved in June 1973, when the IASC was formally established with joint representation from nine countries: Australia, Canada, France, Germany, Japan, Mexico, the Netherlands, the United Kingdom, Ireland, and the United States. Serving as IASC founder members, they subsequently admitted a fairly impressive list of associate members. With the withdrawal of Costa Rica in 1981, the IASC total membership currently stands at sixty professional accounting organizations from forty-six countries.[10]

In signing the IASC Agreement and Constitution, these bodies have consented to "formulate and publish in the public interest, standards to be observed in the presentation of audited financial statements, . . . promote their worldwide acceptance and observance," and to use their best endeavors to "ensure that published accounts comply with these standards or that there is disclosure of the extent to which they do not. . . ."[11]

Completed Projects

Sixteen IASC standards have been issued to date. They are shown here.

SIXTEEN IASC STANDARDS

Standards	Date Of Issue
IAS No. 1, "Disclosure of Accounting Policies"	January 1975
IAS No. 2, "Valuation and Presentation of Inventories" in the Context of the Historical Cost System"	October 1975
IAS No. 3, "Consolidated Financial Statements"	June 1976
IAS No. 4, "Depreciation Accounting"	October 1976
IAS No. 5, "Information to Be Disclosed in Financial Statements"	October 1976
IAS No. 6, "Accounting Responses to Changing Prices"	June 1977
IAS No. 7, "Statement of Changes in Financial Position"	October 1977
IAS No. 8, "Unusual and Prior Period Items and Changes in Accounting Policies"	February 1978
IAS No. 9, "Accounting for Research and Development Activities"	July 1978
IAS No. 10, "Contingencies and Events Occurring after the Balance Sheet Date"	October 1978
IAS No. 11, "Accounting for Construction Contracts"	March 1979
IAS No. 12, "Accounting for Taxes on Income"	July 1979
IAS No. 13, "Presentation of Current Assets and Current Liabilities"	November 1979
IAS No. 14, "Reporting Financial Information by Segment"	August 1981
IAS No. 15, "Information Reflecting the Effects of Changing Prices"	November 1981
IAS No. 16, "Accounting for Property, Plant, and Equipment"	March 1982

Analysis of Standards

An examination of the foregoing list of IAS standards reveals that seven are concerned exclusively with disclosure, the other nine with accounting measurements and disclosure. In terms of alternative practices permitted, only one disclosure requirement permits an alternative—the changing prices information called for by IAS No. 15 which supercedes IAS No. 6. In contrast, eight of the nine measurement standards permit alternative treatments as follows:

1. Some flexibility in applying the basic principles of (a) inventory valuation (IAS No. 2), (b) the allocation of the cost of depreciable assets over their useful lives (IAS No. 4), and (c) computing tax expense (IAS No. 12).
2. Some flexibility in determining whether two specific types of enterprise should be consolidated (IAS No. 3).
3. Alternatives in reporting prior-period adjustments and accounting policy changes (IAS No. 8).
4. Alternatives permitted in accounting for development expenses meeting certain specified criteria (IAS No. 9).
5. Accounting for long-term construction contracts under the percentage of completion or completed-contract method (IAS No. 11).
6. Accounting for property, plant, and equipment as historical cost or a revalued amount (IAS No. 16).

As can be seen, IASC measurement standards cannot be described as "definitive." Mason observes that as a practical matter, the IASC cannot take a position contrary to that of a national pronouncement in a country whose support is vital to the international acceptance of an IAS standard on that topic. To quote him directly,

> *. . .On a continuing basis, therefore, we may expect to see IAS's [IASC standards] which are worded sufficiently broadly to be compatible with the position taken by the FASB and the standard-setting bodies of certain other influential countries. While national standards on some topics, e.g., foreign currency translation, appear to be moving closer together, on others they regrettably seem to be diverging, e.g., accounting for income taxes.*
> *. . .However, the intent has always been that, as the years go by, existing IAS's will be "tightened and strengthened." Presumably, one of the ways of strengthening them will be to reduce, wherever possible, the situations where alternatives are provided.*[12]

Acceptance of International Standards

As intimated earlier, support of IASC dicta has not been uniformly high. Consider some findings.

1. Thomas reports that some professional accounting bodies have formally declared that IASC standards are to be accorded the same status as domestic

standards. Some have strongly urged their members to embrace them. Others, however, have taken no formal stand on the issue.[13]

2. The Canadian Institute of Chartered Accountants (CICA) *Handbook* states, "For companies that report in an international environment . . . it is desirable that they disclose conformity with or identify deviations from International Accounting Standards. . . ." A recent CICA survey of the financial reports of 325 large Canadian enterprises finds, however, that none did so.[14]
3. In conducting a computerized search (NAARS) of annual report data on the U.S. Fortune 500 for the years ended between 1978 and June 1980, Mason found no reference whatever to the IASC or its pronouncements.[15]
4. IASC standards are reportedly accorded more recognition in the United Kingdom. Still, of the fifteen property companies included in the 1979 *Survey of Published Accounts* by the Institute of Chartered Accountants in England and Wales, which did not provide for depreciation on their properties, only three disclosed noncompliance with IAS No. 4.[16]
5. In a *Financial Times* survey of the annual reports of 100 major European firms, Lafferty observes that references to IASC standards are "few and far between."[17]

What may account for this state of affairs? D. de Bruyne, president of the Royal Dutch Shell Company and managing director of the Royal Dutch/Shell Group, offers some candid reasons.

> *First, some highly significant standards-setting bodies such as the FASB are not members of IASC. Second, IASC finds itself having often to pick up what has become accepted practices in a number of countries, sifting the best parts of such existing practice and refining it. It sometimes has to allow alternatives of treatment and tends, in view of its small resources, to have to follow the national bodies rather than show them a lead. Its work tends not, therefore, to be of direct significance to multinationals, which are obliged to follow national standards and rules as they emerge, in advance of their being taken up by IASC.*[18]

Topical Priorities: A Reassessment

Disenchantment with the IASC at a time when interest in global accounting norms is at a high gives genuine cause for concern. International political bodies, such as the United Nations and Organization for Economic Cooperation and Development, have made no secret of their interest in seeking increased comparability and harmonization of accounting measurement rules. Their original interest in accounting harmony was limited to corporate financial disclosure. However, both groups are again studying the wisdom of attempting to harmonize corporate transparency when many of the amounts disclosed are still determined by the use of different accounting principles. While governmental initiatives in the standards-setting process could be helpful, there is always the danger that the objectives of general-purpose accounting standards will receive less attention than those which reflect the views of governments and their special-purpose needs for information.

What are some possible remedies? We argue that the time has come for IASC to "shift gears" and adopt an operating mode more consistent with the current stage of development of the international standards movement.

During its formative years, an overriding concern of IASC—one common to all nascent organizations—was that of survival. In hindsight, the operating procedure adopted was consistent with this concern. The IASC has, thus far, concentrated on rationalizing accounting procedures presently used in countries around the world in terms of a limited number of acceptable alternatives.[19] With IASC now a going concern, attention should appropriately turn to breaking new ground to assure its long-run survival. Specifically, the IASC should directly address the issue of financial reporting objectives. Failing this, it should at least identify accounting subjects on which uniform accounting standards are needed most urgently.[20]

While others have suggested ways of accomplishing the first issue,[21] little work has been devoted to the latter. The balance of this paper focuses on the identification of accounting subjects.

Corporate Accounting Standards: A Multinational Synthesis

The quest for topical priorities prompts the following research questions, "Can one identify key differences in corporate financial accounting standards internationally? If so, what are they?"

Previous Research

A fairly extensive amount of descriptive literature concerning international accounting practices exists as a basis for identifying international accounting differences. They range from booklets describing practices in individual countries which are published by professional accounting firms, government departments of commerce, and banks, to reference books dealing with regional or international practices.[22] While these sources are useful, the current authors preferred to rely primarily on information derived directly from the financial statements of more than 1,000 leading industrial firms from twenty-four countries. Several reasons dictated this choice:

1. Accounting anthologies based on principles and practices codified by local professional accountancy bodies, international accounting organizations, or national laws generally present minimum standards. Accordingly, corporate reporting practices that exceed such minimums are not captured.
2. Many accounting surveys published by professional accounting firms are based on personal assessments by field office personnel of current accounting practices. In addition to problems relating to subjectivity and bias, such assessments usually are based on small samples.
3. With a few exceptions, existing literature is generally dated.
4. Most surveys of international accounting principles do not isolate key differences.

Research Methodology

Countries selected for inclusion in this study were limited to those for which corporate annual report data could be obtained. Annual reports were solicited exclusively from large as opposed to small enterprises on the presumption that the former would more likely attract investor interest internationally and be affected by international accounting pronouncements.

To ensure that the sample included the world's largest industrial companies, firms selected from industrially advanced countries had to have consolidated sales in excess of $500 million as of year-end 1980. Those selected from small industrialized and developing countries had to have sales in excess of $100 million. These selection criteria yielded a sample of 1,000 firms, 413 of which were U.S.-based and the remaining 587 headquartered in twenty-three other countries.

Companies whose operating results were consolidated with those of another firm were not included. Inclusion of subsidiary companies would not have provided a true picture of the practices in a particular country since subsidiaries normally mirror parent-company policies.

Other salient points relating to sample selection include the following:

1. Government-controlled industrial companies were included if separate annual reports were published by the firms.
2. Cooperatives were excluded, since investors at large would not be able to acquire an ownership interest in these firms.

A geographic profile of companies included in this study appears in exhibit 1.

The published annual reports issued by U.S. and non-U.S. companies were secured from each firm in the sample for 1980. Financial statements appearing in

Exhibit 1

NUMBER OF COMPANIES INCLUDED IN THE STUDY BY COUNTRY

Country	Number	Country	Number
Australia	17	South Korea	4
Austria	9	Malaysia	8
Belgium	13	Mexico	4
Brazil	11	Netherlands	21
Canada	36	Norway	9
Denmark	11	South Africa	9
Finland	18	Spain	5
France	49	Sweden	31
West Germany	66	Switzerland	18
India	14	United Kingdom	107
Ireland	5	United States	413
Italy	11	24 Total	1,000 Total
Japan	111		

these reports together with explanatory notes were the sole source of data on accounting principles employed. An exhaustive content analysis was conducted for all countries except Japan, the United Kingdom, and the United States where relative sample sizes were 50, 50, and 100, respectively.

English versions of non-U.S. annual reports were requested when available. Assistance was obtained to translate the relevant accounting sections of foreign-language reports of seventy-seven companies from the following countries: Austria, seven companies; Belgium, six; Brazil, five; France, thirty; Switzerland, one; and West Germany, twenty-eight.

Differences in financial accounting principles internationally were assessed by means of an accounting principles checklist. Construction of this checklist was based on the following considerations:

1. Items chosen for inclusion were accounting principles appearing in a representative sample of U.S. and non-U.S. annual reports as well as those obtained from a survey of existing literature. An item was selected if it was deemed to have material valuation or income determination implications (see exhibit 2).
2. To minimize the number of cross-country comparisons (total possible combinations were 23 × 23 or 529), the reporting practices of all twenty-four countries chosen for the analysis were compared with a single benchmark. In the absence of a definitive set of international accounting standards, U.S. practices were used as a proxy norm.
3. To simplify cross-country analysis, matrix cells of the checklist contain discrete yes/no responses to signify adherence or nonadherence to a given accounting principle.

Research Findings

Several salient points follow from the multinational survey (see Appendices 1–5). One major finding is that fundamental differences in accounting standards between each of the twenty-four countries examined are not as extensive as one would expect. Major differences observed relate to consolidation practices, and accounting for goodwill, deferred taxes, long-term leases, discretionary reserves, inflation, and foreign-currency translation.

Specifically, most countries, with the exception of Finland and Italy, prepare consolidated financial statements when the parent company enjoys majority ownership or operating control of an investee. While most companies appear to employ the equity method of accounting for unconsolidated subsidiaries, German, Norwegian, Japanese, Swedish, and Swiss companies continue to adhere to the cost method. Companies domiciled in Australia, Denmark, and South Africa appear evenly divided in employing the cost and equity methods for unconsolidated subsidiaries. In preparing consolidated accounts, German companies appear to be the only ones that omit foreign subsidiaries; neither do they amortize purchased goodwill. This is also true of U.K. and Malaysian companies. For companies in Finland, Norway, Italy, South Africa, and Switzerland, amortization of goodwill constitutes a minority practice.

Although accounting for deferred taxes was traditionally associated with companies in Canada, the United Kingdom, and the United States, it appears to be

Exhibit 2

SYNTHESIS OF ACCOUNTING DIFFERENCES

1. Marketable securities recorded at the lower cost of market?
2. Provision for uncollectible accounts made?
3. Inventory costed using FIFO?
4. Manufacturing overhead allocated to year-end inventory?
5. Inventory valued at the lower of cost or market?
6. Accounting for long-term investments: less than 20 percent ownership: cost method?
7. Accounting for long-term investments: 21–50 percent ownership: equity method?
8. Accounting for long-term investments: more than 50 percent ownership: full consolidation?
9. Both domestic and foreign subsidiaries consolidated?
10. Acquisitions accounted for under the pooling of interest method?
11. Intangible assets: goodwill amortized?
12. Intangible assets: other than goodwill amortized?
13. Long-term debt includes maturities longer than one year?
14. Discount/premium on long-term debt amortized?
15. Deferred taxes recorded when accounting income is not equal to taxable income?
16. Financial leases (long-term) capitalized?
17. Company pension fund contribution provided regularly?
18. Total pension fund assets and liabilities excluded from company's financial statement?
19. Research and developoment expensed?
20. Treasury stock deducted from owner's equity?
21. Gains or losses on treasury stock taken to owner's equity?
22. No general purpose (purely discretionary) reserves allowed?
23. Dismissal indemnities accounted for on a pay-as-you-go basis?
24. Minority interest excluded from consolidated income?
25. Minority interest excluded from consolidated owners' equity?
26. Are intercompany sales/profits eliminated upon consolidation?
27. Basic financial statements reflect a historical cost valuation (no price-level adjustment)?
28. Supplementary inflation-adjusted financial statements provided?
29. Straight-line depreciation adhered to?
30. No excess depreciation permitted?
31. Temporal method of foreign-currency translation employed?
32. Currency translation gains or losses reflected in current income?

gaining general acceptance internationally. Companies not subscribing to this treatment were limited to those in Belgium, Finland, Italy, Norway, Sweden, and Switzerland. In contrast, the practice of capitalizing long-term leases is rarely practiced by companies outside Canada and the United States, and by some companies in Belgium.

The use of discretionary balance sheet reserves is generally frowned upon by security analysts and other readers of financial statements since their use can significantly distort income and other ratio comparisons between countries. Reserve movements impacting income statement items above the bottom line (that is, before deriving net income) was observed in many countries, but not in Australia, Canada, Malaysia, Mexico, South Africa, South Korea, the United Kingdom, and the United States.

While unadjusted historical cost is assumed to be the basic valuation framework of most countries, the present survey reveals that revaluation of fixed assets above cost is becoming quite common. Companies adhering to the unadjusted cost principle in their basic financial statements were those in Canada, Germany, Japan, the United States, and the Netherlands (by a majority of companies). Supplementary inflation accounting disclosures were predominant among U.K. and U.S. companies and increasingly present in Australia, Canada, the Netherlands, Finland, Norway, and Switzerland.

Finally, despite the popularity of the temporal method of foreign-currency translation in the United States (recently revised) and Canada, companies in most countries in Europe and the Far East prefer the current-rate method. The accounting treatment of translation gains and losses varied, however. As of year-end 1980, U.S., Canadian, and South Korean companies were the only ones to recognize consistently such gains and losses in current income.

Summary and Policy Implications

In September 1975, the IASC published for general distribution a booklet entitled *The Work and Purpose of the International Accounting Standards Committee.* The concluding paragraph to the booklet (par. 23) contains the following prediction:

> *Provided that the initial enthusiasm and thrust with which the IASC was started is continued, its impact in the years to come will be important. It will take perhaps five to ten years before its full effects are recognized but after that they will increase each year. Accounts issued in every important nation of the world will comply with the standards promulgated by the IASC or will disclose the extent to which there has been non-compliance. . . .*

The time span of that forecast has almost elapsed, but the prediction has yet to materialize. A major conclusion of the current study is that the fulfillment of such a prophecy is dependent on the IASC's assuming more of a leadership role in setting world accounting standards. This, in turn, will necessitate a shift of emphasis from maintaining the status quo to identifying and ruling on accounting subjects on which standardization is most urgent.

The foregoing posture is supported by the findings of the multinational survey. Contrary to what is normally presumed, fundamental differences in national accounting principles, as gleaned from the reporting practices of the world's leading industrial companies, are not that great. Hence, attention to areas where commonalities currently abound are not likely to prove fruitful except for those countries desiring guidance in formulating their own standards. Major differences appear to revolve around such issues as consolidation, as well as accounting for goodwill, deferred taxes, long-term leases, discretionary reserves, inflation, and foreign exchange (translation) gains and losses. The IASC should concentrate its attention on these subjects.

Suggestions For Future Research

Having identified some of the major differences in worldwide accounting principles, a natural progression in this line of inquiry would be to examine the impact of these observed measurement differences on the measurement of income and financial position. While studies of this nature have been conducted in the past, they have typically been confined to some of the major industrial countries in North America and Europe. The data set provided here increases significantly the scope of inter-country comparisons. Going a step further, studies assessing the impact of international measurement differences on accounting-based financial ratios appear extremely useful given the high level of interest in the international diversification of securities investments.

The purpose in identifying key international accounting differences was to provide international standard setters, notably the IASC, with a focus. What would be even more useful at this stage would be to assist the IASC in prioritizing these differences. That is, which of the observed accounting measurement differences do users (investors) feel are most critical to their decisions? Which the least? Studies of this nature would aid the IASC in deciding which subject areas to attack first, which second, and so on.

The scope of the present study was limited to twenty-four countries. Since IASC's international membership now totals forty-six, there is an obvious need to extend the comparative framework to more countries. Little is known, for example, concerning accounting measurement rules in spheres of the world, such as South and Central America, Africa, and the Far and Middle East.

Just ten years ago, research in international accounting employing the method of content analysis was regarded as highly risky, especially by doctoral candidates in search of dissertation topics. One of the current authors can attest to the fact that the constraints of data availability, timeliness, and comprehensibility, owing to the language and currency problem, was very real indeed. Our experiences today contrast markedly with those of a decade ago. Such favorable experiences suggest that very exciting and feasible research opportunities await those with a scholarly interest in international financial statement analysis.

Notes

1. Frederick D. S. Choi and Gerhard G. Mueller, *An Introduction to Multinational Accounting* (Englewood Cliffs, N.J.: Prentice-Hall, 1978), p. 153.
2. U.N. Center on Transnational Corporations, *Toward International Standardization of Corporate Accounting and Reporting* (New York: UNCTC, 1982), p. 36.

3. Michael Lafferty and David Cairns, *Financial Times World Survey of Annual Reports 1980* (London: *Financial Times,* 1980), p. 18.
4. For examples, see Robert Hampton, III, "A World of Differences in Accounting and Reporting," *Management Accounting* (September 1980):14–28.
5. Morris Mendelson and Sydney Robbins, *Investment Analysis and Securities Markets* (New York: Basic Books, 1976), p. 89.
6. Werner G. Frank, "An Empirical Analysis of International Accounting Principles," *Journal of Accounting Research* (Autumn 1979):593–605.
7. Reference to size considerations can be found in the pronouncements/proposals of such international accounting organizations as the United Nations, U.N. GEISAR Group, *International Standards of Accounting and Reporting for Transnational Corporations* (New York: United Nations Economic and Social Council, 1977); Organization for Economic Cooperation and Development, *International Investment and Multinational Enterprises* (Paris: OECD, 1976); European Communities, "EEC Fourth Directive," in *International Statements, Guidelines on Accounting and Auditing, Omnibus Edition* (Stockholm: Swedish Institute of Authorized Public Accountants, 1981); and the IASC, *IAS 14,* "Reporting Financial Information by Segment" (March 1981), and *IAS 15,* "Information Reflecting the Effects of Changing Prices" (November 1981).
8. Alister K. Mason, "The Evolution of International Accounting Standards," in *Multinational Accounting: A Research Framework for the Eighties,* ed. Frederick D.S. Choi (Ann Arbor, Mich.: UMI Research Press, 1981), pp. 155–70.
9. Ibid., p. 156.
10. International Accounting Standards Committee, *IASC News* (London: IASC, 1981), p. 4.
11. International Accounting Standards Committee, *Preface to Statements of International Accounting Standards* (London: IASC, 1978), par. 19.
12. Mason, "International Accounting Standards," p. 160.
13. R. Douglas Thomas, "International Accounting Standards," *CA Magazine* (October 1977):49–50.
14. Canadian Institute of Chartered Accountants, *Financial Reporting in Canada,* 13th ed. (Toronto: CICA, 1979), p. 14.
15. Mason, "International Accounting Standards," p. 164.
16. Institute of Chartered Accountants in England and Wales, *Survey of Published Accountants 1979* (London: ICAEW, 1980), pp. 283–84.
17. Michael Lafferty, David Cairns, and James Carty, *100 Major European Companies' Reports and Accounts* (London: *Financial Times,* 1979), p. 19.
18. D. de Bruyne, "International Harmonization of Accounting and Disclosure Standards" (address delivered at the 10th World Congress of the International Association of the Financial Executives Institute, Atlanta, Georgia, October 15, 1979) published by the Royal Dutch/Shell Group of Companies, 7 pp.
19. International Accounting Standards Committee, *Preface to Statements,* par. 9.
20. Authors who have recently raised this research issue include R. D. Nair and Werner G. Frank, "The Impact of Disclosure and Measurement Practices on International Accounting Classifications," *Accounting Review* (July 1980):449; and Mason, "International Accounting Standards," p. 169.

21. D. de Bruyne, "Harmonization," pp. 6–7.
22. Examples include American Institute of Certified Public Accountants, *Professional Accounting in Thirty Countries* (New York: AICPA, 1975), 792 pp.; Michael Lafferty, *Accounting in Europe* (Cambridge, England: Woodhead Faulkner, 1975), 425 pp.; OECD, *International Investment and Multinational Enterprises: Accounting Practices in OECD Member Countries* (Paris: OECD, 1980), 250 pp.; and R. D. Fitzgerald, A. D. Stickler, and T. R. Watts, *International Survey of Accounting Principles and Reporting Practices* (Ontario, Canada: Butterworths, 1979), 47 pp. and appendices.

APPENDIX A
SYNTHESIS OF ACCOUNTING DIFFERENCES

Accounting Principles	U.S.	Canada	Brazil	Mexico	U.K.
1. Marketable securities recorded at the lower cost or market?	Yes	Yes	Yes(A)	Yes	Yes
2. Provision for uncollectible accounts made?	Yes	Yes	Yes	Yes	Yes
3. Inventory costed using FIFO?	Mixed	Mixed	No(F)	Mixed	Yes
4. Manufacturing overhead allocated to year-end inventory?	Yes	NF	Yes	Yes	Yes
5. Inventory valued at the lower of cost or market?	Yes	Yes	Mixed	Mixed	Yes
6. Accounting for long-term investments: less than 20% ownership: cost method?	Yes	Yes	Yes	Yes	Yes
7. Accounting for long-term investments: 21–50% ownership: equity method?	Yes	Yes	Yes	Yes	Yes
8. Accounting for long-term investments: more than 50% ownership: full consolidation?	Yes	Yes	Yes	Yes	Yes
9. Both domestic and foreign subsidiaries consolidated?	Yes	Yes	Yes	Yes	Yes
10. Acquisitions accounted for under the pooling of interest method?	Yes	No(C)	NF	NF	No(C)
11. Intangible assets: goodwill amortized?	Yes	Yes	NF	Yes	No**
12. Intangible assets: other than goodwill amortized?	Yes	Yes	Yes	Yes	No**
13. Long-term debt includes maturities longer than one year?	Yes	Yes	Yes	Yes	Yes
14. Discount/premium on long-term debt amortized?	Yes	Yes	NF	Yes	No
15. Deferred taxes recorded when accounting income is not equal to taxable income?	Yes	Yes	Yes	Yes	Yes

LIQUIDITY RATIOS

Current Ratio → Current Assets / Current Liability

ACID TEST RATIO → Current Assets - stock / Current Liabilities

DEBITORS COLLECTION PERIOD → TRADE DEBITORS x 365 / CREDIT SALES

EFFICIENCY RATIOS

Stock Turnover Ratio

Cost of Goods Sold / Average Stock

(AS = opening stock + closing $ / 2)

APPENDIX A CONTINUED

Accounting Principles	U.S.	Canada	Brazil	Mexico	U.K.
16. Financial leases (long-term) capitalized?	Yes	Yes	No	Yes	No
17. Company pension fund contribution provided regularly?	Yes	Yes	Yes	Yes	Yes
18. Total pension fund assets and liabilities excluded from company's financial statement?	Yes	Yes	Yes	Yes	Yes
19. Research and development expensed?	Yes	Yes	Yes	Yes	Yes
20. Treasury stock deducted from owner's equity?	Yes	Yes	No**	NF	NF
21. Gains or losses on treasury stock taken to owner's equity?	Yes	Yes	No**	NF	NF
22. No general purpose (purely discretionary) reserves allowed?	Yes	Yes	No	Yes	Yes
23. Dismissal indemnities accounted for on a pay-as-you-go basis?	Yes	Yes	No**	Yes	Yes
24. Minority interest excluded from consolidated income?	Yes	Yes	Yes	NF	Yes
25. Minority interest excluded from consolidated owners' equity?	Yes	Yes	Yes	NF	Yes
26. Are intercompany sales/profits eliminated upon consolidation?	Yes	Yes	Yes	Yes	Yes
27. Basic financial statements reflect a historical cost valuation (no price-level adjustment)?	Yes	Yes	No	No	No
28. Supplementary inflation-adjusted financial statements provided?	Yes	No**	No	No	Yes
29. Straight-line depreciation adhered to?	Yes	Yes	Yes	Yes	Yes
30. No excess depreciation permitted?	Yes	Yes	No	No	No
31. Temporal method of foreign-currency translation employed?	Yes	Yes	N/A	Mixed	No(E)
32. Currency translation gains or losses reflected in current income?	Yes	Yes	N/A	Mixed	No

Key: Yes — Predominate practice. Yes* — Minor modifications, but still predominant practice. No** — Minority practice. No — Accounting principle in question not adhered to. NF — Not found. N/A — Not applicable. Mixed — Alternative practices followed with no majority.

Notes: A — Adjusted for monetary correction. B — Cost method is used. C — Purchase method is used. D — Long-term debt includes maturities longer than four years. E — Current rate method of foreign currency translation. F — Weighted average is used. G — Cost or equity. H — Translation gains and losses are deferred. I — Market is used. J — Owners' equity. K — Equity.

APPENDIX B

SYNTHESIS OF ACCOUNTING DIFFERENCES

Accounting Principles	U.S.	Germany	France	Belgium	Neth.
1. Marketable securities recorded at the lower cost or market?	Yes	Yes	Yes	Yes	Yes
2. Provision for uncollectible accounts made?	Yes	Yes	No	No	Yes
3. Inventory costed using FIFO?	Mixed	Yes	Mixed	Mixed	Mixed
4. Manufacturing overhead allocated to year-end inventory?	Yes	Yes	NF	Yes	Yes
5. Inventory valued at the lower of cost or market?	Yes	Yes	Yes	Yes	Yes
6. Accounting for long-term investments: less than 20% ownership: cost method?	Yes	Yes	Yes*	Yes	No(K)
7. Accounting for long-term investments: 21–50% ownership: equity method?	Yes	No(B)	Yes*	No(B)	Yes
8. Accounting for long-term investments: more than 50% ownership: full consolidation?	Yes	Yes	Yes*	Yes	Yes
9. Both domestic and foreign subsidiaries consolidated?	Yes	No**	Yes	Yes	Yes
10. Acquisitions accounted for under the pooling of interest method?	Yes	No(C)	No(C)	No(C)	No(C)
11. Intangible assets: goodwill amortized?	Yes	No	Yes	Yes	Mixed
12. Intangible assets: other than goodwill amortized?	Yes	Yes	Yes	Yes	Yes
13. Long-term debt includes maturities longer than one year?	Yes	No(D)	Yes	Yes	Yes
14. Discount/premium on long-term debt amortized?	Yes	No	No	No**	NF
15. Deferred taxes recorded when accounting income is not equal to taxable income?	Yes	Yes	Yes	No**	Yes
16. Financial leases (long-term) capitalized?	Yes	No	No	No**	No
17. Company pension fund contribution provided regularly?	Yes	Yes	Yes	Yes	Yes
18. Total pension fund assets and liabilities excluded from company's financial statement?	Yes	No	Yes	Yes	Yes

APPENDIX B CONTINUED

Accounting Principles	U.S.	Germany	France	Belgium	Neth.
19. Research and developoment expensed?	Yes	Yes	Yes	No**	Yes
20. Treasury stock deducted from owner's equity?	Yes	No	Yes	NF	Mixed
21. Gains or losses on treasury stock taken to owner's equity?	Yes	No	Yes	NF	Mixed
22. No general purpose (purely discretionary) reserves allowed?	Yes	No	No	No	No
23. Dismissal indemnities accounted for on a pay-as-you-go basis?	Yes	Yes	Yes	NF	NF
24. Minority interest excluded from consolidated income?	Yes	No	Yes	Yes	Yes
25. Minority interest excluded from consolidated owners' equity?	Yes	No	Yes	Yes	Yes
26. Are intercompany sales/profits eliminated upon consolidation?	Yes	Yes	Yes	Yes	Yes
27. Basic financial statements reflect a historical cost valuation (no price-level adjustment)?	Yes	Yes	No	No	No**
28. Supplementary inflation-adjusted financial statements provided?	Yes	No	No	No	No**
29. Straight-line depreciation adhered to?	Yes	Mixed	Mixed	Mixed	Yes
30. No excess depreciation permitted?	Yes	Yes	No	No	No
31. Temporal method of foreign-currency translation employed?	Yes	No(E)	No(E)	Mixed	No(E)
32. Currency translation gains or losses reflected in current income?	Yes	Mixed	Mixed	Mixed	No(J)

Key: Yes — Predominate practice. Yes* — Minor modifications, but still predominant practice. No** — Minority practice. No — Accounting principle in question not adhered to. NF — Not found. N/A — Not applicable. Mixed — Alternative practices followed with no majority.

Notes: A — Adjusted for monetary correction. B — Cost method is used. C — Purchase method is used. D — Long-term debt includes maturities longer than four years. E — Current rate method of foreign currency translation. F — Weighted average is used. G — Cost or equity. H — Translation gains and losses are deferred. I — Market is used. J — Owners' equity. K — Equity.

APPENDIX C
SYNTHESIS OF ACCOUNTING DIFFERENCES

Accounting Principles	U.S.	Switz.	Ireland	Austria	Sweden
1. Marketable securities recorded at the lower cost or market?	Yes	Yes	Yes	Yes	Yes
2. Provision for uncollectible accounts made?	Yes	Yes	Yes	Yes	Yes
3. Inventory costed using FIFO?	Mixed	Yes	Yes	Mixed	Yes
4. Manufacturing overhead allocated to year-end inventory?	Yes	No	Yes	Yes	Yes
5. Inventory valued at the lower of cost or market?	Yes	Yes	Yes	Yes	Yes
6. Accounting for long-term investments: less than 20% ownership: cost method?	Yes	Yes	Yes	Yes	Yes
7. Accounting for long-term investments: 21–50% ownership: equity method?	Yes	No(B)	Yes	No(B)	No(B)
8. Accounting for long-term investments: more than 50%ownership: full consolidation?	Yes	Yes	Yes	Yes	Yes
9. Both domestic and foreign subsidiaries consolidated?	Yes	Yes	Yes	Yes	Yes
10. Acquisitions accounted for under the pooling of interest method?	Yes	NF	No(C)	NF	No(C)
11. Intangible assets: goodwill amortized?	Yes	No**	No**	NF	Yes
12. Intangible assets: other than goodwill amortized?	Yes	No**	NF	NF	Yes
13. Long-term debt includes maturities longer than one year?	Yes	Yes	Yes	Yes	Yes
14. Discount/premium on long-term debt amortized?	Yes	NF	No	NF	No
15. Deferred taxes recorded when accounting income is not equal to taxable income?	Yes	No	Yes	No	No
16. Financial leases (long-term) capitalized?	Yes	No	No	No	No
17. Company pension fund contribution provided regularly?	Yes	Yes	Yes	Yes	Yes
18. Total pension fund assets and liabilities excluded from company's financial statement?	Yes	Yes	Yes	Yes	Yes
19. Research and development expensed?	Yes	Yes	Yes	Yes	Yes

APPENDIX C CONTINUED

Accounting Principles	U.S.	Switz.	Ireland	Austria	Sweden
20. Treasury stock deducted from owner's equity?	Yes	NF	NF	No	NF
21. Gains or losses on treasury stock taken to owner's equity?	Yes	NF	NF	No	NF
22. No general purpose (purely discretionary) reserves allowed?	Yes	No	Yes	Yes	No
23. Dismissal indemnities accounted for on a pay-as-you-go basis?	Yes	NF	Yes	Yes	Yes
24. Minority interest excluded from consolidated income?	Yes	Yes	Yes	NF	Yes
25. Minority interest excluded from consolidated owners' equity?	Yes	Yes	Yes	NF	Yes
26. Are intercompany sales/profits eliminated upon consolidation?	Yes	Yes	Yes	NF	Yes
27. Basic financial statements reflect a historical cost valuation (no price-level adjustment)?	Yes	No	No	No	No
28. Supplementary inflation-adjusted financial statements provided?	Yes	No**	Yes	No	No
29. Straight-line depreciation adhered to?	Yes	Yes	Yes	Mixed	Yes
30. No excess depreciation permitted?	Yes	No	No	Yes	No
31. Temporal method of foreign-currency translation employed?	Yes	No(E)	No(E)	NF	No
32. Currency translation gains or losses reflected in current income?	Yes	No(H)	No	NF	Mixed

Key: Yes — Predominate practice. Yes* — Minor modifications, but still predominant practice. No** — Minority practice. No — Accounting principle in question not adhered to. NF — Not found. N/A — Not applicable. Mixed — Alternative practices followed with no majority.

Notes: A — Adjusted for monetary correction. B — Cost method is used. C — Purchase method is used. D — Long-term debt includes maturities longer than four years. E — Current rate method of foreign currency translation. F — Weighted average is used. G — Cost or equity. H — Translation gains and losses are deferred. I — Market is used. J — Owners' equity. K — Equity.

APPENDIX D
SYNTHESIS OF ACCOUNTING DIFFERENCES

Accounting Principles	U.S.	Denmark	Finland	Norway	Italy
1. Marketable securities recorded at the lower cost or market?	Yes	No(I)	Yes	Yes	Yes
2. Provision for uncollectible accounts made?	Yes	Yes	Yes	Yes	Yes
3. Inventory costed using FIFO?	Mixed	Yes	Yes	Yes	Mixed
4. Manufacturing overhead allocated to year-end inventory?	Yes	Yes	Yes	Yes	Yes
5. Inventory valued at the lower of cost or market?	Yes	Yes	Yes(B)	Yes	Yes
6. Accounting for long-term investments: less than 20% ownership: cost method?	Yes	NF	No**	Yes	Yes
7. Accounting for long-term investments: 21–50% ownership: equity method?	Yes	NF	No**	No(B)	No(B)
8. Accounting for long-term investments: more than 50% ownership: full consolidation?	Yes	Yes	No**	Yes	No**
9. Both domestic and foreign subsidiaries consolidated?	Yes	Yes	No**	Yes	No**
10. Acquisitions accounted for under the pooling of interest method?	Yes	No(C)	No(C)	No(C)	No(C)
11. Intangible assets: goodwill amortized?	Yes	Yes	No**	No**	No**
12. Intangible assets: other than goodwill amortized?	Yes	NF	Yes	NF	Yes
13. Long-term debt includes maturities longer than one year?	Yes	Yes	Yes	Yes	Yes
14. Discount/premium on long-term debt amortized?	Yes	Yes	NF	No	Yes
15. Deferred taxes recorded when accounting income is not equal to taxable income?	Yes	Yes	No	No	No
16. Financial leases (long-term) capitalized?	Yes	No	No	No	No
17. Company pension fund contribution provided regularly?	Yes	Yes	Yes	Yes	Yes
18. Total pension fund assets and liabilities excluded from company's financial statement?	Yes	Yes	Yes	Yes	Yes

APPENDIX D CONTINUED

Accounting Principles	U.S.	Denmark	Finland	Norway	Italy
19. Research and development expensed?	Yes	Yes	NF	Yes	No**
20. Treasury stock deducted from owner's equity?	Yes	Yes	NF	NF	Mixed
21. Gains or losses on treasury stock taken to owner's equity?	Yes	Yes	NF	NF	Mixed
22. No general purpose (purely discretionary) reserves allowed?	Yes	No	No	No	No
23. Dismissal indemnities accounted for on a pay-as-you-go basis?	Yes	Yes	Yes	Yes	Yes
24. Minority interest excluded from consolidated income?	Yes	Yes	Yes	Yes	No
25. Minority interest excluded from consolidated owners' equity?	Yes	Yes	Yes	Yes	No
26. Are intercompany sales/profits eliminated upon consolidation?	Yes	Yes	Yes	Yes	No**
27. Basic financial statements reflect a historical cost valuation (no price-level adjustment)?	Yes	No	No	No	No
28. Supplementary inflation-adjusted financial statements provided?	Yes	No	No**	No**	No
29. Straight-line depreciation adhered to?	Yes	Yes	Yes	Yes	Yes
30. No excess depreciation permitted?	Yes	No	No	No	No
31. Temporal method of foreign-currency translation employed?	Yes	No	No	No	NF
32. Currency translation gains or losses reflected in current income?	Yes	No	Mixed	Mixed	NF

Key: Yes — Predominate practice. Yes* — Minor modifications, but still predominant practice. No** — Minority practice. No — Accounting principle in question not adhered to. NF — Not found. N/A — Not applicable. Mixed — Alternative practices followed with no majority.

Notes: A — Adjusted for monetary correction. B — Cost method is used. C — Purchase method is used. D — Long-term debt includes maturities longer than four years. E — Current rate method of foreign currency translation. F — Weighted average is used. G — Cost or equity. H — Translation gains and losses are deferred. I — Market is used. J — Owners' equity. K — Equity.

APPENDIX E
SYNTHESIS OF ACCOUNTING DIFFERENCES

Accounting Principles	U.S.	India	S. Korea	S. Africa
1. Marketable securities recorded at the lower cost or market?	Yes	Yes	Yes	Yes
2. Provision for uncollectible accounts made?	Yes	No	Yes	No**
3. Inventory costed using FIFO?	Mixed	Mixed	Mixed	Mixed
4. Manufacturing overhead allocated to year-end inventory?	Yes	No	Yes	Yes
5. Inventory valued at the lower of cost or market?	Yes	Yes	Yes	Yes
6. Accounting for long-term investments: less than 20% ownership: cost method?	Yes	Yes	Yes	Yes
7. Accounting for long-term investments: 21–50% ownership: equity method?	Yes	No(B)	No(B)	No(G)
8. Accounting for long-term investments: more than 50% ownership: full consolidation?	Yes	No(B)	No	Yes
9. Both domestic and foreign subsidiaries consolidated?	Yes	No(B)	N/A	Yes
10. Acquisitions accounted for under the pooling of interest method?	Yes	NF	No(C)	No(C)
11. Intangible assets: goodwill amortized?	Yes	NF	Yes	No**
12. Intangible assets: other than goodwill amortized?	Yes	NF	Yes	Yes
13. Long-term debt includes maturities longer than one year?	Yes	Yes	Yes	Yes
14. Discount/premium on long-term debt amortized?	Yes	Yes	Yes	Yes
15. Deferred taxes recorded when accounting income is not equal to taxable income?	Yes	No	No	Yes
16. Financial leases (long-term) capitalized?	Yes	No	No	No
17. Company pension fund contribution provided regularly?	Yes	Yes	Yes	Yes
18. Total pension fund assets and liabilities excluded from company's financial statement?	Yes	Yes	Yes	Yes
19. Research and development expensed?	Yes	Yes	No	Yes
20. Treasury stock deducted from owner's equity?	Yes	NF	Yes	NF
21. Gains or losses on treasury stock taken to owner's equity?	Yes	NF	Yes	NF

APPENDIX E CONTINUED

Accounting Principles	U.S.	India	S. Korea	S. Africa
22. No general purpose (purely discretionary) reserves allowed?	Yes	No	Yes	Yes
23. Dismissal indemnities accounted for on a pay-as-you-go basis?	Yes	Yes	No	Yes
24. Minority interest excluded from consolidated income?	Yes	NF	NF	Yes
25. Minority interest excluded from consolidated owners' equity?	Yes	NF	NF	Yes
26. Are intercompany sales/profits eliminated upon consolidation?	Yes	NF	Yes	Yes
27. Basic financial statements reflect a historical cost valuation (no price-level adjustment)?	Yes	No	No	No
28. Supplementary inflation-adjusted financial statements provided?	Yes	No	No	No
29. Straight-line depreciation adhered to?	Yes	No	No	Yes
30. No excess depreciation permitted?	Yes	No	No	No
31. Temporal method of foreign-currency translation employed?	Yes	No	No	No
32. Currency translation gains or losses reflected in current income?	Yes	No	Yes	No

Key: Yes — Predominate practice. Yes* — Minor modifications, but still predominant practice. No** — Minority practice. No — Accounting principle in question not adhered to. NF — Not found. N/A — Not applicable. Mixed — Alternative practices followed with no majority.

Notes: A — Adjusted for monetary correction. B — Cost method is used. C — Purchase method is used. D — Long-term debt includes maturities longer than four years. E — Current rate method of foreign currency translation. F — Weighted average is used. G — Cost or equity. H — Translation gains and losses are deferred. I — Market is used. J — Owners' equity. K — Equity.

APPENDIX F

SYNTHESIS OF ACCOUNTING DIFFERENCES

Accounting Principles	U.S.	Spain	Japan	Australia	Malaysia
1. Marketable securities recorded at the lower cost or market?	Yes	Yes	Yes	Yes	Yes
2. Provision for uncollectible accounts made?	Yes	No**	Yes	Yes	Yes
3. Inventory costed using FIFO?	Mixed	Yes	Mixed	Yes	Mixed
4. Manufacturing overhead allocated to year-end inventory?	Yes	Yes	NF	Yes	No
5. Inventory valued at the lower of cost or market?	Yes	Yes	Yes	Yes	Yes
6. Accounting for long-term investments: less than 20% ownership: cost method?	Yes	Cost	Yes	Yes	Yes
7. Accounting for long-term investments: 21–50% ownership: equity method?	Yes	No(B)	No(B)	No(G)	Yes
8. Accounting for long-term investments: more than 50% ownership: full consolidation?	Yes	Yes	Yes	Yes	Yes
9. Both domestic and foreign subsidiaries consolidated?	Yes	Yes	Yes	Yes	Yes
10. Acquisitions accounted for under the pooling of interest method?	Yes	NF	NF	No(C)	No(C)
11. Intangible assets: goodwill amortized?	Yes	No	Yes	Yes	No
12. Intangible assets: other than goodwill amortized?	Yes	Yes	Yes	Yes	Yes
13. Long-term debt includes maturities longer than one year?	Yes	Yes	Yes	Yes	Yes
14. Discount/premium on long-term debt amortized?	Yes	Yes	Yes	Yes	Yes
15. Deferred taxes recorded when accounting income is not equal to taxable income?	Yes	No	Yes	Yes	Yes
16. Financial leases (long-term) capitalized?	Yes	No	No	No	No
17. Company pension fund contribution provided regularly?	Yes	Yes	Yes	Yes	Yes
18. Total pension fund assets and liabilities excluded from company's financial statement?	Yes	Yes	Yes	Yes	Yes
19. Research and development expensed?	Yes	No	Yes	Yes	No**

APPENDIX F CONTINUED

Accounting Principles	U.S.	Spain	Japan	Australia	Malaysia
20. Treasury stock deducted from owner's equity?	Yes	Yes	Yes	NF	NF
21. Gains or losses on treasury stock taken to owner's equity?	Yes	Yes	No**	NF	NF
22. No general purpose (purely discretionary) reserves allowed?	Yes	No	No	Yes	No
23. Dismissal indemnities accounted for on a pay-as-you-go basis?	Yes	Yes	Yes	Yes	Yes
24. Minority interest excluded from consolidated income?	Yes	NF	Yes	Yes	Yes
25. Minority interest excluded from consolidated owners' equity?	Yes	NF	Yes	Yes	Yes
26. Are intercompany sales/profits eliminated upon consolidation?	Yes	Yes	Yes	Yes	Yes
27. Basic financial statements reflect a historical cost valuation (no price-level adjustment)?	Yes	No	Yes	Yes	No
28. Supplementary inflation-adjusted financial statements provided?	Yes	No	No	No**	No
29. Straight-line depreciation adhered to?	Yes	Mixed	Mixed	Yes	Yes
30. No excess depreciation permitted?	Yes	No	Yes	No	No
31. Temporal method of foreign-currency translation employed?	Yes	No	No	Mixed	N/A
32. Currency translation gains or losses reflected in current income?	Yes	No	Mixed	Mixed	N/A

Key: Yes — Predominate practice. Yes* — Minor modifications, but still predominant practice. No** — Minority practice. No — Accounting principle in question not adhered to. NF — Not found. N/A — Not applicable. Mixed — Alternative practices followed with no majority.

Notes: A — Adjusted for monetary correction. B — Cost method is used. C — Purchase method is used. D — Long-term debt includes maturities longer than four years. E — Current rate method of foreign currency translation. F — Weighted average is used. G — Cost or equity. H — Translation gains and losses are deferred. I — Market is used. J — Owners' equity. K — Equity.

5. TRANSLATED FINANCIAL STATEMENTS CAN BE MEANINGFUL

THOMAS W. HALL and H. JIM SNAVELY

Thomas W. Hall and H. Jim Snavely are Associate Professor and Professor of Accounting, respectively, at the University of Texas at Arlington.

At the present time, application of commonly used translation methodologies results in financial statements which are of limited usefulness. Translation gains or losses do not represent real gains or losses except by coincidence; balance sheet translation adjustments are no more than numbers needed to make the translated balance sheets balance; and real and nominal income effects are mixed, precluding a rational interpretation of income. This situation need not exist. The translation of foreign currency financial statements can and should produce meaningful results.

This paper will (1) explain why current translation methodologies produce numbers which are of limited usefulness, (2) develop, through a series of basic examples, a method which produces meaningful numbers, and (3) present a comprehensive example comparing the results of the different methods. Even if translated financial statements cannot be corrected, investors, creditors, and managers of firms with foreign operations need to understand the method described in the following pages because its application produces numbers which are useful in evaluating the results of foreign operations and planning hedging activities.

The Deficiency In Current Translation Methodologies

Available evidence indicates that domestic and foreign inflation rates play a major, though not complete, role in determining exchange rate changes. Studies by Aliber and Stickney[1] and Giddy[2] confirm a significant relationship between inflation and changes in exchange rates. A recent study by Hall[3] suggests that during periods of high inflation and floating exchange rates, relative inflation rates may account for as much as 82 percent of the variations in exchange rates.

This relationship between inflation and exchange rate changes is described by the purchasing power party (PPP) theory. The PPP theory predicts that a change in the country-to-country ratio of commodity price levels results in a proportional change in the exchange rate.[4] Mathematically, the relationship can be expressed as follows:

$$E_t = E_{t-1}\left[\frac{P_{d,t} \div P_{d,t-1}}{P_{f,t} \div P_{f,t-1}}\right],$$

Thomas W. Hall and H. Jim Snavely, "Translated Financial Statements Can Be Meaningful," *International Journal of Accounting* 20.1 (Fall 1984):153–70. Reprinted by permission.

where

E_t; E_{t-1} = exchange rates at times t and t − 1 denominated in domestic currency units per foreign currency unit,

P_{dt}; $P_{d,t-1}$ = domestic price levels at times t and t − 1, and

$P_{f,t}$; $P_{f,t-1}$ = foreign price levels at times t and t − 1.

In spite of the significant relationship between changes in exchange rates and inflation rates, present translation methodologies ostensibly ignore inflation in translating foreign currency financial statements. However, the exchange rates are an integral part of statement translation procedures. Thus, while inflation is explicitly ignored, it implicitly affects the statements.

Since the effects of foreign and domestic inflation are not considered, reported translation gains and losses are not meaningful—they are the uninterpretable result of various economic events and accountants' calculation rules. Failure to consider the effects of foreign inflation also precludes the identification of purchasing power gains/losses from holding a foreign net monetary position. Finally, failure to consider domestic inflation makes it impossible to distinguish between real and nominal amounts. In sum, current translation methodologies produce results of limited usefulness because they ignore the effects of changes in domestic and/or foreign price levels.

To produce meaningful results, therefore, a translation method must consider the effects of both domestic and foreign inflation. The next section presents a series of examples which illustrate how information regarding foreign and domestic inflation rates can be used to prepare meaningful translated foreign currency financial statements.

Some Basic Examples

The following basic examples highlight some differences between meaningful numbers that should be reported and what is reported under translation methodologies which are currently in widespread use. We use results of applying the current rate (CR) and the temporal rate (TR) methods[5] as benchmarks. The discussion begins with cases in which the foreign operation holds only monetary assets and concludes with an example in which nonmonetary assets are held. Included are cases where only the foreign price level changes, where only the domestic price level changes, and where both foreign and domestic price levels change.

Holding Monetary Assets with a Changing Foreign Price Level

Assume that a parent corporation established a foreign subsidiary by investing 2,000 domestic currency units (DC) when the exchange rate was 2 DC for 1 foreign currency unit (FC). The subsidiary held the FC for a year, and at year end, the exchange rate was 1.667 DC for 1 FC. The foreign country incurred 20 percent inflation, while the domestic price level remained unchanged. At the end of the year, the subsidiary's 1,000 FC were exchanged for 1,667 DC for a loss of 333 DC.

What type of loss did the firm sustain? Because the firm held monetary assets, FC units, in a period when the purchasing power of those FC units was decreasing, the firm sustained a purchasing power loss calculated as follows:

Monetary assets in FC units	1,000 FC
Foreign inflation rate	× .20
Purchasing power loss in FC	200 FC
Ending exchange rate (DC/FC)	× 1.667
Purchasing power loss in DC	333 DC

Both the CR and TR translation methods would report this 333 DC loss, but the loss would be incorrectly identified as an exchange loss rather than as a purchasing power loss.

To change the example slightly, assume that the year-end exchange rate was 1.50 DC for 1 FC unit. The 1,000 FC units were exchanged for 1,500 DC units. Here, the firm sustained a loss of 500 DC (2,000 DC − 1,500 DC). A portion of the 500 DC loss relates to exchange rate exposure, and part relates to the holding of monetary assets during inflation. The 500 DC total loss should be reported in two components: a 300 DC purchasing power loss and a 200 DC exchange rate loss.

The loss in purchasing power is calculated as in the first example.

Monetary assets in FC units	1,000 FC
Foreign inflation rate	× .20
Purchasing power loss in FC	200 FC
Ending exchange rate (DC/FC)	× 1.50
Purchasing power loss in DC	300 DC

In this instance, however, the actual exchange rate at year end was 1.50 DC for 1 FC.

In the calculation of the exchange rate loss, an exchange rate of 1.667 DC to 1 was used. This exchange rate is an "expected" rate; it is the rate of exchange that would have existed had the rate changed exactly in proportion to the change in purchasing power of the moneys involved. This expected exchange rate is calculated using the purchasing power parity formula given earlier:

$$2\ \text{DC/FC} \times \frac{1.0}{1.2} = 1.667\ \text{DC/FC}$$

The exchange rate loss is calculated as the product of the firm's net asset position in price-level-adjusted FC units and the difference in the actual exchange rate at year end as compared to the expected rate due to inflation.

Net asset position in nominal FC units	1,000 FC
Foreign inflation adjustment	× 1.2
Price-level-adjusted net assets in FC units	1,200 FC
Real change in exchange rate (difference between actual and expected ending exchange rate)	× (1.5 − 1.667)
Exchange rate loss	200 DC

In this instance, the CR and TR translation methods would report the 500 DC as an exchange loss. No distinction would be made between that portion of the loss due to exchange risk and that portion due to the changing foreign price level.

These examples illustrate an approach to reporting exchange rate gains/losses which considers the effect of foreign inflation. This approach segregates the currently reported translation gain/loss into two components: (1) the purchasing power gain/loss incurred from holding a FC net monetary position during a period of changing FC prices and (2) an exchange rate gain/loss. This exchange rate gain/loss reflects the effect of a real change in value of one currency relative to another.

Holding Monetary Assets with a Changing Domestic Price Level

In the previous examples, there were no real differences between real and nominal amounts because it was assumed that the domestic price level remained unchanged. To explore the potential differences between real and nominal amounts, the facts are changed. Assume the same initial investment, but reverse the inflation rate assumptions. Now the domestic country is assumed to experience a 20 percent inflation rate, while the foreign country price level remains unchanged. Further, assume that the year-end exchange rate was 2.40 DC to 1 FC unit (which is a rate change exactly in proportion to the relative inflation rates). In this example, the 1,000 FC at year end can be exchanged for 2,400 DC. The firm has incurred what might appear to be a gain of 400 DC (2,400 DC − 2,000 DC), and present translation methods would report this gain. Actually, this gain is only a nominal gain since DC units decreased in purchasing power by 20 percent. In real terms, the firm has not incurred a gain but has only maintained the purchasing power of its original investment. In addition, the firm has not incurred a purchasing power gain or loss since the monetary FC units held were not subject to inflation in the foreign country.

Changing the example slightly, assume that at year end the exchange rate was 2.30 DC to 1 FC. The 1,000 FC units at year end could be exchanged for 2,300 DC. In real terms, the firm has sustained a loss of 100 DC calculated as follows:

Initial DC investment	2,000 DC
Domestic inflation adjustment	× 1.2
Constant dollar investment	2,400 DC
Year end worth of 1,000 FCs	−2,300 DC
Loss	100 DC

The loss is an exchange rate loss and can be calculated as the product of the firm's net asset position in FC units and the difference in the actual ending exchange rate as compared to the rate that would have existed had the exchange rate changed exactly in proportion to the relative inflation rates.

Beginning exchange rate (DC/FC)	2	
Inflation effect	×1.2/1	
Expected ending exchange rate based on relative inflation rates (DC/FC)	2.40	
Actual ending exchange rate (DC/FC)	2.30	
Difference (DC/FC)	.10	
FC net asset position	×1,000	FC
Exchange rate loss	100	DC

No gain or loss in purchasing power took place since there was no inflation in the foreign country.

Application of the CR or TR translation methods, however, would require the firm to report a 300 DC gain. This gain has two components: (1) a 400 DC nominal gain due to a decrease in the purchasing power of DC units as compared to FCs and (2) a 100 DC real loss resulting from an exchange rate change which was not proportional to the changes in the purchasing power of the two moneys. Thus, present inflation methods result in not disclosing a real exchange loss of 100 DC and, instead, in reporting a nominal gain of 300 DC when, in fact, the firm is worse off at year end than at the beginning.

Holding Monetary Assets When Both Domestic and Foreign Price Levels Change

To illustrate another point, assume that both the domestic and foreign country incur 20 percent inflation. The exchange rate would not change unless other factors cause a change. If the exchange rate remained 2 DC for 1 FC, in real terms the firm would incur a 400 DC purchasing power loss calculated as 1,000 FC units × 20 percent inflation × 2 DC. Present translation methods, however, would report no gain or loss since the beginning and ending exchange rates remained unchanged.

If the ending exchange rate was 1.90 DC to 1 FC, in real terms the firm incurred a purchasing power loss of 380 DC and an exchange loss of 120 DC calculated as follows:

Purchasing Power Loss		
Monetary Assets in FC units	1,000	FC
Foreign inflation rate	× .20	
Purchasing power loss in FC	200	FC
Ending exchange rate (DC/FC)	× 1.90	
Purchasing power loss in dollars	380	DC

Exchange Loss		
Beginning exchange rate (DC/FC)	2.00	
Inflation effect	×1.2/1.2	
Expected ending exchange rate based on relative inflation rates (DC/FC)	2.00	
Actual ending exchange rate (DC/FC)	1.90	
Difference (DC/FC)	.10	
FC net asset position adjusted for foreign inflation (1,000 × 1.2)	×1,200	FC
Exchange rate loss	120	DC

Using the CR and TR translation methods, the firm would report only a 100 DC exchange loss.

Holding Nonmonetary Assets

Had the parent used the 2,000 D units to purchase land in the foreign nation instead of holding FC units of money, how would the previous examples change? First, no purchasing power gains or losses would have occurred since land is a nonmonetary item. Purchasing power gains/losses result only when monetary assets/liabilities are held. Instead of being exposed to possible purchasing power gains/losses, the firm would be exposed to possible gains/losses from changes in the market value of the land. Second, the exchange rate losses would have been exactly the same as the previous examples. The type of asset held does not affect the exchange rate gain or loss. An exchange rate gain or loss results when the exchange rate does not change in proportion to the inflation rates of the countries involved, and the foreign operation has a non-zero net asset position (assets do not equal liabilities).

Application of the TR method when holding nonmonetary assets would, appropriately, not report any purchasing power gain or loss. The TR method would fail to report exchange gains or losses, however, because nonmonetary assets would be translated at historical exchange rates.

A strict application of the CR method to land or other fixed assets results in neither a purchasing power gain or loss, nor an exchange rate gain, nor any balance sheet translation adjustment since present and all previous balance sheet amounts and income statement related amounts are translated at the current rate. Thus, all amounts maintain the same relationship to the other statement amounts as reported in the FC statements. Modification of the CR method so that prior balance sheet figures are translated at the exchange rate in existence at those prior balance sheet dates (rather than the exchange rates at the current balance sheet date) and/or income statement related numbers are translated at rates other than the rates as of the end of the latest balance sheet (e.g., average rates for the year reported) results in either translation gain/loss amounts on the income statement or translation adjustment figures on the balance sheet (which sometimes are reported as adjustment figures on the balance sheet (which sometimes are reported as adjustments to various named reserves). These amounts would not be the same exchange gain/loss amount as calculated in the previous examples because the CR method fails to consider the effects of foreign and domestic inflation.

Summary of Examples

The previous examples indicate that a firm experiences real purchasing power gains/losses whenever monetary liabilities or assets denominated in FC units are held, while at the same time, the FC unit is subject to inflation/deflation. Also, the firm experiences real exchange gains/losses whenever exchange rate movements are only partially accounted for by foreign and domestic relative inflation rates. On the other hand, nominal gain/losses may exist when there are no real gains/losses and, conversely, nominal gains/losses may not exist even though real gains/losses are incurred. In addition, sometimes nominal gains/losses correspond with real gains/losses.

Since the gains/losses which present translation methods require to be reported are nominal gains/losses, since the required methods do not distinguish between exchange gains/losses and purchasing power gains/losses, and since the nominal figures have no reliable relationship to the real amounts, the results of applying current translation methods appear to be of little value and potentially misleading.

A Comprehensive Example

In this section, we use a comprehensive example to illustrate more fully a new approach to translation foreign currency financial statements. This new approach identifies both purchasing power gains/losses and exchange gains/losses resulting from foreign investments. All amounts are stated in real terms. For identification purposes, the new method shall be referred to as the restate-translate-rollforward (RTR) method.[6]

For comparison purposes, results for the comprehensive example will also be calculated using a variation of the temporal method (explained in SFAS No. 8[7]) and a variation of the current rate method (explained in SFAS No. 52[8]). Brief summaries of each method follow.[9]

The RTR method would (1) comprehensively restate FC statements for any inflation/deflation in the foreign currency, (2) translate year-end assets and liabilities using the actual exchange rate at the year end, (3) translate the capital stock by using the number of DC units invested adjusted only for domestic inflation, (4) translate the revenue, expenses, gains, and losses for the year at the actual year-end exchange rate, (5) determine the exchange rate gain or loss by multiplying the beginning net assets of the price-level-adjusted foreign currency balance sheet times the difference between the actual ending exchange rate and what the ending rate would have been had it changed exactly in accord with the inflation rates in the two countries,[10] and (6) rollforward prior period statements which had been translated into DC units by the procedures described above using only information regarding domestic inflation for the rollforward period.

SFAS No. 8 methodology required that (1) monetary balance sheet items be translated at the exchange rate as of the balance sheet date (current rate), (2) nonmonetary balance sheet assets and liabilities be translated at the relevant historical translation rate (rate which existed at the transaction date), (3) income statement items which relate to nonmonetary assets/liabilities (e.g., depreciation) are translated at the historical rate, (4) the remaining income statement items are translated at a rate which existed when the transactions occurred (average calculations are encouraged), and (5) the amount needed to make the balance sheet balance is reported on the income statement as a translation gain or loss.

SFAS No. 52 requires (1) translation of all assets and liabilities at the rate which existed at the balance sheet date (current rate), (2) translation of income statement items at rates which existed at the transaction dates (averages are encouraged), and (3) the amount needed to make the balance sheet balance is reported as a separate component (translation adjustment) of stockholders' equity.[11] This translation adjustment will be used later in the calculation of a gain/loss upon sale, substantially complete liquidation, or partial sale of the investment in the foreign entity. (However, if the firm's foreign operations are in a highly inflationary economy, e.g., one incurring a three-year cumulative inflation of over 100 percent, SFAS No. 52 requires application of the SFAS No. 8 method.)

Assumptions for the Comprehensive Example

Assume a U.S. company initially invested $2,000 in a foreign subsidiary at the beginning of year 1. The subsidiary purchased a building with a three-year life for 1,000 FC and used straight-line depreciation with no salvage value. The building was leased to a client for 450 FC a year, and the lease stipulated that at the beginning of each new year, the lease payment was to be adjusted for the prior year's foreign country inflation. Due to a 20 percent annual inflation, actual FC cash flows were as follows:

Year 1		450 FC
Year 2	1.2×450 FC =	540 FC
Year 3	1.2×540 FC =	648 FC

Lease payments were received uniformly throughout the year. At the end of year 3, the building was abandoned, the related accounts eliminated, and the subsidiary was liquidated.

Comparative statements in nominal FC units based on the foregoing assumptions are presented in Exhibit 1. These statements indicate that the subsidiary earned a cumulative three-year profit of 638 nominal FC.

Also, assume that over the three-year period, the foreign country incurred inflation of 9.545 percent each six-month period (20 percent per year) while the United States incurred inflation of 4.881 percent each six-month period (10 percent per year). After adjusting for differences in relative inflation rates, it is assumed the foreign currency lost 5 percent of its value relative to the U.S. dollar each year. Relevant general price indices and exchange rates were as follows.

	US price index	FC price index	Actual exchange rate	Expected exchange rate based on beginning of year exchange rate and current year relative inflation rates[12]
Beg yr 1	100	100	$2-1 FC	
Mid yr 1	104.881	109.545	1.871-1	
End yr 1	110	120	1.742-1	1.833 -1
Mid yr 2	115.69	131.453	1.630-1	
End yr 2	121	144	1.517-1	1.597 -1
Mid yr 3	126.906	157.744	1.419-1	
End yr 3	133.1	172.8	1.321-1	1.390 -1

Exhibit 2 presents comparative price-level-adjusted FC statements prior to roll-forward to end of year 3 FCs. Information regarding yearly beginning price-level-adjusted equity, presented in this exhibit, is used in later sections in the determination of the yearly exchange gain/loss under the RTR method.

Results

Income statement results of applying the RTR, SFAS No. 8, and SFAS No. 52 methodologies are presented in Exhibit 3. Translated balance sheet amounts are presented in Exhibit 4. A comparison of the results yields several interesting and very significant differences.

In reporting results of operations, both SFAS No. 8 and SFAS No. 52 methodologies report the same nominal revenue amounts, and these amounts shown an upward trend. This upward trend is present because the example assumed rental payments were adjusted for inflation. The RTR method reports real amounts and a slowly

Exhibit 1

COMPARATIVE STATEMENTS IN NOMINAL FC UNITS

Balance Sheets (FC)	Beg Yr 1	End Yr 1	End Yr 2	End Yr 3
Cash	0 FC	450 FC	990 FC	1,638 FC
Building	1,000	1,000	1,000	0
Accumulated depreciation	0	(333)	(666)	0
Total assets	1,000	1,117	1,324	1,638
Initial equity	1,000	1,000	1,000	1,000
Retained earnings	0	117	324	638
Total equity	1,000 FC	1,117 FC	1,324 FC	1,638 FC
Income statements (FC)				
Revenues		450 FC	540 FC	648 FC
Depreciation expense		(333)	(333)	(334)
Operating income		117	207	314
		117	207	314

declining trend. This slowly declining trend more accurately reflects economic reality because, although the rental payments were adjusted for inflation, suggesting a stable trend, in real terms the foreign currency lost value relative to the U.S. dollar, thus resulting in a declining trend. Had the exchange rate changed in exact proportion to the relative inflation rates, the RTR method would have reported constant revenues.

The SFAS No. 8 method reports a constant amount of depreciation expense, while SFAS No. 52 reports a rapidly declining depreciation expense. The RTR method reports a slowly declining depreciation expense due to the foreign currency's reduction in value relative to the dollar in real terms.

Exhibit 2
COMPARATIVE PRICE-LEVEL-ADJUSTED FC STATEMENTS (PRIOR TO ROLLFORWARD TO END OF YEAR 3)

Balance Sheets (FC)	**Year**			
	1-beginning (beginning of year 1 FCs)	1-end (end of year 1 FCs)	2-end (end of year 2 FCs)	3-end (end of year 3 FCs)
Cash	0 FC	450 FC	990 FC	1,638 FC
Building	1,000	1,200	1,440	0
Accumulated depreciation	0	(400)	(959)	0
Total assets	1,000	1,250	1,471	1,638
Initial equity	1,000	1,200	1,440[a]	1,728[c]
Increments from prior years' operations	—	—	60[b]	37[d]
Beginning equity	1,000	1,200	1,500	1,765
Current year income/loss	—	(50)	(29)	(127)
Total equity	1,000	1,250 FC	1,471 FC	1,638 FC
Income statements (FC)				
Revenues		493 FC	592 FC	710 FC
Depreciation expense		(400)	(480)	(577)
Operating income		93	112	133
Purchasing power gain (loss)		(43)	(141)	(260)
Net income (loss)		50 FC	(29) FC	(127) FC

[a] 1,000 FC × 144/100
[b] 50 FC × 144/120
[c] 1,000 FC × 172.8/1,000
[d] (50 FC × 172.8/120) + (−29 FC × 172.8/144)

Because of the foregoing, the SFAS No. 8 and SFAS No. 52 methods report an increasing trend for operating income; under the RTR method, however, operating income shows a declining trend. As with revenue, this declining trend is appropriate because the foreign currency lost value in real terms relative to the U.S. dollar.

Both the SFAS No. 8 and RTR methods report translation or exchange losses. Under SFAS No. 8, these translation losses increase each year, although real equity exposed to exchange fluctuations slowly declines and the foreign currency declines

Exhibit 3

COMPARATIVE INCOME STATEMENTS IN U.S. DOLLARS PRESENTED AS OF THE END OF YEAR 3

	Year		
	1	2	3
RTR method			
Revenues	$1,039[a]	$ 988	$ 938[e]
Depreciation expense	(843)[b]	(801)	(762)[f]
Operating income	196	187	176
Purchasing power loss	(91)[c]	(235)	(343)[g]
Exchange rate loss	(133)[d]	(132)	(123)[h]
Net income (loss)	$ (28)	$(180)	$(290)
SFAS No. 8 method			
Revenues	$ 842	$ 880	$ 920
Depreciation expense	(666)	(666)	(668)
Operating income	176	214	252
Purchasing power loss	—	—	—
Translation loss	(58)	(162)	(258)
Net income (loss)	$ 118	$ 52	$ (6)
SFAS No. 52 method			
Revenues	$ 842	$ 880	$ 920
Depreciation expense	(623)	(543)	(474)
Operating income	219	337	446
Purchasing power loss	—	—	—
Translation adjustment	—	—	(838)
Net income (loss)	$ 219	$ 337	$(392)

[a] 450 FC (see Exhibit 1) × 120/1.09545 × 1.742 $/FC × 133.1/110
[b] 333 FC (see Exhibit 1) × 120/100 × 1.742 $/FC × 133.1/110
[c] 450 FC (see Exhibit 1) × .09545 × 1.742 $/FC × 133.1/110
[d] 1,200 FC (see Exhibit 2) × (1.742 $/FC − 1.833 $/FC) × 133.1/110
[e] 648 FC (see Exhibit 1) × 172.8/157.744 × 1.321 $/FC
[f] 334 FC (see Exhibit 1) × 172.8/100 × 1.321 $/FC
[g] [(990 FC (see Exhibit 1) × .2) + (648 FC (see Exhibit 1) × .09545)] × 1.321 $/FC
[h] 1,765 FC (see Exhibit 2) × (1.321 $/FC − 1.390 $/FC)

Exhibit 4

COMPARATIVE BALANCE SHEETS IN U.S. DOLLARS PRESENTED AS OF THE END OF YEAR 3

	Beginning of Year 1	End of Year 1	End of Year 2	End of Year 3
RTR method				
Cash	$ 0	$ 948	$ 1,652[b]	$2,164
Building	2,662[a]	2,529	2,402[c]	0
Accumulated depreciation	0	(843)	(1,600)	0
Total assets	$2,662	$2,634	$ 2,454	$2,164
Initial equity	2,662	2,662	2,662[d]	2,662
Retained earnings	0	(28)	(208)[e]	(498)
Total equity	$2,662	$2,634	$2,454	$2,164
SFAS No. 8 method				
Cash	$ 0	$ 784	$ 1,502	$2,164
Building	2,000	2,000	2,000	0
Accumulated depreciation	(0)	(666)	(1,332)	0
Total assets	2,000	2,118	2,170	2,164
Initial equity	2,000	2,000	2,000	2,000
Retained earnings	0	118	170	164
Total equity	$2,000	$2,118	$ 2,170	$2,164
SFAS No. 52 method				
Cash	$ 0	$ 784	$ 1,502	$2,164
Building	2,000	1,742	1,517	0
Accumulated depreciation	(0)	(580)	(1,010)	0
Total assets	2,000	1,946	2,009	2,164
Initial equity	2,000	2,000	2,000	2,000
Retained earnings	0	219	556	164
Translation adjustment	0	(273)	(547)	0
Total equity	$2,000	$1,946	$ 2,009	$2,164

[a]1,000 FC (see Exhibit 1) 100/100 × 2 $/FC × 133.1/100
[b]990 FC (see Exhibit 1) × 1.517 $/FC × 133.1/121
[c]1,000 FC (see Exhibit 1) × 144/100 × 1.517 $/FC × 133.1/121
[d]$2,000 (initial dollar investment) × 133.1/100
[e]From Exhibit 3 (28) + (180)

relative to the dollar at a constant rate. On the other hand, actual exchange rate losses reported by the RTR method are of approximately the same magnitude and slowly decline. This slowly declining trend is appropriate since the foreign currency lost value relative to the U.S. dollar at a constant rate and at the same time real equity exposed to exchange fluctuations slowly declined. The SFAS No. 52 method reports no gain or loss related to translation on the income statement until the third year. A translation adjustment is reported as part of equity until the subsidiary is liquidated. At that time, the accumulated adjustments are reported as part of income. Had the parent continued its investment, the translation adjustment would have continued to be reported on the balance sheet even after the sale/abandonment of the building, and the income statement for year three would have reported net income of $446.

Neither the SFAS No. 8 nor SFAS No. 52 method reports purchasing power gains/losses incurred by holding net monetary items during a period of changing prices. The RTR method reports such gains/losses. Because the RTR method distinguishes between purchasing power gains/losses and exchange rate gains/losses, users of the financial statements should better understand the distinct types of risks facing a foreign operation. Such information would also be useful to management in its attempt to measure and limit such exposure through hedging activities.

Net income for all three years totals $164 under both SFAS No. 8 and SFAS No. 52 (assuming liquidation of the subsidiary), but the income patterns vary. The SFAS No. 8 method reports a declining trend each year, while the SFAS No. 52 method reports an increasing trend until the year of liquidation when the equity translation adjustments are passed through income. In that year, a large loss is reported. The RTR method reports a three-year real loss of $498. The yearly patterns reflect increasing losses—due principally to holding an ever-larger net monetary asset position during an inflationary period, thus incurring purchasing power losses.

Turning to the balance sheet information presented in Exhibit 4, the accumulated depreciation under the SFAS No. 8 methodology equals the total of depreciation expense reported in the income statements, while similar results are not obtained under either SFAS No. 52 or the RTR method. SFAS No. 52 requires the assets in the balance sheet (and related accumulated depreciation) to be translated at year-end rates, while the expense in the income statement is translated at average rates for the year. The difference becomes part of the translation adjustment in the stockholders' equity. While the RTR method uses year-end rates for both calculations (i.e., accumulated depreciation at year end and depreciation expense), the accumulated depreciation at the *beginning* of the year is translated at beginning-of-the-year rates. The difference becomes part of the reported exchange rate loss or gain when the exchange rate changes are not in proportion to the inflation rates.

The building is reported on the balance sheets at the same figure each year (excluding depreciation) under SFAS No. 8 methodology, while SFAS No. 52 and the RTR methods reflect (in this example) decreasing figures for the building. The SFAS No. 52 method figures for the building decrease to a much greater extent than under the RTR method since SFAS No. 52 uses exchange rates in effect at each balance sheet date, ignoring the fact that a large proportion of the exchange rate changes was due to inflation. In the RTR method, the building amounts decrease only because the value of the foreign currency relative to the U.S. dollar decreased more than could be attributed to the 20 percent foreign inflation versus the 10 percent U.S. inflation. Had the exchange rates varied exactly in proportion to the inflation rates, the RTR method would reflect the building at the same amount each year. The change in the building figures is reflected as part of the exchange rate loss.

A Variation of the RTR Method

We suggest translating income statement accounts by using the actual exchange rate at the end of the period. Average rates would not be appropriate since the foreign currency statements have been price level adjusted to end-of-year amounts.

It would be possible, and conceptually supportable, to translate the income statement accounts using the expected end-of-year rates that would have existed had the exchange rates varied exactly in proportion to the changes in the inflation rates of the nations involved. If such a course were followed, the exchange rate gain or loss would be calculated by using the end-of-year (rather than beginning) price-level-adjusted net asset position times the difference between the actual ending exchange rate and the expected rate. The exchange rate gain or loss under this approach would include the gain or loss incurred during the year, related to the average net assets earned or lost during the year; however, the revenues, expenses, gains, and losses reflected on the income statement would be hypothetical amounts (e.g., what the revenue for the year, in DC units, would have been had the exchange rates varied exactly in proportion to the related inflation rates). We chose to use actual rates so that the revenues, expenses, and so forth are reflected at the amounts actually earned during the period even though such an approach reports only the exchange rate loss related to the beginning net assets (or additional investments made during the year).

Conclusion

Translation methods in widespread use yield, in many instances, results which do not reliably reflect significant economic events which affect foreign subsidiaries. Purchasing power gains and losses are not reported; amounts are labeled translation gains or losses or translation adjustments which resemble real exchange rate gains or losses only by accident; real gains or losses can be ignored, yet nominal gains or losses are reported; and year-to-year data on the balance sheet and income statement cannot be reliably compared in making decisions concerning the firms involved. These deficiencies arise primarily because current translation methods ignore the effect of domestic and foreign inflation on currency exchange rates.

In this paper, we have presented a new approach to the translation problem which has much appeal. Real gains and losses are separated from nominal gains and losses, and exchange rate gains and losses are defined, thus becoming directly calculable instead of being some number needed to make a balance sheet balance. Perhaps, with greater understanding of the issues, progress can be made toward a more generally accepted solution to the foreign currency statement translation problem.

Notes

1. R. Z. Aliber and C.P. Stickney, "Accounting Measures of Foreign Exchange Exposure: The Long and Short of It," *Accounting Review* (January 1975), 44–57.
2. I. H. Giddy, "Exchange Risk: Whose View?" *Financial Management* (Summer 1977), 23–33.
3. Thomas W. Hall, "Inflation and Rates of Exchange: Support for SFAS No. 52," *Journal of Accounting, Auditing & Finance* (Summer 1983), 299–313.
4. Significant evidence suggests that not all exchange rate changes can be attributed to the change in purchasing power of the moneys involved. Interest rates, political risks, and restrictions on the flow of money are examples of other factors affecting exchange rates. Published works by M. R. Darby, "Does Purchasing Power Parity Work?" *National Bureau of Economic Research Working Paper No. 607* (December 1980) and J.A. Frenkel, "The Collapse of Purchasing Power Parities during the 1970s," *European Economic Review* (1981), 145–65, explore deviations from the purchasing power parity theory.
5. Information reported in Frederick D. S. Choi and Gerhard G. Mueller, *International Accounting* (Englewood Cliffs, N.J.: Prentice-Hall, 1984), 157–61, indicates that the current rate method and temporal method represent the most widely used translation methodologies.
6. The RTR method should not be confused with the restate-translate method. The restate-translate method does not identify exchange gains/losses, nor does it report results of operations in real terms. For a more comprehensive review of the restate-translate approach, see Paul Rosenfield, "General Price-Level Accounting and Foreign Operations," *Journal of Accountancy* (February 1971), 58–65.
7. Financial Accounting Standards Board, *Statement of Financial Accounting Standards No. 8,* "Accounting for the Translation of Foreign Currency Transactions and Foreign Currency Financial Statements" (Stamford, Conn.: FASB, 1975).
8. Financial Accounting Standards Board, *Statement of Financial Accounting Standards No. 52,* "Foreign Currency Translation" (Stamford, Conn.: FASB, 1981).
9. Jon R. Nance and Roger A. Roemmich, "Foreign Currency Translation: An Evaluation," *International Journal of Accounting* (Spring 1983), 29–48, provide an interesting review of five translation methods including the approach set forth by SFAS No. 52.
10. Additional investments or disinvestments would require a similar treatment.
11. SFAS No. 52 is not clear as to whether capital stock (and paid-in capital) accounts should be translated at current or historical rates. Our example uses the historical rate. If current rates are required, both the capital accounts and the translation adjustment would change by the same amount.

12. The expected exchange rates were calculated as follows:

$$\text{Year 1:2} \times \frac{110/100}{120/100} = 1.833$$

$$\text{Year 2:1.742} \times \frac{121/110}{144/120} = 1.597$$

$$\text{Year 3:1.517} \times \frac{133.1/121}{172.8/144} = 1.390$$

6. MANAGING MULTINATIONAL EXCHANGE RISKS

JAMES G. S. YANG

Because of inconsistencies in the accounting treatment of foreign currency transactions, multinationals should not rely upon information in their income statements when doing business abroad.

A purchase or sale transaction between a U.S. multinational corporation and a foreign country can be done on a cash basis, on credit, or a forward exchange contract with an international bank. Regardless of the method of payment used, because of the future fluctuation of exchange rates, a certain amount of risk is inherent in any purchase or sale. This risk is manageable, however, if companies understand the various methods of payment available, and how each method is affected by foreign currency fluctuations.

Measuring Multinational Exchange Risks

When merchandise is purchased from, or sold to a foreign country, the valuation is dependent upon whether the transaction is immediate or if it contains a future commitment that determines when funds are received. Also, the transaction could mean dealing with an international bank to guarantee the value of the foreign currency or the U.S. dollar. How much risk is involved when companies do business abroad depends on two key factors: the nature of the transaction, and to what extent exchange rates are expected to fluctuate.

A U.S. multinational corporation may engage in a cash sale (Table 2, Case A), a credit sale (Case B), a current sale with a forward exchange contract (Case C), or a future sale with a forward exchange contract (Case D). Let's assume that on December 1, of year 1, a U.S. multinational corporation sells merchandise to Britain for the price of BP1,000. What is the risk involved in this sale transaction when the exchange rates fluctuate as shown in Table 1? The answers depend on the terms of the transaction and to what extent the currency fluctuates. The results for each case are summarized in Table 2.

The Cash Sale: A cash sale is an exchange of inventory for U.S. dollars. The risk results from the possible decline in the value of the currency held. Another business uncertainty is the loss of the increased value of the inventory which may have been realized if the inventory had not been relinquished but sold at a later date and is called a "sale risk." In Table 1, the sales revenue is recorded and measured immediately at the spot buying rate of BP1 = US$1.98. By January 31, of year 2, the rate has increased from BP1 = US$1.98 to BP1 = US$2.13. No transaction gain or loss is recognized in the accounting income statement. The transaction has

Table 1
FOREIGN EXCHANGE RATES

	Spot Rate		Forward Rate	
BP1 =	Buying	Selling	Buying	Selling
December 1, year 1	US$1.98	US$2.00	US$1.88	US$2.10
December 31, year 1	2.16	2.18	2.06	2.28
January 31, year 2	2.13	2.15	2.03	2.25

incurred a US$150 (US$2,130 – US$1,980) loss or "sale risk." Therefore, had the merchandise been sold two months later, it would have been valued at US$2.130 instead of US$1.980. The loss, of course, is perceived as an opportunity cost and is not shown in the income statement. But when management must decide how to handle the transaction, the opportunity cost is an important factor to consider and yet accepted accounting practice fails to reveal this significant information. Essentially, it means the cash sale transaction is a loss-free event, but not a risk-free deal. According to Case A in Table 2, if the value of the U.S. dollar is expected to decline (the value of the foreign currency rises), the cash sale is not the most suitable exchange risk strategy for the U.S. company selling goods overseas.

The Credit Sale: If the BP1,000 worth of merchandise is sold on credit to a foreign country on December 1, year 1, and is received on January 31, year 2, the recording and measuring of the sales revenue takes place on December 1, year 1. However, accounts receivable will not be settled until the January 31 final due date in year 2. If the value of the British pound increases (the value of the U.S. dollar decreases), the accounts receivable will have a gain; whereas, if it were to decrease, a loss.

In Table 1, the rate increased from BP1 = US$1.98 to BP1 = US$2.13. The effect is for accounts receivable to realize a US$150 (US$2,130 – US$1,980) "transaction gain" and it is treated as current income. Why? Because by delaying the receipt of the British pound, the value actually has increased by that particular amount. But management should not be misled and believe the credit sale transaction resulted in a US$150 gain. The sales revenue was recorded and measured on December 1 of year 1. If the sale had taken place two months later, then there would have been a realization of US$2,130 sales revenue. As a consequence, what has been incurred is a US$150 (US$2,130 – US$1,980) "sale risk" loss for not having sold the merchandise at a later date. Thus, the US$150 gain from accounts receivable is offset by the US$150 loss from sales revenue, and the company experiences neither a gain nor loss. (Case B in Table 2). The credit sale transaction is a risk-free deal, but not a loss-free event. It is risk-free because the credit transaction delays the settlement until the due date; so whenever a loss occurs, there is an automatic gain offsetting the loss. The credit sale is always a promising strategy for conservative managers. However, it is not for managers who plan to increase earnings by taking advantage of fluctuations in exchange rates.

Table 2
THE SALE RISK

Case	A	B	C	D
	Cash Sale	Credit Sale	Current Sale With Forward Exchange Contract	Future Sale With Forward Exchange Contract
Sales revenue	US$1,980	US$1,980	US$1,980	US$1,880
Interest expense			(100)	
Transaction gain		150		
Total revenue	1,980	2,130	1,880	1,880
Sale risk	Loss 150	0	Loss 250	Loss 250
Sum	2,130	2,130	2,130	2,130

The case of the credit sale reveals inconsistencies in accounting practices and why accounting data should not be used for management decision-making purposes. The US$150 transaction gain from accounts receivable is recognized in the accounting income statement, but the US$150 loss of sale risk from sales revenue is not.

A Current Sale with a Forward Exchange Contract: As previously demonstrated, a credit sale may create a transaction gain or loss due to a fluctuation in the exchange rate. In order to hedge against a loss, the corporation may enter into an agreement with a bank to sell the future foreign currency at a pre-determined rate, which is referred to as a current sale with a forward exchange contract. The sale risk involved in this case constitutes the difference between the forward buying rate and the spot buying rate. If the future value of foreign currency decreases (the value of the U.S. dollar increases), the corporation will realize a gain. Or, if the value of the foreign currency increases, a loss is present.

In Table 1, the spot buying rate is BP1 = US$1.98. However, the corporation is willing to accept a lower forward buying rate of BP1 = US$1.88 by absorbing a US$0.10 initial loss. Its legal rights and future cash receipt are now fixed at the given rate of US$1.88. How is the sales revenue determined? Because the merchandise is delivered immediately, the earning process is considered complete. The sales revenue is recorded and measured at the time of the transaction when the spot buying rate of BP1 is at US$1.98.

Don't be misled into believing the US$100 initial loss is the only loss involved. The US$1,880 cash will not be received until two months have passed, when the value of the British pound has increased from BP1 = US$1.98 to BP1 = US$2.13. The corporation will suffer an opportunity cost loss totaling US$150 (US$2,130 − US$1,980).

Thus, by signing the forward exchange contract, the firm loses the US$150 profit. Again, the accounting income statement fails to reveal the loss. Therefore, the "sale risk" consists not only of the US$100 initial loss but includes the US$150 loss of the opportunity cost. Thus, the total loss is actually US$250 (Table 2, case C) because of the immediate sale of merchandise and signing of the forward exchange contract, as opposed to selling merchandise at a later date.

UNDERSTANDING MULTINATIONAL EXCHANGE RISK TERMS

BANK SELLING RATE VS. BANK BUYING RATE

Foreign currency is a form of commodity that is traded on the foreign exchange markets, and the exchange rate of each currency is subject to the law of supply and demand. International banks buy and sell foreign currencies as their major business. Thus, when a U.S. multinational corporation purchases goods from abroad, it is required to relinquish U.S. dollars to an international bank in exchange for foreign currency. At this point, the bank sells the foreign currency to the corporation at the current selling rate. Therefore, the value of the inventory and the accounts payable resulting from the purchase must be measured at the bank's selling rate.

In contrast, when a U.S. multinational sells to foreign markets the company is expected to receive foreign currencies and sell them to banks for U.S. dollars. The bank purchases the foreign currency from the corporation at the buying rate. Therefore, accounts receivable and sales revenue from a sale transaction must be measured at the bank's buying rate.

As one can expect, the bank selling rate is usually a more lofty rate than the buying rate. The difference between the two rates is the commission the bank earns from the transaction.

SPOT RATE VS. FORWARD RATE

If the purchase or the sale transaction involves cash, the measurement is at the prevailing market price of the foreign currency, or "the spot rate." However, if the terms are on credit, the valuation of accounts payable and accounts receivable cannot be determined until the final due date. What follows is that, because of constant fluctuations in foreign exchange rates, accounts payable and accounts receivable will definitely produce a transaction gain or loss.[1] In order to hedge against this kind of risk, a U.S. multinational corporation may enter into an agreement with an international bank, to purchase or sell foreign currency on a specified future date at a predetermined rate in effect when the contract was made. The bank assumes all future risks and benefits from any gains. This is recognized as a "forward exchange contract," and the rate agreed upon is referred to as the "forward rate."

A forward exchange contract is only one of the many devices available for risk management. Deferring the collection of accounts due between subsidiaries, granting intersubsidiary loans, borrowing or lending in local capital market are used by multinationals to measure risk.[2] Table 1 illustrates the relationship between spot and forward rates using the British pound. The value of the pound is expressed in terms of the U.S. dollar. Because there are bank selling rates and buying rates, there are, likewise, spot selling rates and buying rates, forward selling rates and buying rates. Under any circumstance, the selling rate is above the buying rate. However, is the forward rate always higher than the spot rate? The answer depends on whether it is a selling rate or buying rate. For a bank to sell foreign currency in advance at a predetermined rate, the rate charged must be greater than the current spot rate. The difference in the rates is the bank's financial protection fees. Corporations, in their desire to protect the value of the U.S. dollar from further decline in the future, willingly absorb a certain amount of initial loss. This is why the forward selling rate is perpetually higher than the spot selling rate.

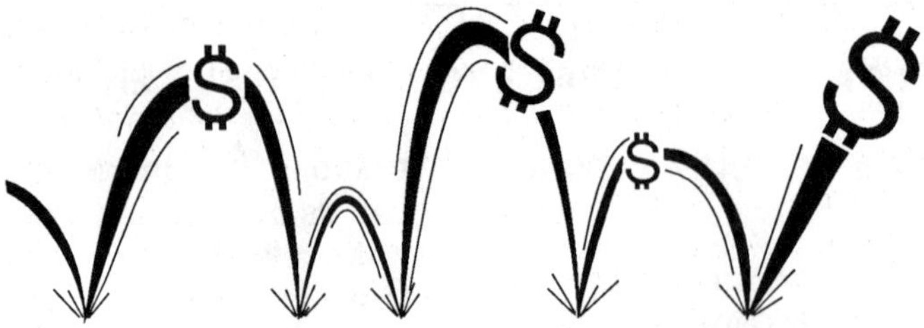

Conversely, for the bank to acquire foreign currency at a predetermined rate, it must pay a rate lower than the current spot rate. Once again the rate differences are the fees the bank assumes to compensate for future uncertainty. From the corporation's standpoint, in order to insure the value of foreign currency in the future, it must initially bear a certain amount of loss. Thus, the forward buying rate for banks is always less than the spot buying rate.

Current Sale vs. Future Sale

As we know, the sale of merchandise to a foreign country involves two currencies. Consequently, the value of the sale depends on the exchange rate. A sale is considered current if the merchandise sold abroad is delivered immediately, and if at the same time of the delivery a U.S. multinational corporation enters into a forward exchange contract with a bank. According to FAS 52, the contract is not intended to hedge an identifiable foreign currency commitment, or in short it is a current sale.

Nevertheless, in expectation of a steady decline in the value of foreign currency, management may decide to make a commitment to sell merchandise in advance, of a delivery date. At the same time, the corporation enters into a forward exchange contract with its bank. FAS 52 calls this "the contract intended to hedge an identifiable foreign currency commitment," or in short "a future sale."

Current Purchase vs. Future Purchase

In contrast to a sale, if the merchandise purchased is delivered immediately, and if a forward exchange contract is signed, it can be termed "a current purchase." However, due to a steady decline in the value of the U.S. dollar, management may make a commitment to purchase merchandise in advance of a planned delivery date and will sign a forward exchange contract. This transaction is termed "a future purchase."

The Transaction Gain or Loss vs. the Sale Risk or Purchase Risk

Credit sales create accounts receivable, and credit purchases give rise to accounts payable. The sale of future currency to a bank in advance of the transaction generates a forward exchange contract payable, and the purchase of future currency from a bank results in a forward exchange contract receivable. As the exchange rates fluctuate, these receivables and payables result in "a transaction gain or loss," and these gains or losses are shown in the current accounting income statement.

However, the accounting income statement does not recognize losses for not having sold or purchased merchandise through another medium. The loss is considered an opportunity cost, and is referred to as a "sale risk" or "purchase risk."

Another important aspect of the sale risk for companies to consider involves the detailed components of each loss from one period to another as the exchange rates fluctuate. The initial US$100 loss is actually a financial service fee for protecting the value of the foreign currency and is equal to interest expense amortized over the two month-period (US$50 a month).

By December 31, year 1, the rate has increased from BP1 = US$1.98 to BP1 = US$2.16 (Table 1). The forward exchange contract payable results in a US$180 (US$2,160 − US$1,980) loss, and the accounts receivables have realized a gain of US$180—cancelling out the loss. The gain and loss are treated as current income for the month of December, year 1, because the sale is considered a completed transaction. As a result, the December, year 1, income statement will show US$1,980 sales revenue, US$50 interest expense, US$180 loss, and US$180 gain, ending with US$1,930 net revenue. (See Table 3, column 1).

As time progresses to January 31 of year 2, the rate has decreased from BP1 = US$2.16 to BP1 = US$2.13 and a US$30 (US$2,130 − US$2,160) gain from the forward exchange contract and loss from accounts receivable results. Moreover, in January of year 2, there is the continuation of the US$50 interest expense to be amortized, without any additional sale revenue to be realized. Consequently, the January, year 2, income statement consists only of US$50 interest expense, a US$30 gain, and a US$30 loss, ending with a net loss of US$50. Table 3 shows the breakdown of the sale risk, and for managerial decisions a company should consider only the total as shown in the last column.

A Future Sale with a Forward Exchange Contract: In view of the steady decline in the value of foreign currency, a U.S. multinational corporation may commit itself to sell to a foreign country prior to the delivery date of the merchandise. At the same time, in order to protect the value of the foreign currency, the corporation enters into an agreement with a bank to sell the foreign currency at a future date and at a pre-determined rate. The sale risk involved in the case of a future sale with a forward exchange contract is the same as a current sale with a forward exchange contract. An important difference is that all sales revenue, interest expense, and the gains and losses from the forward exchange contract payable will not be rec-

Table 3

GAINS AND LOSSES FROM A CURRENT SALE WITH A FORWARD EXCHANGE CONTRACT

	December year 1	January year 2	Total
Sales revenue	US$1,980		US$1,980
Interest expense	(50)	(US$50)	(100)
Transaction gain (loss) from forward exchange contract payable	(180)	(30)	(150)
Transaction gain (loss) from accounts receivable	180	(30)	150
Net Revenue	1,930	(50)	1,880

ognized as current income until the final inventory delivery date. Because only at that time can the earning process be considered completed. Any gain or loss occurring before final delivery must be deferred to the final contract date to serve as an adjustment of sales revenue.

As in the example shown in Table 1, although the sales commitment is made on December 1 of year 1, there will be no sales revenue or accounts receivable recorded. The initial US$100 loss is deferred. The forward exchange contract payable has accrued a US$180 loss in December of year 1, and a US$30 gain in January of year 2. However, they too are deferred. When the inventory delivery date is scheduled for January 31 of year 2, there is a realization of US$2,130 sales revenue at the spot buying rate, US$100 interest expense, and US$150 net loss from the forward exchange contract payable. As a result, the net sales revenue is US$1,880 (Table 4).

It is significant that the deferred gain or loss from the forward exchange contract payable did not result in offsetting the exact amount of that gain or loss from the accounts receivable, as presented in Case C because of the absence of accounts receivable in this particular case.

The sale risk in this case is the difference between the actual cash received at the forward buying rate of BP1 = US$1.88, and the cash that would have been received had the merchandise been sold two months later at the spot buying rate of BP1 = US$2.13, and there is a US$250 loss (US$2,130 − US$1,880).

A purchase transaction also carries with it the risk of not having purchased merchandise in another manner. Assuming a U.S. multinational corporation purchased a BP1,000 worth of merchandise from Britain on December 1 of year 1, what is the purchase risk involved when the exchange rate fluctuates as shown in Table 1? The answer depends on the settlement of the transaction (see Table 5). The corporation may engage in a cash purchase (Case E), a credit purchase (Case F), a current purchase with a forward exchange contract (Case G), or a future purchase with a forward exchange contract (Case H).

The Cash Purchase. If the merchandise is purchased from a foreign country by paying immediate cash, there is an exchange of U.S. dollars for inventory. Should the value of the U.S. dollar increase (the value of the foreign currency decreases), the action of the cash purchase will produce a loss. If there is a decrease, a gain

Table 4

GAINS AND LOSSES FROM A FUTURE SALE WITH A FORWARD EXCHANGE CONTRACT

	December year 1	January year 2	Finally recognized
Sales revenue			US$2,130
Deferred interest expense	(US$100)		(100)
Deferred transaction gain (loss) from forward exchange contract payable	(180)	US$30	(150)
Net Revenue			1,880

Table 5

THE PURCHASE RISK

Case	E	F	G	H
	Cash Purchase	Credit Purchase	Current Purchase With Forward Exchange Contract	Future Purchase With Forward Exchange Contract
Inventory	US$2,000	US$2,000	US$2,000	US$2,100
Interest expense			100	
Transaction loss		150		
Total cost	2,000	2,150	2,100	2,100
Purchase risk	gain 150	0	gain 50	gain 50
Sum	2,150	2,150	2,150	2,150

results. In the example shown in Table 1, the inventory is recorded and measured immediately at the spot selling rate of BP1 = US$2.00 on December 1 of year 1. Two months later on January 31 of year 2, the value of the U.S. dollar has decreased from BP1 = US$2.00 to PB1 = US$2.15; the resultant effect is a US$150 gain (US$2,150 − US$2,000). This gain is considered a type of opportunity cost. Therefore, if the goods were purchased two months later on January 31 of year 2, it would have been necessary to declare the purchase at US$2,150. The ordinary accounting function is incapable of expressing this kind of penalty or reward for performance measurement which is realized. Thus, although a cash purchase is gain or loss-free, it is not risk-free. From the viewpoint of risk management, the indication is that, if the value of the U.S. dollar is expected to rise, a cash purchase is not the best strategy, but if a decline is anticipated, companies may be advised to pursue this strategy.

The Credit Purchase. When merchandise is purchased on credit and payable in two months, the amount of inventory and accounts payable is increased. The inventory is recorded and measured at the date of delivery when the transaction is considered complete. However, the accounts payable will not be settled until the final due date. Should the value of the foreign currency rise (the value of the U.S. dollar shall fall), the accounts payable will result in a loss. If the value of the foreign currency falls, there will be a gain. Whatever the case, inventory need not be adjusted.

As shown in Table 1, the inventory was measured immediately at the spot selling rate of BP1 = US$2.00, two months later, the rate increased from BP1 = US$2.00 to BP1 = US$2.15. Thus, the accounts payable have incurred a US$150 (US$2,150 − US$2,000) transaction loss, but the inventory is intact. The accounting treatment may mislead companies to believe that the transaction has indeed produced a US$150 loss. The truth is, if one considers what the inventory value would have been, had it been purchased two months later, this is not true. The inventory value would have increased by a US$150 gain. This gain is, of course, considered in the sense of an opportunity cost and the traditional accounting system fails to recognize it. The

US$150 loss from accounts payable cancels out the US$150 gain from inventory, and the bottom line is that neither a gain nor a loss has occurred. The accounting income statement is misleading. The current value of inventory remains equal to the liability of accounts payable on the due date. Therefore, a credit purchase is a risk-free deal, although it is not a loss-free transaction.

When managing risk, a credit purchase may be the optimum strategy for a conservative-minded individual, but not for the speculator.

A Current Purchase with a Forward Exchange Contract. A U.S. multinational corporation concerned with protecting the value of the U.S. dollar will immediately arrange with a bank to buy future foreign currency at a pre-determined rate. The purchase risk involved in the case of the current purchase with a forward exchange contract is the difference between the current forward selling rate and the spot selling rate during the two-month period. If the future value of the U.S. dollar rises (the value of foreign currency decreases), the corporation has a loss. If there is a decrease in the value, the company will have a gain.

For example in Table 1, the spot selling rate is shown as BP1 = US$2.00, but the corporation is willing to pay BP1 = US$2.10 to protect itself from currency fluctuations. The initial US$100 loss (US$2,100 – US$2,000) to the company is similar to an insurance premium that is amortized over the next two-month period at US$50 per month. The loss also may be interpreted as interest expense because payment of accounts payable is delayed.

By December 31 of year 1, when the currency rate has increased from BP1 = US$2.00 to BP1 = US$2.18, the accounts payable has incurred a US$180 loss (US$2,180 – US$2,000), and the forward exchange contract receivable has realized the same US$180 gain. Although the gain is offset by the loss, they are recorded separately in the accounting income statement of December 31 of year 1. At the January 31, year 2 due date, the rate has decreased from BP1 = US$2.18 to BP1 = US$2.15. The gain and loss situation has been reversed as shown in Table 6. There is a gain of US$30 (US$2,150 – US$2,180).

Table 6

GAINS AND LOSSES FROM A CURRENT PURCHASE WITH A FORWARD EXCHANGE CONTRACT

	December year 1	January year 2	Total
Inventory	US$2,000		US$2,000
Interest expense	50	US$ 50	100
Transaction loss (gain) from forward exchange contract receivable	(180)	30	(150)
Transaction loss (gain) from accounts payable	180	(30)	150
Total	2,050	50	2,100

As a result of these detailed measurements of gain and loss, the financial statement shows inventory valued at US$2,000, interest expense at US$100, a net gain of US$150 from the forward exchange contract receivable, and the same US$150 as a net loss from the accounts payable. The accounting statement may mislead users of financial statements to believe there is a final net loss of US$100. In fact, because no cash is disbursed for two months, the inventory account was never adjusted. If the merchandise had been purchased on January 31 of year 2, there would have been a measurement of US$2,150 instead of US$2,000. A US$150 (US$2,150 − US$2,000) gain has been accrued. Again this amount is considered the opportunity cost for not having purchased the merchandise at a later date and the accounting income statement fails to express this consequence. However, the opportunity cost is an important factor to be considered when it is time for a company to decide on the method of paying for foreign goods. As a result of the US$100 interest expense and the US$150 gain of the opportunity cost, the transaction actually results in a US$50 gain of a purchase risk. In other words, because the company had a forward exchange contract, it prevented a loss of US$50. Without the agreement, the company would have had to pay US$2,150 to the seller, instead of US$2,100 to the bank.

A Future Purchase with a Forward Exchange Contract. If the U.S. dollar declines in value, management may decide to make a commitment to purchase merchandise from a foreign country, but will arrange for the merchandise to be delivered at some future date. At the same time, the corporation is advised to protect itself against further declines in the dollar's value through an agreement to purchase foreign currency in the future at a pre-determined rate. The purchase risk involved in the case of a future purchase with a forward exchange contract is identical to the case of a current purchase with a forward exchange contract. What is noteworthy about the future purchase, however, is that the value of inventory will not be recorded and measured until the final delivery date, and all gains and losses incurred during the interim must be deferred to the final contract date to serve as an adjustment of inventory.

In Table 1, neither the amount of inventory nor the accounts payable had been established at the beginning of the transaction. The initial US$100 loss from the forward exchange contract is now deferred. By December 31 of year 1, the forward exchange contract receivable has a realized gain of US$180 to be deferred. Note, there were no accounts payable established and, therefore, no losses incurred. The US$180 gain is not offset by the same US$180 loss as it was in the previous case. By January 31 of year 2, the forward exchange contract receivable has incurred a US$30 loss, but once again, it will be deferred. Finally, when the date arises for the merchandise to be delivered, inventory will be recorded and measured at the spot selling rate of BP1 = US$2.15. When the initial US$100 deferred loss and the US$150 net deferred gain from the forward exchange contract receivable are finally realized to serve as an adjustment of inventory, the true value of inventory is only US$2,100 (US$2,150 + US$100 loss − US$150 gain). In this case, no transaction is considered complete until the merchandise delivery date. Therefore, no gain or loss is recognized during the interim. Instead, it is finally incorporated into the inventory account (Table 7).

Table 7

GAINS AND LOSSES FROM A FUTURE PURCHASE WITH A FORWARD EXCHANGE CONTRACT

	December year 1	January year 2	Finally Recognized
Inventory			US$2,150
Deferred interest expense	US$ 100		100
Deferred transaction loss (gain) from forward exchange contract receivable	(180)	US$30	(150)
Total			2,100

It's true that the value of inventory must eventually depend on the US$2,100 cash paid for the goods. However, the accounting statement fails to convey the purchase risk involved. Had there been no forward exchange contract, there would have been a required payment of US$2,150 to the seller instead of US$2,100 to the bank. Consequently, a US$50 gain has resulted from a purchase risk. Management's decision to make a purchase commitment and sign the forward exchange contract has prevented a US$50 loss.

Future purchases with forward exchange contracts differ from current purchases with forward exchange contracts because in the case of a current purchase when the gain or loss is incurred it is immediately recognized as opposed to being deferred. With a current purchase, inventory is recorded on day one, and with a future purchase it is recorded on the final date. These differences have some effect on periodical accounting income measurements, but not on the ultimate data management bases its decisions on. The consideration of a purchase risk and a sale risk provides a common ground for evaluating the alternative strategies.

How to Manage Multinational Exchange Risks

So far we have demonstrated how to measure the sale risk and the purchase risk for all forms of transactions, such as cash, credit, and a forward exchange contract. The measurement of these risks reveals the true sense of a gain or loss and enables management to compare viable alternatives. Based on this analysis, management is able to determine how the transaction should be paid for, whether merchandise should be sold or purchased, and whether the corporation should deal with a foreign country or with the domestic market.

When selling abroad should a company use cash, credit, or a forward exchange contract? Both the cash sale and the sale with a forward exchange contract always carry the "sale risk." If the future value of foreign currency increases (the value of the U.S. dollar decreases), both will incur a loss. Both will have a gain if the future value of foreign currency decreases (value of the U.S. dollar increases). On the other hand, the credit sale is always indifferent—fluctuations in exchange rates will not cause a gain or loss because the accounts receivable are always protected by the current value of a foreign currency. In other words, the credit sale is equivalent to a delayed current sale. The ultimate choice from among these three alternatives depends upon the future fluctuation of the rates.

In principle, if the value of the foreign currency rises above the spot buying rate, the credit sale is the best strategy because it is risk-free, and yet both the cash sale and the sale with a forward exchange contract definitely incur losses at this point. Conversely, if the value falls between the spot buying rate and the forward buying rate, the cash sale is most preferable because of the realization of a gain, and while the sale with a forward exchange contract takes a loss, the credit is neutral. Finally, if the value falls lower than the forward buying rate, the sale with a forward exchange contract becomes acceptable, but the cash sale is exceptional. The indication is that the cash sale, under any circumstances, is more acceptable than the sale with a forward exchange contract simply because it does not absorb an initial loss. In fact, decision making becomes easier when the "sale risk" is considered. For instance, in Table 2 the value of the British pound increases from BP1 = US$1.98 to BP1 = US$2.13. The sale risks for a cash sale are US$100 loss, for a credit sale US$10 loss, and a sale with a forward exchange contract US$250 loss. Companies should simply select the transaction that results in the minimum amount of loss at the best strategy, and in this case it is the credit sale.

When purchasing goods from abroad should a company use cash, credit or a forward exchange contract? The cash purchase and the purchase with a forward exchange contract always involve the "purchase risk." If the future value of the U.S. dollar rises (the value of the foreign currency decreases), both will incur a loss. If the value of the currency drops, there is a gain. If we reverse the situation, the credit purchase is always neutral because no gain or loss occurs. It is a risk-free transaction. The choice from among the three alternatives depends on the future fluctuation of exchange rates.

In principle, if the value of the foreign currency drops below the spot selling rate, the credit purchase offers the most preferable strategy because it is risk-free, while both the cash purchase and the purchase with a forward exchange contract definitely suffer a loss at this point. On the other hand, if the value falls between the spot selling rate and the forward selling rate, the cash sale is a better choice because it realizes a gain, and the purchase with a forward exchange contract still incurs a loss. Finally, if the value rises above the forward selling rate, the purchase with a forward exchange contract becomes acceptable, but still not as adequate as a cash purchase. The credit purchase is of course least preferable because it does not produce a gain in any circumstance.

Management can use the concept of "purchase risk" to determine strategy. For the example shown in Table 5, the value of the British pound rises from BP1 = US$2.00 to BP1 = US$2.15. The purchase risks for a cash purchase, a credit purchase, and a purchase with a forward exchange contract are US$150 gain, US$0 gain, and US$50 gain, respectively. The method with the greatest gain is the best strategy and in this case it is the cash purchase.

Deciding Between a Sale and Purchase. The decision to either sell or purchase merchandise depends on how exchange rates are expected to fluctuate. If the future value of foreign currency is expected to increase (the value of the U.S. dollar decreases), the cash seller will lose and the purchaser will win. If the U.S. dollar increases the cash seller will be the winner. A credit sale and credit purchase are always indifferent because of their risk-free nature.

Whether to sell with a forward exchange contract or purchase with a forward exchange contract, depends on how much currency fluctuates. The forward selling rate is always above the forward buying rate, and the mid-point between these two rates is where the decisions are made. If the future value of foreign currency is expected to rise above the mid-point, the purchaser is the winner and the seller is the loser. If the value declines then the seller gains.

An easier way to determine strategy is to compare the sale risk with the purchase risk. For instance, in Table 2 and Table 5, each of the sale risks are losses while all purchase risks are gains and indicates that, if the value of the U.S. dollar is expected to decrease, it is more beneficial for companies to purchase goods from a foreign country than to sell at this time. If the dollar is expected to increase, companies should sell to foreign markets.

How should a U.S. multinational corporation decide between a foreign country and the domestic market? The answer depends on the future fluctuation of the rates. If the future value of the U.S. dollar is expected to rise (the value of the foreign currency decreases), it is more advantageous to purchase from a foreign country at a later date than from the domestic market. The reasoning is because the purchasing power of the U.S. dollar has more value in the foreign market than in the domestic market. However, given the identical circumstances it is more beneficial to sell merchandise to the domestic market than to a foreign country. This is because foreign currency now holds a lower value than it previously did. Conversely, if the value of the U.S. dollar is expected to decrease in the future, it is more profitable to purchase merchandise from the domestic market and sell it to a foreign country at a later date.

The forward exchange contract is a management device to stabilize the values of the U.S. dollar and a foreign currency. Theoretically, the forward rates must be equivalent to the domestic prices. Therefore, the forward exchange contract is effectively neutralized between a foreign country and the domestic market. In other words, the scheme of a forward exchange contract makes it possible to purchase or sell merchandise anywhere in the world, domestic or foreign, without incurring different levels of concern over the risk involved in the transaction. For a conservative-minded individual, the forward exchange contract is the optimum strategy in choosing between the domestic market and a foreign country. It is a risk-free device for managing foreign exchange risks.

Predicting Foreign Currency Fluctuations

Simply stated, risk management of multinational operations involves deciding between the purchase and the sale, between a foreign country and the domestic market, between the current transaction and the future commitment, and whether it will be a cash deal, credit arrangement, or a forward exchange contract. The best strategy results from management's ability to predict the direction and the extent of currency fluctuations in foreign exchange rates.

Notes

1. Statement of Financial Accounting Standards No. 32, "Foreign Currency Translation," FASB, 1982.
2. Bruce Sangstet, "International Funds Management," *Financial Executive,* Dec. 1977, p. 30.

III MANAGERIAL ACCOUNTING: GLOBAL PRACTICES

7. THE EFFECTS OF FOREIGN OPERATIONS ON DOMESTIC AUDITOR SELECTION

JOHN W. EICHENSEHER

John W. Eichenseher, Ph.D., is Assistant Professor of Accounting at the University of Wisconsin-Madison.

This article considers the effects of foreign operations on the domestic auditor selections of U.S. corporations. Brief arguments are presented supporting the notion of multinational scale economies available to a small number of large U.S. CPA firms. Empirical tests, utilizing FASB Statement No. 14 geographical disclosures of New York Stock Exchange corporations, yield support for these arguments. Sample corporations with substantial foreign assets exhibit a higher propensity to select an identifiable subset of Big 8 auditors than their primarily domestic counterparts. These results, which appear largely independent of client industry and the specific location of foreign assets, are important for worldwide audit firm structures. The final section of the article discusses the implications of the findings for public and private policy formulations.

Recent accounting research has focused on the effects of various corporate attributes on external auditor selections. Typically this research delineates two broad classes of CPA firms, large national auditors (the Big 8) and all other CPA firms. Within this context, empirical evidence has been presented to support the effects of corporate size [1] and capital structure [2] on choices between these two broad auditor classes. Analytical arguments have also been presented to support the notion of differences in perceived independence between these groups of CPA firms [3]. A complementary approach to this line of inquiry has been the attempt to determine the effects of client industry on auditor selections, motivated by either cost [4] or demand arguments [5]. In general, empirical evidence from this research points to substantial effects for client industry on the auditor selection process.

This article explicitly considers the effects of one additional corporate dimension—the geographical location of operations—on auditor selections. In particular, the following questions are considered:

1. Does the existence of material non-U.S. operations affect a corporation's choice of auditor class (Big 8 versus other CPA firms)?
2. Does the existence of material non-U.S. operations affect a corporation's choice of auditors within the class of Big 8 CPA firms?

Reprinted with permission from: *Journal of Accounting, Auditing, and Finance* 8.3 (Spring 1985).

3. Does the actual location of non-U.S. operations (e.g., Europe, South America, Asia) affect a corporation's choice of auditors within the class of CPA firms with an apparent advantage in auditing foreign operations?

These questions are addressed empirically by examining the auditor selections of large publicly held U.S. corporations.

The Economics of External Audits

Prior Research

As with any free[1] market, buyer/seller alignments in the U.S. market for audit services result from the interaction of conditions of supply and demand. Any factors that systematically affect either supply or demand conditions can likewise alter observed corporation/CPA-firm alignments, giving rise to differential market structures. Three corporate attributes have been suggested in prior research as affecting either CPA-firm cost differentials or corporate preferences across CPA firms.

First, company size can affect both demand and supply conditions. Besides the obvious argument that small CPA firms are simply unable to bring enough resources to bear to audit large clients, one can argue that audit technologies are such that larger CPA firms have a cost advantage in auditing larger corporations. If audits of larger companies involve relatively higher percentages of auditor hours devoted to more routinized tasks, smaller partner-to-staff ratios in larger CPA firms may induce cost advantages to these firms in auditing larger corporations. The result of this condition, higher propensities to choose large auditors for larger corporations, also flows from a demand-based argument which asserts lower levels of perceived independence as the importance of any given client to its external auditor exceeds some threshold amount. At the extreme, one would expect little audit benefit from an external auditor who was perceived to rely solely on one client for professional revenues. This size effect, whatever its underlying source may be, has been amply demonstrated empirically. As of 1981, non-Big 8 CPA firms audited 50 percent of publicly held companies with annual sales less than $100 million, but only 8 percent of such companies with sales over $100 billion [6].

Second, a corporation's capital structure may alter conditions of supply and demand in the audit market. From a cost point of view, high levels of capital market activity involve the corporation in a realm of complex, regulated financial disclosures. In dealing with this environment, the CPA firm must develop specialized knowledge which gives rise to scale opportunities. Empirical evidence to this effect is provided by the observation that publicly held U.S. corporations are more likely to employ Big 8 auditors than their privately held counterparts, even when corporate size is held constant [7]. From a demand point of view, one can appeal to agency theory to deduce the same observable market behavior. The magnitude of agency costs should increase as the outside (nonmanagerial) interests in the firm increase [8]. If larger CPA firms are more effective monitors of managerial actions because of their enhanced independence [3], publicly held corporations or, more generally, companies with higher debt and nonmanagerial equity levels, should exhibit greater preferences for large CPA firms.

Third, audit market conditions of supply can be affected by corporations' activities in different product or service markets. Similar to scale advantages accruing to the CPA firm highly active in servicing publicly held clients, scale opportunities can arise in the acquisition of industry-specific knowledge germane to the audit process. Eichenseher and Danos [2] point to higher auditor concentration levels in regulated client industries (e.g., public utilities) as support for such scale effects. Scale effects of this nature differ somewhat from the effects related to client size and capital structure. While large size and diverse ownership appear common enough in the U.S. economy to support minimally efficient scale operations on the part of many CPA firms, industry-specific scale opportunities frequently lack a broad enough base of application to support efficient exploitation by all large CPA firms. This implies that industry effects in the audit market may serve to differentiate not only between large and small CPA firms but also among large CPA firms.

Geographical Effects

This article adds a fourth corporate attribute, geographical location, to the set of attributes affecting audit market structure. The effect of client geographical dispersion on CPA-firm costs has previously been suggested by Benston [9], who argues for scale economies in servicing dispersed clients. In auditing a multiple-location client, a CPA firm can use three approaches:

1. It can temporarily transport personnel from one office to the client's various locations;
2. It can enter into contracts with other CPA firms to audit the client's outlying operations; or
3. It can operate offices in each of the clients' localities and utilize its own local personnel throughout the audit.

These alternative approaches involve different cost structures. The first alternative can give rise to substantial variable travel costs. The second alternative involves variable subcontracting costs. And the third alternative, while presumably reducing variable costs, gives rise to additional fixed costs in operating more offices.

Clearly all three approaches to the auditing of multiple-location clients are currently pursued in the United States, but this does not imply that all are equally effective from a cost point of view. It can be argued that trends in the U.S. audit market over the past several decades, such as mergers of local and regional firms with national firms, provide evidence of the superiority of the multiple-office approach. In short, scale economies in the form of lower variable transportation costs achieved with the incurring of additional fixed operating costs appear quite plausible in the domestic U.S. audit market.

When one moves to the domain of multinational corporate operations, the above arguments for scale effects become even stronger. Variable costs increase substantially when personnel must be transported around the world to audit client locations.

Subcontracting costs, particularly costs of quality control, also increase substantially when non-U.S. CPA firms are employed to audit client operations [10]. And additional fixed costs from operating new offices outside the United States also presumably exceed amounts required to operate new domestic offices. Since all potential cost components are increased in the multinational environment [11:181], scale effects become more pronounced. Variable cost advantages accruing to the multinational CPA firm exceed those accruing to the national firm in the domestic environment.

Indirect evidence of the importance of multinational scale economies in auditing is provided by recent trends in international mergers and growth by large U.S. CPA firms [12]. It remains unclear, however, which CPA firms are or can be exploiting such scale opportunities. In general, one would expect large domestically diversified U.S. CPA firms to be more likely to attempt to exploit multinational geographical scale economies than their smaller U.S. counterparts.

> H_1: *The existence of foreign operations makes a U.S. corporation more likely to select a Big 8 CPA firm as its domestic auditor.*

U.S. corporations with multinational operations are presumably more likely to have geographically dispersed operations in this country. In short, multinational cost advantages can be more effectively exploited if they are not offset by domestic geographical cost disadvantages.

If all large U.S. CPA firms exploit these opportunities, their effects on cost differentials and, therefore, auditor selections within the Big 8 may be negligible. On the other hand, cost structures resulting from multinational operations may be such that only a subset of these firms can achieve minimally efficient scale through extensive foreign office development. Multinational geographical scale effects may be similar to domestic industry scale effects in forcing differentiation among CPA firms within the class of large U.S. CPA firms.

> H_2: *Given a Big 8 auditor selection, propensities to choose specific Big 8 CPA firms as auditors are affected by the extent of a corporation's non-U.S. operations.*

More completely analogous to domestic industry scale effects, multinational scale opportunities may be mutually independent. Different large U.S. CPA firms may develop foreign offices in different locations.

> H_3: *Given a Big 8 auditor selection and non-U.S. operations, propensities to choose specific Big 8 CPA firms as auditors are affected by the location of a corporation's non-U.S. operations.*

The Sample

To test the above hypotheses, attributes and auditor identities for all U.S.-based corporations with securities listed on the New York Stock Exchange (NYSE) as of

1981 were sought. Thus, only relatively large, publicly held corporations were considered. These corporations were identified from listings in the seventh edition of *Who Audits America* [6]. Auditors, size, industry, and the extent of foreign operations for each corporation were obtained by inspecting 1981 annual reports on file at the University of Illinois. Foreign operations were measured as the percentage of total assets reported for non-U.S. operations in FASB Statement No. 14 [13] mandated segmental disclosures. Assets were chosen as a basis of measurement because asset locations are typically more relevant than sales locations in the allocation of audit resources. Since percentages of foreign assets and sales are highly correlated across corporations, it is unlikely that the utilization of sales-based measures of foreign operations would yield test results significantly different from those reported below.

FASB Statement No. 14 dictates an arbitrary cutoff of 10 percent in the disclosure of foreign operations. Thus, one cannot distinguish between a corporation with no foreign operations and one with limited foreign operations by reference to disclosures in annual reports. Therefore, only corporations with foreign asset levels in excess of 10 percent are considered as having foreign operations in this research. Substantial problems also arise in identifying the location of foreign assets from FASB Statement No. 14 mandated disclosures. Vast differences in the fineness of geographical partitioning are observed. While such differences undoubtedly arise partially from differences in corporate organization and geographical diffuseness, clearly different policies are followed by corporations in reporting foreign operations. These policy differences weaken empirical tests aimed at detecting CPA-firm differences across geographical areas and may induce biases in statistical tests if they are not randomly distributed across auditors. Results of tests for such biasing effects are provided below.

Full information was obtained for 1,424 sample corporations, 98.3 percent of the NYSE population identified in *Who Audits America* [6].

For purposes of identifying the location of a corporation's foreign assets, three broad geographical areas were defined—Europe/Africa, Western Hemisphere, and Asia/Pacific. This segmentation is typical of partitioning followed in FASB Statement No. 14 disclosures although, as indicated above, wide variations are frequently observed. Table 2 provides the distribution of sample corporations across these areas, where dominant foreign area is defined as the area with more than 50 percent of total foreign assets.

Inspection of Tables 1 and 2 yields several insights into the foreign operations of large U.S. corporations. Corporations with primarily manufacturing operations (SIC codes 200 through 399) appear much more likely to have significant foreign holdings. Seventy-five percent of NYSE companies with at least 10 percent foreign assets are classified as manufacturers, while only 53 percent of all NYSE companies are so classified. These manufacturing corporations also appear much more likely to have a dominant foreign domicile in Europe. Such differences across industry categories underscore the need to control for the industry variable in subsequent tests for the effects of foreign operations on auditor selections. These operations are clearly not randomly distributed across all industries. If industry itself is a significant factor in auditor selections, failure to control for this variable can significantly bias test results.

Table 1

SAMPLE POPULATION

Industry Category	1-Digit SIC Codes	Foreign Assets Less Than 10%		Foreign Assets Greater Than 10%		Total	
		N	%	N	%	N	%
Agriculture, mining construction	0,1	32	51.6	30	48.4	62	100.0
Manufacturing	2,3	370	49.1	384	50.9	754	100.0
Transportation, utilities	4	210	92.1	18	7.9	228	100.0
Trade	5	123	89.8	14	10.2	137	100.0
Financial services, real estate	6	135	73.8	48	26.2	183	100.0
Other services	7,8	43	71.7	17	28.3	60	100.0
Overall		913	64.1	511	35.9	1,424	100.0

Table 2

DOMINANT FOREIGN LOCATIONS

Industry Category	Europe/ Africa		Western Hemisphere		Asia/ Pacific		Undeter-minable		Total	
	N	%	N	%	N	%	N	%	N	%
Agriculture, mining construction	7	23.3	5	16.7	3	10.0	15	50.0	30	100.0
Manufacturing	186	48.4	43	11.2	7	1.8	148	38.6	384	100.0
Transportation, utilities	1	5.6	7	38.9	0	0.0	10	55.5	18	100.0
Trade	3	21.4	7	50.0	2	14.3	2	14.3	14	100.0
Financial services, real estate	9	18.7	2	4.2	1	2.1	36	75.0	48	100.0
Other services	5	29.4	2	11.8	0	0.0	10	58.8	17	100.0
Overall	211	41.3	66	12.9	13	2.6	221	43.2	511	100.0

Test Results

H_1: The existence of foreign operations makes a U.S. corporation more likely to select a Big 8 CPA firm as its domestic auditor.

Underlying this hypothesis is the expectation of scale effects primarily exploited by large CPA firms (the Big 8) in the auditing of clients with multinational operations. Table 3 presents data germane to this hypothesis.

For both manufacturing and nonmanufacturing corporations the propensity to employ non-Big 8 auditors declines when the corporation has at least 10 percent of its assets outside of the United States. This decline appears most significant in manufacturing where the hypothesis that non-Big 8 client percentages are unaffected by such foreign holdings can be rejected at the 98 percent confidence level.

H_2: Given a Big 8 auditor selection, propensities to choose specific Big 8 CPA firms as auditors are affected by the extent of a corporation's non-U.S. operations.

Table 3
AUDITOR SELECTIONS AND FOREIGN OPERATIONS—THE BIG 8 VS. ALL OTHERS

	Big 8		Others		Total		Chi-Square
	N	%	N	%	N	%	Statistic[a]
Manufacturing clients							
Less than 10% foreign assets	343	92.7	27	7.3	370	100.0	
Greater than 10% foreign assets	371	96.6	13	3.4	384	100.0	5.74*
All other clients							
Less than 10% foreign assets	509	93.7	34	6.3	543	100.0	
Greater than 10% foreign assets	123	96.9	4	3.1	127	100.0	1.86
All clients							
Less than 10% foreign assets	852	93.3	61	6.7	913	100.0	
Greater than 10% foreign assets	494	96.7	17	3.3	511	100.0	7.12*

[a]These statistics in this and all subsequent tables provide tests of the hypothesis of no difference in auditor selection propensities across corporate subpopulations.
*Indicates that the no-difference hypothesis can be rejected with at least 95% confidence.

This hypothesis expands upon H_1, asserting that multinational scale opportunities can be exploited by only a subset of Big 8 CPA firms.

Once again significant differences appear in auditor selections when manufacturing corporations are partitioned around 10 percent foreign asset levels. In short, Tables 3 and 4 lend support to a theory of multinational scale effects in auditing, where such effects serve to differentiate not only between Big 8 and all other U.S. CPA firms, but also among Big 8 firms. Nonetheless, two opportunities for a finer partitioning of the sample domain appear worthy of pursuit.

First, Tables 3 and 4 consider only one class of foreign holdings—asset levels above 10 percent. One might logically expect the magnitude of multinational scale effects to increase with the magnitude of foreign operations. To test this hypothesis, manufacturing corporations with at least 10 percent foreign assets were partitioned

Table 4

AUDITOR SELECTIONS AND FOREIGN OPERATIONS—WITHIN BIG 8 DIFFERENCES PERCENTAGE OF CLIENTS IN EACH ROW[a]

	AA	AY	CL	EW	DHS	PMM	PW	TR	Total	Chi-Square Statistic
Manufacturing clients										
Less than 10% foreign assets	19.8	8.4	12.0	19.0	7.6	8.7	12.5	12.0	100.0	
Greater than 10% foreign assets	16.2	10.8	14.5	11.6	12.1	12.7	18.9	3.2	100.0	38.64*
All other clients										
Less than 10% foreign assets	24.8	6.3	11.8	9.2	12.4	15.3	10.8	9.4	100.0	
Greater than 10% foreign assets	21.1	10.6	12.2	7.3	8.1	19.5	14.7	6.5	100.0	8.36
All clients										
Less than 10% foreign assets	22.8	7.2	11.9	13.1	10.4	12.7	11.5	10.4	100.0	
Greater than 10% foreign assets	17.4	10.7	14.0	10.5	11.1	14.4	17.8	4.1	100.0	37.53*

[a]In this and subsequent tables, AA = Arthur Andersen; AY = Arthur Young; CL = Coopers and Lybrand; EW = Ernst and Whinney; DHS = Deloitte, Haskins and Sells; PMM = Peat, Marwick, Mitchell; PW = Price Waterhouse; and TR = Touche Ross.

*Indicates that the no-difference hypothesis can be rejected with at least 95% confidence.

around a 25 percent foreign asset level. No significant difference was found in the auditor selections of these two groups of multinational manufacturing corporations. In short, foreign asset holdings of the lower level (10-24%) seem to fully induce alterations in auditor selections associated with any multinational scale effects in auditing.

Second, the confounding effects of corporate size on auditor selections can be more fully pursued. While the sampling strategy eliminates from consideration small U.S. corporations, even within the realm of NYSE corporations size per se may be a significant factor in selections among Big 8 auditors. If the likelihood of foreign holdings is not independent of company size, observed relationships between foreign assets and auditor selections may merely reflect size effects in the auditor selection process. Or, alternatively observed size effects may primarily reflect multinational scale opportunities. To sort out confounding effects of size and foreign asset holdings, sample manufacturing corporations were placed in three size categories of total assets: (1) less than $200 million; (2) between $200 million and $750 million; and (3) over $750 million. Table 5 indicates Big 8 client percentages for foreign and domestic corporations within each of these categories.

These results clearly support two assertions. Corporate size appears highly correlated with foreign asset holdings, and size also appears to affect auditor selections. The hypothesis of no size effects in the auditor selections of domestic corporations can be rejected at the 97 percent confidence level. Despite these conditions, foreign holdings still appear significant per se in auditor selections. Particularly in

Table 5

AUDITOR SELECTIONS AND FOREIGN OPERATIONS—CLIENT SIZE CATEGORIES—WITHIN BIG 8 DIFFERENCES—MANUFACTURING CLIENTS ONLY

PERCENTAGE OF CLIENTS IN EACH ROW

Total Assets	Foreign Asset %	N	AA	AY	CL	EW	DHS	PMM	PW	TR	Total	Chi-Square Statistic
Less than $200 million	Less than 10	157	19.9	5.8	16.0	17.9	7.1	11.5	7.7	14.1	100.0	
	Greater than 10	75	16.0	12.0	20.0	14.7	5.3	9.4	17.3	5.3	100.0	11.98
$200-$750 million	Less than 10	116	21.6	11.2	11.2	14.7	10.3	6.9	13.8	10.3	100.0	
	than 10	111	14.3	9.8	13.4	14.3	11.6	14.3	20.5	1.8	100.0	13.35
Greater than $750 million	Less than 10	70	17.1	8.6	4.3	28.6	4.3	5.7	21.4	10.0	100.0	
	Greater than 10	185	17.2	11.3	13.4	8.6	15.1	12.9	18.3	3.2	100.0	30.85*

*Indicates that no-difference hypothesis can be rejected with at least 95% confidence.

the context of the largest size category (total assets greater than $750 million), auditor selections seem significantly affected by the existence of foreign holdings.

> H_3: *Given a Big 8 auditor selection and non-U.S. operations, propensities to choose specific Big 8 CPA firms as auditors are affected by the location of a corporation's non-U.S. operations.*

Underlying this hypothesis is the expectation that multinational scale effects may be location-specific. Different CPA firms may exploit scale advantages in different areas of the world. Once again, chi-square tests for differences in auditor selections conditioned on differences in the location of foreign assets can be employed. A fundamental problem, however, arises in the identification of dominant foreign areas from publicly available (FASB Statement No. 14) information. As indicated in Table 2, for many sample clients with foreign assets (43%), such identification is impossible. The ability to perform unbiased tests related to foreign locational effects is, therefore, conditioned on an assumption of random unidentifiability across CPA firms. A check for the reasonableness of this assumption was obtained by testing the following model:

$$n_i = f\,(A_i,\ CPA_i)$$

where n_i = the number of identifiable foreign segments reported by corporation i in its 1981 annual report

A_i = the ratio of foreign assets to total assets for corporation i

CPA_i = corporation i's external auditor

ANOVA results for this model support the notion of random unidentifiability across CPA firms. While A_i levels explain a significant amount of variance in n_i (17%), the incremental explanatory power of the CPA variable is negligible (F-state = 1.15, $\alpha > .20$).

Thus, tests for locational effects were performed given the available information and consideration of two possible dominant foreign areas—Europe/Africa and the Western Hemisphere—as shown in Table 6.

While these tests are much less powerful than those in Table 4 due to smaller sample sizes, results provide little support for H_3. The existence of significant foreign holdings does appear to significantly alter auditor selections (Table 4), but additional modifications based on the general location of foreign assets appear insignificant in this sample of NYSE clients.

The following section summarizes empirical findings and considers their implications for both policy formulations and the development of a comprehensive theory of audit market structure.

Summary and Implications

Taken in total, the empirical results presented in this article provide strong support for a relationship between foreign asset positions and domestic auditor selections in

Table 6
AUDITOR SELECTIONS AND FOREIGN OPERATIONS—DOMINANT AREA STRATIFICATION —WITHIN BIG 8 DIFFERENCES—
PERCENTAGE OF CLIENTS IN EACH ROW

Dominant Foreign Area	N	AA	AY	CL	EW	DHS	PMM	PW	TR	Total	Chi-Square Statistic
Manufacturing clients											
Europe/Africa	180	16.1	10.6	15.0	9.4	11.7	12.2	21.1	3.9	100.0	
Western Hemisphere	42	9.5	16.7	19.1	14.3	19.0	9.5	9.5	2.4	100.0	9.06
All other clients											
Europe/Africa	25	28.0	16.0	8.0	4.0	8.0	4.0	24.0	8.0	100.0	
Western Hemisphere	19	21.1	10.5	21.1	5.3	10.5	26.2	0.0	5.3	100.0	10.54
All clients											
Europe/Africa	205	17.6	11.2	14.1	8.8	11.2	11.2	21.5	4.4	100.0	
Western Hemisphere	61	13.1	14.7	19.7	11.5	16.4	14.7	6.6	3.3	100.0	9.78

the United States. It appears that such positions both increase the propensity to select a Big 8 auditor and confer advantages upon a subset of Big 8 firms in the auditor selection process. In particular, the market positions of two CPA firms (Peat Marwick Mitchell and Price Waterhouse) appear more positively affected by foreign holdings by domestic corporations, although other CPA firms also appear to reap foreign advantages in certain industries or locations.

Such results are consistent with a theory of audit market structure which posits substantial scale opportunities available in the auditing of geographically dispersed corporations. To exploit these opportunities, a CPA firm must develop a multilocation structure. In the context of multinational clients, this implies the development of foreign offices integral to the firm. The inability to find support for hypothesis H_3 in the current research indicates a probable efficiency to worldwide structure for the CPA firm. Empirical support for hypothesis H_2, on the other hand, suggests that the magnitude of foreign operations required to exploit multinational scale economies is such that less than eight CPA firms currently exploit these opportunities.

These results bear implications for policy formulations within the CPA firm. If U.S. investment abroad continues to grow, as it has over the past several decades, the ability of the U.S. CPA firm to compete for large clients will increasingly become a function of the firm's development of offices outside the United States. It appears, however, that only a small number of CPA firms can achieve a minimally efficient scale of operations in many specific foreign areas. If worldwide firm structures are more efficient, these conditions call into question the long-run viability of the Big 8 in the U.S. and world audit markets. Two factors appear crucial in determining the long-run equilibrium number of large CPA firms: (1) conditions in organizational technology which determine the costs of monitoring and controlling diverse worldwide professional organizations [12]; and (2) the extent to which the auditing of multinational clients in their various locations can be combined with domestic audit practices in these locations. The ability to fully integrate the servicing of purely domestic and multinational clients allows for smaller efficient scales and, thus, increases the number of firms that can effectively compete in the worldwide audit market.

This naturally leads to consideration of the role of national barriers to entry in auditing. Public policy formulators at the national level affect the costs of integrating domestic and multinational audit practices by their decisions on licensing and standards. Unique licensing requirements and auditing standards make it more costly for large multinational CPA firms to enter domestic audit markets. Current barriers to entry into foreign markets may well explain the results of this research (i.e., the apparent ability of fewer than eight U.S. CPA firms to fully exploit multinational scale economies).

Finally, this research points to the need to explicitly consider the role of multinational scale effects in developing comprehensive theories of audit market structure. Past research has focused on the effects of other corporate attributes on the auditor selection process. Since many of these attributes are not independent of foreign asset levels, the results of past research may be misleading in drawing inferences about differentiated demand or cost structures in the audit market.

References

1. N. Dopuch and D. Simunic, "The Nature of Competition in the Auditing Profession," in J. Buckley and J. Weston, eds., *Regulation and the Accounting Profession* (Los Angeles: Lifetime Learning, 1980), pp. 77–94.
2. J. Eichenseher and D. Shields, "Corporate Monitoring Decisions and Capital Structure," Unpublished Manuscript, Rice University, 1983.
3. L. DeAngelo, "Auditor Size and Audit Quality," *Journal of Accounting and Economics,* Dec. 1981, pp. 183–200.
4. J. Eichenseher and P. Danos, "The Analysis of Industry-Specific Auditor Concentration: Towards an Explanatory Model," *The Accounting Review,* July 1981, pp. 479–492.
5. Z. Palmrose, "Quality-Differentiated Audit Services and Size-Related Surrogates for Quality," Unpublished Manuscript, University of California-Berkeley, 1982.
6. S. Harris, *Who Audits America* (New York: Data Financial Press, 1981).
7. P. Danos and J. Eichenseher, "Market Conditions and Temporal Adjustments Affecting Auditor/Client Alignments," Unpublished Manuscript, University of Michigan, 1982.
8. M. Jensen and W. Meckling, "Theory of the Firm: Managerial Behavior, Agency Costs and Ownership Structure," *Journal of Financial Economics,* Oct. 1976, pp. 305–360.

9. G. Benston, "The Market for Public Accounting Services: Demand, Supply and Regulation," *The Accounting Journal,* Winter 1979–1980, pp. 2–46.
10. M. Tipgos, "Potential Liabilities in International Accounting Practice," *Journal of Accountancy*, April 1981, pp. 24–30.
11. D. Simunic, "The Pricing of Audit Services: Theory and Evidence," *Journal of Accounting Research,* Spring 1980, pp. 161–190.
12. W. Luck and H. Holzer, "Multinationale Wirtschaftsprufungs-gesellschaften," *Der Betrieb,* Oct. 1981, pp. 1989–1993 and 2037–2041.
13. Statement of Financial Accounting Standards No. 14, "Financial Reporting for Segments of a Business Enterprise" (Stamford, Conn.: FASB, 1976).

Notes

1. The term "free" is used here to indicate freedom of choice for buyers across sellers. Free, in this context, is not synonymous with unregulated. Clearly the U.S. audit market is regulated, but buyer choice across a wide range of suppliers remains free.

8. WHY INTERNATIONAL COST ACCOUNTING PRACTICES SHOULD BE HARMONIZED

MAUREEN H. BERRY

Maureen H. Berry is assistant professor of accountancy at the University of Illinois at Urbana-Champaign. *Research assistance was provided by contributions from the Investors in Business Education, College of Commerce and Business Administration, University of Illinois, for which the author expresses her appreciation. The author thanks officials of the U.K. and West German governments, as well as several West German aerospace firms, for their kind cooperation. She is also indebted to certain colleagues, notably Professors Peter Holzer and Hanns-Martin Schoenfeld, for their valuable assistance. This article summarizes two papers presented at the European Accounting Association's conventions held in Cologne, West Germany, in March 1979 and in Amsterdam in March 1980.*

Countries involved in coproduction ventures need a mutually agreeable method of resolving their cost-sharing problems.

International coproduction programs, which are increasing in both size and scope, have had a significant impact on United States procurement and military equipment foreign sales policy. Nationally sponsored firms in different countries are working together on civil and defense programs, with their governments both assisting the production financing and possibly purchasing the end product. The fact that firms operate under different public contract costing arrangements presents problems in measuring the costs and benefits associated with each coproducer's efforts.

Two major European Participating Governments (EPG) are the United Kingdom and West Germany. Their public costing procedures can be contrasted with those of the United States to show the international differences that exist in philosophy and practice with respect to setting "fair" prices for publicly needed goods and services. What is called for is the harmonizing of international cost accounting practices.

The Evolution of Coproduction

In the past decade, U.S. domination of the civilian and defense aerospace industry has been challenged by the steady growth of international coproduction ventures, particularly in Europe. Coproduction refers to investment and production projects, other than agreements involving production under license, carried out cooperatively by firms in two or more countries under the sponsorship of their respective governments. Such projects frequently originate in Memoranda of Understanding (MOUs) entered into on a government-to-government basis, each government nominating national firms which form industrial consortia. Because of their obvious benefits of economies of scale, sharing of research and development costs, and technology transfer, coproduction ventures today represent economic necessity as well as political strategy.

In the mid-1970s, the impact of these structural changes in the European aerospace industry reached across the Atlantic when the United States was drawn into collaborative efforts in the F–16 jet fighter program. Under an MOU signed in June 1975 by the United States, Belgium, the Netherlands, Denmark, and Norway, European contractors were awarded production and assembly contracts for the equivalent of 10% of the original 650 aircraft ordered by the U.S. government, 40% of the aircraft ordered by European governments, and 15% of any sales to third countries.[1] The U.S. Congress recognized the political reality that European production was indispensable for European procurement when it passed "two-way street" legislation in 1976 identifying coproduction as the preferred method of increasing inter-Allied purchases.[2] By that time, the U.S. volume of military equipment sales to foreign buyers had reached $8.7 billion, about half of this amount involving sales to NATO countries.[3]

The F–16 program involved more than 4,000 suppliers in the United States and Europe.[4] There were, however, delays in issuing contracts and subcontracts to the European Participating Government firms:

> *"Before these contracts could be awarded, a number of basic differences in EPG and U.S. contractual and business practices had to be resolved. These differences included patent rights, royalties, customs and duties, governing law, cost and pricing requirements, cost accounting standards, progress payments, termination, default, quality control standards, and contract audits. Negotiations of these issues contributed to a delay in awarded EPG subcontracts."*[5]

The MOUs called for all aircraft to be built for the prime contractor, General Dynamics, which would in turn transfer them to the U.S. government. The U.S. government then would sell aircraft to the purchasing EPGs on a government-to-government basis.[6] Because of the contractual relationships established between the EPG firms and the U.S. government prime contractor, the Cost Accounting Standards Board (CASB) undertook a review of various issues concerning the application of its standards, rules and regulations to foreign concerns. It concluded that:

> *". . . the cost accounting practices which foreign concerns follow vary substantially from country to country and contractor to contractor. The review also indicates that because of the requirements of individual countries, the application of some Standards may cause significant administrative problems."*[7]

As a result, the CASB exempted foreign concerns and foreign governments from most of its requirements effective November 14, 1978.[8]

In the case of the Tornado program, coproduced by Italy, the United Kingdom and West Germany, the problem of public contracting differences were dealt with by a special legal and contract subcommittee of the venture's independent management organization—Panavia Aircraft GmbH. The need for this type of organization was impressed on the United Kingdom as a result of its experiences with France in attempting to determine the development and production costs on the Concorde program. Officials from both countries "found it impossible to make any meaningful comparison of development or production costs in the two countries or even, in fact, to select an agreed basis of comparison from a number of possibilities."[9] Because of the increase in the number of international civil and defense collaborative agreements, the U.K.'s Committee of Public Accounts felt that "it should be possible for collaborating governments to identify the major areas in which cost-sharing problems will arise and to devise, in advance, mutually acceptable formulae for resolving those differences."[10] A more efficient approach would be to establish some generally accepted cost accounting practices for use in publicly supported programs. Generally speaking, the United Kingdom, West Germany and the United States follow the format shown in Table 1 in preparing a cost proposal.

Basic Criteria for Reimbursable Costs

In all three countries, costs claimed under government contracts have to meet certain basic criteria such as reasonableness of amount, allocability to government work, and compliance with tax regulations and/or generally accepted accounting principles (GAAP). For example, distinctions have to be made between revenue and capital expenditures, and costs have to be recognized in appropriate (benefitting) accounting

Table 1
PREPARING A COST PROPOSAL

Direct materials		
Material overhead		
Dir. engineering labor		
Engineering overhead		
Dir. manufacturing labor		
Manufacturing overhead		
Other direct costs	= Factory cost	
	Design & development (IR&D)	
	Selling & marketing	
	General and administrative	
	Expenses (G&A)	= Total cost input
		Profit
		Proposed contract price

periods. While there is general agreement as to what constitutes allocability and meeting GAAP, each nation has different views or tax regulations affecting the concept of reasonableness.

The United States[11] takes the view that "a cost is reasonable if, in its nature or amount, it does not exceed that which would be incurred by an ordinarily prudent person in the conduct of competitive business."[12] West Germany, on the other hand, applies "the principle of efficiency," and the U.K. assesses reasonableness by defining what is unreasonable.

West Germany's Regulations

Two sets of basic contracting regulations exist in West Germany: the VOL (Verdingungsordnung fuer Leistungen) for supplies and the VOB (Verdingungsordnung fuer Bauleistungen) for construction. These regulations apply to all public contracts issued at all levels of government. The Federal Ministry of Economic Affairs has jurisdiction over the regulations governing the pricing of public contracts, while responsibility for the supervision of compliance with price control regulations lies with the State-level (Laender) Ministries of Economic Affairs.

The standard conditions for pricing public contracts are contained in the LSP (Leitsaetze fuer die Preisermittlung aufgrund von Selbstkosten).[13] As expressed in PR 30/53, Section 1, heavy emphasis is placed on the general principle that market prices are to be given preference over cost prices and that fixed prices are to be negotiated where the nature of the contract permits. The rules for determining cost prices are contained in the Schedule to PR No. 30/53. The efficiency principle, mentioned earlier, is defined as:

> *"In the determination of prices on the basis of cost as defined in these Rules, only those costs will be considered which, in their nature and amount, do not exceed those which, given efficient operation of the enterprise, would be incurred in the performance of the contract." [LL.4.(2)]*

Regarding how "efficient operation" is measured, several West German government contractors said that because of price regulation surveillance, government auditors have considerable comparative data at their disposal concerning operating costs of different firms at varying operating capacities. Intra-industry comparisons are facilitated by individual versions of standard charts of accounts which these firms use—usually versions of the GKR (Gemeinschafts-Kontenrahmen der Industrie) issued by the German Industry Association (BDI).

The United Kingdom's Regulations

The public contracting system in the U.K. is neither comprehensive nor as clearly defined as in West Germany. The rules and procedures governing the placement and administration of public contracts do not emanate from a single authoritative source but have developed within the various government contracting departments in "case law" fashion.

The chief mechanism for coordinating the contracting experience of these departments is the Committee of Public Accounts. Assisting in the process is the Treasury, long recognized for its expertise in contract work. It issues various procurement policy statements and rulings for consideration or compliance by government buyers. The Public Accounts Committee reports and the Treasury minutes on these reports, which include the opinions and actions of the departments involved as well as the Treasury's position, constitute an authoritative body of contract principles and practice which all departments acknowledge.[14]

The two principal sets of standards used in government contracts are GC/Stores/1 for stores supplies other than "off-the-shelf" purchases and GC/Wks/1 for building and civil engineering works. Both booklets contain standard conditions adopted by the principal government purchasing departments. The pricing of noncompetitive stores contracts is discussed in Form GC/Stores/2.[15] This booklet contains several documents which do not constitute standard conditions but which provide information for government contractors, including: review of the profit formula; the Memorandum of Agreement reached between the government and the Confederation of British Industry (CBI) in 1968, which established the Review Board for Government Contracts (the Review Board); and, in Appendix to Annexure 3, the Statement of Government Accounting Conventions.

The Review Board is an independent body of five members nominated by the CBI and the Treasury whose chief function is to review and rule on referred government profit formula risk contracts and subcontracts. It reviews industry's overall average earnings on government contracts and sends a report of its findings and recommendations to the Treasury at three-year intervals.[16] A main channel of communication between the Review Board and government contractors is the Joint Review Board Advisory Committee, whose membership includes CBI representatives and interested trade associations.

In the United Kingdom, as in West Germany, the government reviews each firm individually. The Ministry of Defense (MOD) goes a step further than the West German government, however, by requiring a firm to complete a questionnaire, similar in concept to the disclosure statement filed by U.S. defense contractors,[17] describing its cost allocation methods.

The existing Government Accounting conventions, used in pricing noncompetitive government contracts[18] deal with two topics: the allowability and allocability of overhead costs attributable to government work and determination of profit through application of a formula based on capital employed for government work.

Allowable overhead costs include those applicable specifically to government work and those applicable to both government and nongovernment work. Excluded are those costs which are identifiable only to nongovernment work, certain costs which are treated for tax purposes as capital expenditures and are otherwise not allowable for tax purposes, and those costs which are not regarded as occurring in the same periods as allowable for tax purposes. The criterion of reasonableness is covered by item 11, paragraph 2A of the Conventions which lists "unnecessary, extravagant or wasteful outlays" as items which normally would be excluded from overhead claims. All costs are presumed to be "reasonable" in amount, however, if government contracts constitute only a small proportion of the contractor's sales volume.

Direct materials and labor costs are not dealt with in the U.K.'s Government Accounting Conventions.

Some Indirect Expenses Are Not Allowable

In all three countries, certain types of indirect expenses are not allowed under government contracts because the government does not benefit from the incurrence of a certain type of cost and because certain costs should be charged directly to the work which generates them rather than being classified as indirect expenses.

Table 2 summarizes the indirect expenses which are explicitly unallowable, wholly or partially, under cost-type contracts in the United Kingdom and West Germany. Because unwritten cost accounting understandings are followed by government suppliers and auditors in both countries, however, it is possible that other cost items not mentioned in Table 2 also are inadmissible.

Table 2

COST WHOLLY OR PARTIALLY UNALLOWABLE UNDER GOVERNMENT CONTRACTS

Types of Costs	References	
	West Germany*	U.K.**
Advertising		
Of a "goodwill" nature	III.H.34	2(B)2
After sales service		
Attributable to a specific product		2(A)9
Agent's commissions		
Chargeable against civil sales		2(A)7
Not required in preparing, making or performing contract	III.I.35	
Bad debts		
	Not allowable by convention	2(A)4
Certain taxes		
Including income taxes	III.F.30	
Contingencies		
Risks not related to operations of enterprise and/or covered by insurance	III.K.C.48(2)	

*Schedule to Regulation PR 30/53.

**"Statement of government accounting conventions applicable from 1st August 1970 as amended with effect from 30th June 1971", Appendix to Annexure 3, Form GC/Stores/2, Edition October 1970 (published September 1972).

Table 2(*continued*)

Types of Costs	References West Germany*	U.K.**
Donations		
Subscriptions and donations not allowable for tax purposes		2(A)1
Pooling levies or other similar arrangements		2(A)3
Entertainment expenses		
May be partially excludable if "unreasonable"	III.H.34	2(B)1
Fines and penalties		
Resulting from violations of, or failure to comply with, law	Unallowable by convention	
Insurance		
Insurance of credit and goods in transit and any other related to civil work risks		2(A)6
Losses on other contracts	III.H.47(2) III.H.48(1)	
On losses of profits	III.H.48(1)	2(A)12
Interest		
Cost of raising and servicing capital	III.H.43(3)	2(A)2
Interest on borrowings, bond discounts, costs of financing and refinancing capital, and related costs	III.H.43(3)	
Research and Development		
R&D and engineering costs designed to lead to new products for sale to general public	III.D.27	
Royalties, patents,license fees		
Limited allowability as direct costs	III.G.33	2(A)13
Sales discounts		
Should be accounted for as adjustments of selling prices		2(A)5
Shipping (Freight Out)		
Treat as direct charges most government work shipped ex-factory	III.A.18(1)	2(A)8

*Schedule to Regulation PR 30/53.

**"Statement of government accounting conventions applicable from 1st August 1970 as amended with effect from 30th June 1971", Appendix to Annexure 3, Form GC/Stores/2, Edition October 1970 (published September 1972).

The international variability in treating indirect costs is noticed most in advertising, contingencies, contributions and donations, entertainment, notional (imputed) costs, and sales discounts.

Advertising

West Germany does not allow advertising for marketable products nor, like the U.K., does it permit "goodwill" related costs. Both nations subject any remaining types of advertising costs to the "reasonableness" test. The United States, on the other hand, permits only advertising expenses for contract-related personnel recruitment, the purchase of scarce items, or the disposal of scrap or surplus materials (DAR 15.205.1).

Contingencies

West Germany does not permit recovery for contingencies if they are covered by insurance or unrelated to business operations. In the U.K., contingency provisions must be excluded from the basic cost estimate and submitted as a separate item for consideration by the government buyer. They must be "adequately" defined, and the proposal must contain a "reasoned assessment of the probability of occurrence and its consequence for the cost of carrying out the work."[19] In the U.S., contingency provisions for forward pricing purposes are somewhat similar to the U.K.'s requirements. If reasonably accurate estimates of the effects of contingencies arising from "presently known and existing conditions" [DAR 15–205.7(c)(i)] can be made, they may be included in cost estimates. Otherwise, they must be disclosed separately and include the rationale on which they are based.

Contributions, Donations and Entertainment

Compulsory fees and contributions are allowable in West Germany to the extent that they are related to the contractor's operations [III.F.32(1)]. Donations to organizations are allowable "if they are in the interest of the contractor's operations" [III.F.32(ii)], as well as "reasonable" other-than statutory contributions. German firms state that their government interprets these provisions narrowly, and reimbursable donations and contributions are severely limited in practice. The U.K. is more liberal because it only excludes contributions of a political nature. The U.S., therefore, stands alone in its exclusion of all contributions and donations (DAR 15.205.8).

Entertainment expenses allowability follows the same pattern as contributions and donations. West Germany and the U.K. review entertainment expenses for reasonableness whereas all are excluded by the U.S. (DAR 15.205.11).

Notional (Imputed Costs)

In the U.K., notional transactions normally would be excluded from contractors' claims for overheads, and the Conventions cite an imputed rental charge for property owned as an example (2A10). West Germany, in contrast, permits a number of types of imputed costs, including special depreciation charges (III.K.). In the U.S., the

DAR [15–205.9(g)] provides that no rental/use charge shall be allowed on property acquired free from the government or on fully depreciated property, but "a reasonable charge for the use of fully depreciated property may be agreed upon and allowed" [15–205.9(i)].

Sales Discounts

Sales discounts commonly are classified as marketing costs in the U.K. and are grouped together with bad debts, credit and transit insurance; agents' commissions; after-sales service costs; and freight out. They are classified this way in the Review Board's list of marketing costs which should be charged direct to the contracts that generated them.[20] West Germany and the U.S., on the other hand, account for sales discounts as deductions from revenues rather than cost elements.

How to Treat Indirect Expenses

There are certain types of costs for which particular cost accounting treatment or disclosure may be prescribed, namely depreciation, bid and proposal (B&P) costs, independent research and development (IR&D) costs, and marketing and selling expenses.

West Germany's regulations require depreciation charges to be determined by "evenly spreading the cost of acquisition or manufacture of an asset over its useful life" [III.D(a)39(1)], which suggests that only the straight-line method can be used. The most important feature is that the depreciation charge is to be determined "independently of the asset values stated in the balance sheet and in tax statements" [III.K.(a)38(1)], and "where cost of acquisition or manufacture differs substantially from replacement cost, and this is not only a temporary development" [III.K.(a)38(2)], depreciation may be based on replacement cost "provided that the principle of valuation at replacement cost is consistently adhered to" [III.K.(a)38(2)]. These provisions freeing contractors from the historic cost principle provide West German firms with the advantage of claiming higher depreciation charges that more closely measure the economic cost of the fixed asset services consumed.

In the U.K., depreciation charges are required to be consistent, reasonable, and related to the original cost of the asset. Any profit or loss on disposal is to be treated as an adjustment of the relevant depreciation charge [2(D)1], but no particular method is specified other than calculation at the contractor's own rates [2(D)1]. The Review Board has been interested in affording contractors protection against inflation by permitting increased valuation of fixed assets as elements of both contract price and capital employed. The Board has delayed recommending this proposal for government approval, however, because of the lack of uniformity in accounting for price-level changes. This problem may have been resolved by the recent issuance in the U.K of Statement of Standard Accounting Practice (SSAP) No. 16, *Current Cost Accounting,* by the Accounting Standards Committee.

The U.S. also recognized the problem, and in October 1975 the CASB circulated a proposed Standard (CAS 413), aimed at using price-level adjustments for inflation in determining contract costs of depreciation. This proposed Standard was withdrawn in March 1976, however, when it was decided to combine the topic of adjusting historical depreciation costs for inflation with that of the imputed cost of capital employed.

Bid and proposal costs are not identified separately in the West German regulations, but the topic of IR&D is discussed under the heading of "Independent" and "Contract-sponsored" Development (III.D.27). In price calculations, development and design costs must be identified separately as one or the other [III.D.28(2)]. If such work is beyond the scope of the contractor's so-called "independent" development, it is subject to contractual agreement between the firm and the public agency and classifiable as "contract-sponsored" development (III.D.27). All such costs incurred and their allocation must be substantiated separately, the details being determined by agreement with the government customer [III.D.28(1)]. In costing public contracts, product development costs are by convention excluded from overhead.

In the U.K., bid and proposal costs usually are classified as marketing and selling expenses, and no separate accounting guidelines have been developed. The government accounting conventions do not deal with the accounting treatment of IR&D costs, but a full discussion of this topic is contained in the Review Board's survey of "conventions normally followed by Purchasing Departments."[21] IR&D costs are referred to as "private venture" research and development, and all "reasonable" expenditures are generally accepted in overhead except for those incurred for exclusively commercial projects. Related product development costs are allowable overhead items for government purchases of proprietary items, "provided that the costs are reasonable for the industry and are allocated as overheads over all work of the contractor within the relevant product group."[22]

In the United States, CAS 420, *Accounting for Independent Research and Development Costs and Bid and Proposal Costs,* requires that individual IR&D and B&P projects be accounted for separately and treated as if they were final cost objectives.

The most specific requirements regarding accounting for marketing and selling expenses are to be found in the U.K., which provides for their allocation within relevant product groups [2(B)6(c)], thus echoing the IR&D allocation provisions. West Germany does not specify the accounting treatment of marketing and selling expenses in its regulations, but usually after adjustment for unallowable items, they are either allocated on a total cost input basis or as a percentage of total direct labor and manufacturing overhead.

The accounting treatment of marketing and selling expenses is not specified in the DAR either. In September 1978, the CASB circulated for comment a Staff Issues Paper, "Allocation of Selling and Marketing Costs," which presented some major conceptual issues. By 1979, this research project was not complete.

How Cost of Capital Is Handled

The imputed cost of capital is allowable for cost-reimbursement purposes in West Germany and the U.S. In the U.K., the amount of capital employed by the contractor forms part of the profit.

In West Germany, the two basic elements of the cost-of-capital calculation are operating capital and imputed interest on operating capital. In calculating the operating capital, the objective is to determine the amount of those fixed and current assets used in the firm's main operations, thus excluding, in particular, idle facilities except any standby equipment necessary for manufacturing or trading firms. First the average amount of "operating assets" is determined [III.K.(b)45]. Fixed assets are valued according to the provisions governing depreciation, that is, acquisition cost or replacement cost less accumulated depreciation. Current assets are valued at acquisition cost or cost of manufacture. If there is a substantial difference between these historic costs and replacement cost, substitutions are made: current prices instead of acquisition cost and the cost of manufacture of an equivalent asset instead of the actual cost of manufacture of the asset. After adoption, valuation principles have to be applied uniformly and consistently. The amount of "operating capital" is arrived at by reducing the average "operating assets" amount by "any interest-free advance payments and deposits received from the contracting public agency and any credits granted free of interest by suppliers under the agreed terms of payment" [III.K.(b)44(1)].

The maximum allowable imputed interest rate is established by the Federal Ministry of Economic Affairs in agreement with the Federal Ministry of Finance. This rate, applied to the computed operating capital, produces a preliminary cost of capital such as interest or rent [III.K.(b)43(4)]. The adjusted, and final, imputed interest chargeable to any particular contract is based on the proportion of contract cost to total production costs as shown in Table 3.

The U.S. method of computing the cost of facilities capital is specified in Cost Accounting Standard (CAS) 414 and is similar to the German approach in that it multiplies a base figure (facilities capital) by a designated interest rate established at semiannual intervals by the U.S. Secretary of the Treasury. The arithmetic mean

Table 3

DETERMINING IMPUTED INTEREST

Average operating assets (values adjusted)		800,000 DM
Less		
Interest-free advance payments	80,000 DM	
Interest-free credits	40,000	120,000
Average operating capital:		680,000 DM
Imputed interest		
Cost of capital, 680,000 DM, multiplied by currently allowable interest rate, say 6%		40,800 DM
Less interest on operating capital received during year:		5,000
Imputed cost of capital for year:		35,800 DM

of the specified interest rates is used for historical cost purposes, whereas the most recently published rate is used in connection with forward pricing.

The U.S. approach differs in several respects from the West German model: the assets included in the base are restricted to tangible capital assets and those intangible assets subject to amortization, thus excluding working capital; net book values are used for valuation purposes; and an imputed cost of money is calculated for each indirect cost pool which has a significant amount of allocated facilities capital and which is used to allocate indirect costs of final cost objectives.

How Do We Achieve Harmonization?

Whenever public funds provide support to international joint ventures, public contract regulations control the way in which individual firms account for their production efforts. In my brief survey, only some of the main features of public contract pricing in just two of the major EPGs could be compared and contrasted with U.S. practice. Yet a number of troublesome areas were highlighted. Inconsistencies were found in practice with respect to the allowability, or degree of allowability, of certain costs; the treatment of certain items as cost or revenue elements; recognition of imputed costs; adherence to the cost principle; and the extent to which accounting systems are monitored by the government and particular cost accounting practices are mandated. It would seem axiomatic that partners in a joint venture would record their investments consistently so that their contributions could be compared. This is not, however, the case at present.

Because of the symbiotic relationship between public contract costing arrangements and a firm's cost accounting system, the need for harmonization of public contract costing practices extends to cost accounting practices in general.

One recent published argument in favor of setting international cost accounting standards suggested the creation of an international management accounting institute to coordinate such activities.[23] A special public sector committee of such an international organization could provide the institutional framework for the needed harmonization of public contract costing practices. For now, however, the matter remains unresolved.

Notes

1. "European Partners Study F–16 Production Problems," *Aviation Week & Space Technology,* Sept. 22, 1980.
2. Department of Defense Appropriations for 1978. Hearings before a subcommittee of the Committee on Appropriations, House of Representatives, 95th Congress, First Session, Part 2, U.S. Government Printing Office, Washington, D.C., 1977.
3. *Foreign Military Sales—A Potential Drain on the U.S. Posture,* LCD–76–455, General Accounting Office, Washington, D.C., July 25, 1977.
4. "First European F–16 Delivery Scheduled," *Aviation Week & Space Technology,* Jan. 22, 1979.

5. *Sharing the Defense Burden: The Multinational F–16 Aircraft Program,* PSAD–77. 40, GAO, Washington, D.C., Aug. 15, 1977.
6. *Ibid.*
7. U.S., *Federal Register,* vol. 43, July 31, 1978, p. 33252.
8. U.S., *Federal Register,* vol. 43, Nov. 14, 1978, p. 52693. The CASB was disbanded at the end of 1980.
9. Great Britain, *Eighth Report from the Committee of Public Accounts.* Session 1976–77, Her Majesty's Stationary Office, London, 1977.
10. *Ibid.*
11. In the U.S., civilian agencies' procurement is controlled by the Federal Procurement Regulation (FPR) and defense procurement by the Defense Acquisition Regulation (DAR). Defense and nondefense negotiated contracts in excess of $100,000 are subject to standards issued by the CASB.
12. Government Contract Reports, *Defense Acquisition Regulation,* Commerce Clearing House, Chicago, 1979, DAR 15–201.3.
13. From decree PR No. 30/53 of Nov. 21, 1953: Bundesanzeiger No. 244 of Dec. 18, 1953, amended by PR 8.61 of November 9, 1961, and PR 7/67 of Dec. 12, 1967.
14. Colin Turpin, *Government Contracts,* Penguin Books Ltd., Harmondsworth, Middlesex, 1972.
15. Form GC/STORES/2, Oct. 1970 edition, published Sept. 1972, *Pricing of Government Non-Competitive Stores Contracts.*
16. Great Britain, Review Board of Government Contracts, *Report on the First General Review of the Profit Formula for Non-Competitive Government Contracts,* Her Majesty's Stationary Office, London, 1974.
17. U.S., *Federal Register,* vol. 37, p. 4139, Feb. 29, 1972.
18. Form GC/STORES/2, Appendix to Annexure 3.
19. Great Britain, *Report on the Second General Review of the Profit Formula for Non-Competitive Government Contracts,* Her Majesty's Stationary Office, London, 1977.
20. Great Britain, *Report on the First General Review of the Profit Formula for Non-Competitive Government Contracts,* Her Majesty's Stationary Office, London, 1974.
21. Great Britain, Review Board for Government Contracts, *Report on the Interim Review,* Her Majesty's Stationary Office, London, 1972.
22. *Ibid.*
23. Adolph J.H. Enthoven, "International Management Accounting—a Challenge for Accountants," Management Accounting, Sept. 1980.

9. AN INTERNATIONAL STUDY OF ACCOUNTING PRACTICES IN DIVISIONALIZED COMPANIES AND THEIR ASSOCIATIONS WITH ORGANIZATIONAL VARIABLES

ROBERT W. SCAPENS and J. TIMOTHY SALE

Robert W. Scapens is Professor of Accounting, University of Manchester, and J. Timothy Sale is Professor of Accounting, University of Cincinnati. *The authors are grateful to Pantelis Tikkas for assistance in collecting the U.K. data, to Pat Thomson for implementing the Guttman-Lingoes Nonparametric programs, and to Murray Bryant, David Cooper, and David Otley for commenting on earlier drafts of this paper. Any remaining errors or omissions, however, are the responsibility of the authors.*

The measurement of divisional performance is still a subject of some debate. Most accounting researchers appear to favor measures which either include an interest charge on capital employed or relate divisional income to its capital asset base, but some dissenters exist. Various measures are used in practice. The use of particular accounting methods is hypothesized to be influenced by organizational characteristics, such as the extent to which decision making authority has been delegated to divisional managers.

An empirical study of associations between 12 variables reflecting accounting methods and the nature of divisional autonomy was undertaken from questionnaire surveys of large companies in the United States (U.S.) and the United Kingdom (U.K.), and the relationship between accounting methods and the nature of divisional autonomy in the two countries is examined.

Many similarities were observed in the accounting methods used by the responding companies in the U.S. and the U.K. to evaluate divisional performance, analyze divisional capital expenditure proposals, and control authorized divisional capital expenditures. The major difference between the countries was the use of post-completion audits by more than twice as many U.S. companies (84.2 percent) as U.K. companies (36.3 percent).

In both countries, the expected associations between accounting methods and divisional autonomy were not found. Further research is needed to explore the dynamics of accounting systems in divisionalized companies, such as longitudinal studies of individual companies.

The appropriate measurement of divisional performance has been a concern of accountants in recent years. Many accounting researchers have favored measures

Robert W. Scapens and J. Timothy Sale "An International Study of Accounting Practices in Divisionalized Companies and Their Associations with Organizational Variables 60, no. 2 (1985) 231–247.

which include an interest charge on capital employed [Solomons, 1965] or at least on some part thereof [Tomkins, 1973]. Others have supported the use of return on investment (e.g., Shillinglaw [1977]). A review of the debate concerning appropriate measures led Emmanuel and Otley [1976] to conclude that there is a measure of agreement; income should be related to capital employed when assessing divisional performance. Amey [1969 and 1975], however, argued that investment decisions should be reserved for corporate management and the capital asset base need not be introduced into the assessment of divisional operating performance.

Surveys in the United States (U.S.) [Mauriel and Anthony, 1966; Reece and Cool, 1978] and in the United Kingdom (U.K.) [Tomkins, 1973; Scapens, Sale and Tikkas, 1982] indicate that various measures are used in practice. Some companies use measures which reflect divisional capital employed either through an interest charge or by relating income to the capital asset base. Other companies use measures such as cash flow and income before interest and taxes, which do not reflect fully the cost of divisional capital investment.

This paper describes the relationship between accounting practices in divisionalized companies and certain organizational variables. The data were collected in 1980 from a mail survey of companies in the *Fortune* 500 in the U.S. and the *Times* 1000 in the U.K. Two countries were studied in an attempt to explore international differences in accounting methods.

Particular attention was given to the measurement of divisional performance and the control of divisional capital investment in the questionnaire. In addition, questions were asked about the nature of the organization and its divisionalized structure. The questionnaire survey was undertaken primarily to obtain data about the accounting methods used in practice. A subset of the questionnaire data will be used to test hypotheses that organizational variables, in particular the extent of divisional autonomy, contribute to the diversity of accounting methods used in divisionalized companies.

Divisional Performance Measurement

The debate concerning divisional performance measurement has been primarily normative. There is little theoretical or empirical work which attempts to explain the diversity of divisional performance measures observed in practice. As a result, the present study is exploratory. The existing literature, however, provided the background for the hypotheses which were developed. Accordingly, the paper begins by reviewing briefly some normative arguments concerning performance measurement in divisionalized companies.

Divisional managers are aware that their performance will be measured at some later date and that financial and/or non-financial rewards may be obtained if appropriate decisions are made. In this way, performance measurement has the potential to influence decisions. Ideally, performance would be measured and rewarded directly by reference to the decision outcome—e.g., the achievement of the goals which corporate management has set for the division. One difficulty is that a division's goals may be expressed in long-run terms, whereas performance measures are prepared on a periodic (short-run) basis. For periodic reporting to be effective, the performance measure must reinforce the divisional goals.

Periodic performance measures which do not reinforce divisional goals could introduce bias into decision making. Consider a divisional manager who has authority to make decisions regarding expenditures on fixed assets and/or working capital. Performance measures which do not reflect the capital asset base of the division could encourage the divisional manager to make capital investments below the cost of capital. Measures not incorporating the capital asset base may be used, however, because divisional managers do not have the authority to make capital investment decisions (including decisions which affect the level of working capital) or alternatively, because control over such decisions is exercised in some other way, for instance, through a process of authorization, reinforced by *ex post* audits of capital projects [Scapens and Sale, 1981a].

This suggests that divisional performance measurement may be influenced by the extent of delegated authority over capital investment decisions (including operating decisions which affect investment in working capital) and by the use of alternative methods for the control of divisional capital investment decisions. It is possible, however, that the methods of controlling divisional decisions and measuring divisional performance will themselves influence the extent of delegated authority [Otley, 1980]. Accordingly, the causal relationships could be very complex. The issue addressed here, therefore, is the association (rather than causal relationship) between accounting methods and the extent of delegated authority.

It should be recognized that notions such as delegation of authority and divisional autonomy cannot be interpreted in any absolute sense. Since corporate management wants to retain control over the direction of the organization as a whole, some restrictions must be imposed on the actions taken by divisional managers. The nature of these restrictions will give more or less autonomy to divisional managers.

Divisional performance measures may or may not include an explicit adjustment for divisional capital employed. Such an adjustment could either be made through an interest charge on capital employed or reflected in a return on investment ratio. We are concerned with the association between the use of any accounting method which includes an explicit adjustment for divisional capital employed and the extent of divisional autonomy.

The Questionnaire Survey

The data for this paper were collected as part of a wider study of accounting in divisionalized companies. Identical questionnaires were used in both the U.S. and U.K. except for minor amendments for slight differences in terminology and monetary amounts.[1]

The U.K. questionnaires were mailed to the 744 companies in the *Times* 1000 which are not subsidiaries of overseas corporations. Ten questionnaires were undelivered because the company had liquidated or merged, giving a reduced sample size of 734. Replies were received from 331 U.K. companies (a response rate of 45.1 percent), of which 300 were usable (a usable response rate of 40.9 percent).

The unusable responses were from 31 companies who sent a letter indicating their unwillingness to complete the questionnaire due to company policy or lack of time.

The U.S. questionnaires were mailed to all companies in the *Fortune* 500. Four questionnaires were returned undelivered and three companies had been acquired by other companies, giving a reduced sample size of 493. Replies were received from 243 U.S. companies (a response rate of 49.3 percent), of which 227 were usable (a usable response rate of 46.0 percent). The unusable responses were from 16 companies who sent a letter indicating their unwillingness to complete the questionnaire due to company policy or lack of time.

The representativeness of the respondents was confirmed by comparing the total sales, reported net income, and principal activities of the responding companies with the characteristics of the population.

Not all of the responding companies had a divisional structure. The analyses described in this paper are based on the replies from 211 U.K. and 205 U.S. companies which are divisionalized according to the following definition of a division: "A section within the organization where the divisional chief executive has responsibility for costs, revenues, and at least some discretion over capital expenditures (e.g., working capital management, capital projects up to a specified sum, etc.)." This definition is a synthesis of definitions discussed in Solomons [1965] and Tomkins [1973]—see Scapens, Sale and Tikkas [1982, pp. 20–21].

The questionnaires were addressed to the corporate headquarters with instructions that they should be completed by "corporate accounting personnel." Thus, the responses inevitably reflect only the formal systems within the organization. In general, these formal systems apply to all or most divisions within a particular organization. The replies to questions concerning differences in the treatment of individual divisions indicate that standard systems are used with few, if any, exceptions.

A series of interviews with corporate controllers in the U.K. and the U.S. was undertaken prior to the survey. These interviews assisted in the development of the questionnaire. In addition, post-questionnaire interviews were used to test the reliability of the responses. Tests for nonresponse and question-order bias were also performed.

The test for non-response bias of Moser and Kalton [1971, pp. 185–186] was performed by analyzing differences in replies received from the first questionnaire mailing and the follow-up letter. The absence of significant differences indicates that replies were unaffected by the timing of the response. To avoid question-order bias, two versions of the questionnaire were used—each version contained identical questions, but ordered differently. Chi-square tests (corrected for non-continuity) were unable to locate evidence of question-order bias. In general, the non-response and question-order bias tests indicate that the questionnaire data provide a satisfactory database concerning large divisionalized companies in the U.S. and the U.K.

Accounting Practices

The questionnaire asked respondents to supply factual information about practices in their companies. Thirty-nine questions were included in the questionnaire soliciting various types of information from each company, such as total annual capital expenditures, annual sales and profits, bases for divisionalization, interdependencies between divisions, the length of time divisionalized, the criteria used to evaluate the performance of divisional managers, the responsibility of divisional managers for operating and capital expenditures budgets, and the use of post-completion audits of capital investment projects (see Scapens, Sale and Tikkas [1982] for details of the questionnaire).

The financial criteria used to evaluate the performance of divisional managers in the companies responding to the questionnaire are shown in Table 1. A majority of the companies in both the U.S. and the U.K. use a performance measure which reflects divisional capital employed (either through a rate of return or an interest charge). There is, however, a sizable minority not using such performance measures.

Two additional accounting methods will be examined in this paper: discounted cash flow (DCF) analysis of divisional capital expenditure proposals and *ex post* (or post-completion) audits of capital projects. Table 2 summarizes the financial analysis techniques generally used in the responding companies to evaluate divisional capital projects involving an expansion of existing production facilities. Projects involving expansion were specifically mentioned in the question since financial analysis techniques are particularly appropriate for such projects.

Table 3 describes the procedures used by responding companies to control the implementation of divisional capital expenditure decisions. Differences in practices in the U.S. and the U.K. can be seen in both Table 2 and Table 3. The major difference between the U.S. and U.K. companies is that 84.2 percent of U.S.

Table 1
FINANCIAL CRITERIA USED TO EVALUATE THE PERFORMANCE OF DIVISIONAL MANAGERS

	U.S.		U.K.	
	No.	**Percent***	**No.**	**Percent***
1. Achievement of a target rate of return imposed by the corporation	106	51.7	92	44.7
2. Achievement of a target profit after charging interest on total capital employed by the division	59	28.8	77	37.4
3. Achievement of a target profit before interest and taxes	93	45.4	104	50.5
4. Achievement of a target cash flow figure	44	21.5	86	41.7
5. Ability to stay within budget	101	49.3	90	43.7
6. Other	42	20.5	18	8.7
Total Responses	205		206	
No Answer	0		5	
	205		211	

*Percentage of respondents (excluding no answers) using each criterion—multiple responses were permitted.

Table 2

FINANCIAL ANALYSIS TECHNIQUES USED FOR INVESTMENT APPRAISAL

	U.S.		U.K.	
	No.	**Percent***	**No.**	**Percent***
1. Discounted cash flow (NPV or IRR)	172	84.3	106	51.7
2. Payback	115	56.4	113	55.1
3. Accounting rate of return	83	40.7	114	55.6
4. Non-financial criteria used	47	23.0	49	23.9
Total responses	204		205	
No answer	1		6	
	205		211	

*Percentage of respondents (excluding no answers) using each criterion—multiple responses were permitted.

companies use post-completion audits as opposed to 36.3 percent of U.K. companies. Also, very few U.S. companies (6.9 percent) use "other" procedures to control the implementation of divisional capital expenditure decisions, while 23.9 percent of U.K. companies use "other" procedures. The majority of these U.K. companies indicated that they use informal rather than formal procedures. These informal procedures consist of monitoring the original capital authorization requests either prior to or after they are submitted to corporate headquarters by the divisions and then informally comparing the actual outcomes with the expected outcomes.

The following analysis will attempt to determine whether the use of DCF techniques and *ex post* audits is related to the extent of divisional autonomy.

Variable Construction

A subset of the questionnaire data was used to construct the 12 variables listed in Table 4. These variables reflect accounting methods and divisional autonomy. The interconnectedness variables were included because a division's autonomy will be restricted to the extent that it depends upon other sections of the organization. For instance, a division which returns all of its cash flows to corporate headquarters, uses many central services, and is affected by the decisions made in other divisions would be believed, *a priori,* to have little autonomy.

The respondents were not asked to assess explicitly the autonomy of divisional managers. Responses to questions concerning decision making and other procedures were converted into an assessment of divisional autonomy through the variable construction described below. This approach avoids the bias which might be introduced from respondents interpreting the nature of autonomy differently. The scales developed have no established theoretical basis, but are consistent across all of the data, both in the U.S. and the U.K. data. Scales for the divisional autonomy variables,

Table 3

CONTROL OF AUTHORIZED CAPITAL PROJECTS

	U.S. No.	U.S. Percent*	U.K. No.	U.K. Percent*
1. Projects monitored through project accounts	115	56.9	110	54.7
2. Post-completion audits undertaken	170	84.2	73	36.3
3. Other	14	6.9	48	23.9
Total responses	202		201	
No answer	3		10	
	205		211	

*Percentage of respondents (excluding no answers) using each criterion—multiple responses were permitted.

Table 4

VARIABLE LIST

Variable Group	Variable No.	Variable Name	Variable Description	Scale
Interconnectedness	1	INTERDEP	Interdependencies between divisions	0, 1, 2, 3, 4, 5
	2	CENTFNC	Centralization of functions	0, 1, 2, 3, 4, 5
	3	CASHRTN	Extent of cash returns to corporate headquarters	0, 1
Operating Autonomy	4	BUDGET	Delegation of responsibility for operating budgets	0, 1, 2
	5	PURCH	Delegation of responsibility for purchases	0, 1, 2, 3, 4
	6	SELLPR	Delegation of responsibility over sales/selling prices	0, 1, 2
Capital Expenditures Autonomy	7	NEWFIN	Delegation of authority to raise new financing	0, 1
	8	CAPEXP	Delegation of authority over capital investment projects	0, 1, 2, 3
	9	CAPBUD	Delegation of responsibility for capital budgets	0, 1, 2
Accounting Methods	10	PERFEVAL	Use of residual income/return on investment for divisional performance evaluation	0, 1
	11	INVAPP	Use of discounting techniques for investment evaluation	0, 1
	12	EXPOST	Use of accounting methods for ex post control of capital projects	0, 1, 2

1 through 9, were constructed such that a low value indicates decentralization, while a high value indicates centralization in the area in question.

Responses to a question concerning the nature of interdependencies between divisions were used to construct the scales for the first three variables. The particular interdependencies included in the question were suggested by the pre-questionnaire interviews. Interdependencies (variable 1, INTERDEP) and centralization of functions (variable 2, CENTFNC) were both scaled 0 through 5. These scales were obtained by counting the number of interdependencies between divisions and the number of centralized functions provided by corporate headquarters. Values of 0 were assigned to respondents who indicated no interdependencies or centralized functions. Centralized functions which are included in other variables were omitted from CENTFNC.

Cash returns to headquarters (variable 3, CASHRTN) is a dichotomous variable indicating whether divisions do (1) or do not (0) return cash to corporate headquarters.

The scale for the responsibility for operating budgets (variable 4, BUDGET) was constructed using responses to a question which asked: "Are divisional managers responsible for determining operating budget methods (i.e., techniques to be used) and gathering the necessary information?" The following values were assigned to the responses:

0—divisional managers responsible for both determining operating budget methods and gathering the necessary information,
1—divisonal managers responsible for information gathering, but budgeting methods determined centrally, and
2—both operating budget methods and information gathering centrally determined.

The scale for the responsibility for purchases (variable 5, PURCH) was based on the responses to a question concerning the extent to which divisional managers can approve large purchase contracts. With a range of 0 through 4, a value of 0 indicates complete autonomy and 4 indicates no autonomy in this area. The scale for the responsibility for sales/selling prices (variable 6, SELLPR) was constructed in a similar manner using responses to a question concerning the extent to which divisional managers are allowed to change prices of existing products or establish prices for new products. A value of 0 indicates delegation of complete authority for selling prices and 2 indicates corporate responsibility for selling prices. Both PURCH and SELLPR relate to external transactions; the responsibility for pricing internal transactions was dealt with separately in the questionnaire.

Authority for raising new financing (variable 7, NEWFIN) is a dichotomous variable indicating whether divisional managers are (0) or are not (1) allowed to raise external financing. The scale for authority over capital investment projects (variable 8, CAPEXP) ranges from 0 to 3, with the lower value indicating substantial autonomy and the higher value indicating little autonomy. Responsibility for capital budgets (variable 9, CAPBUD) indicates the extent to which divisional managers have responsibility for the preparation of capital expenditure budgets. A value of 0 indicates that the responsibility is at the divisional level, 1 indicates that there is interaction between the divisions and corporate headquarters, and 2 indicates that the responsibility is at the corporate level.

Two of the three accounting variables, PERFEVAL and INVAPP, are dichotomous variables. Although Tables 1 and 2 indicate that a variety of accounting methods are used in both the U.S. and the U.K. and that multiple methods are common, the present analysis is restricted to the use or non-use of performance measures which reflect the capital asset base and discounted cash flow techniques. Variable 10, PERFEVAL, has a value of 0 when corporate headquarters does and 1 when corporate headquarters does not use return on investment and/or residual income to evaluate the performance of divisional managers. Variable 11, INVAPP, indicates whether corporate headquarters does (0) or does not (1) use discounted cash flow techniques in the formal evaluation of divisional capital expenditure proposals which involve an expansion of existing production facilities.

The *ex post* control of capital projects (variable 12, EXPOST) was constructed from a question which asked respondents to indicate the control mechanisms used to monitor the progress of authorized divisional capital projects. A value of 2 indicates that no *ex post* control mechanisms are used, 1 indicates that capital expenditures are monitored through project accounts, and 0 indicates that *ex post* control is exercised through independent evaluation and review, i.e., post-completion audits. This scale for EXPOST implies a rank ordering of project accounts and post-completion audits. It is assumed that the use of project accounts provides only partial *ex post* control over capital investments, primarily monitoring the disbursement for capital expenditures. Post-completion audits, however, are assumed to involve somewhat greater control through the (independent) evaluation of the outcomes of capital projects against the original capital authorization requests. Although a sizable minority of the U.K. companies studied use neither project accounts nor post-completion audits, such a scale was needed because all of the U.S. companies use at least one of these two control techniques. A dichotomy similar to those used for PERFEVAL or INVAPP would have been inappropriate for EXPOST as far as the U.S. data are concerned. A revised scaling of the U.K. EXPOST variable—a value of 1 indicating that neither project accounts nor post-completion audits are used and 0 indicating that at least one of these control techniques is used—did not significantly alter the U.K. statistics discussed below.

Since each of the 12 variables can take an explicit value of 0, the value 9 was used to identify missing values in each case.

It has to be admitted that the scales for all 12 variables are *ad hoc,* and alternative scales could have been used. Furthermore, there could also be problems created by overlap in the characteristics measured by particular variables. For example, the groups of variables representing operating and capital expenditure autonomy are unlikely to be independent of each other and of the interconnectedness group of variables. Yet, the scales should capture the essence of any associations between the accounting methods and the organizational variables included in the study. The results of the analysis must, however, be interpreted cautiously.

Hypotheses

The variables within each of the first three groups represent particular dimensions of the aspect of autonomy which the group is intended to reflect. There may be considerable overlap, however, in these dimensions [Ezzamel and Hilton, 1980], and thus, redundancy in the data may exist. This is necessary to ensure the covergent validity of the selected variables—i.e., that they capture the intended underlying factors of interconnectedness, operating autonomy, and capital expenditure autonomy. The following hypothesis will be tested.

Hypothesis H_1:
The variables within each of the three groups of divisional autonomy variables, individually and collectively, reflect an underlying factor; viz.,
a: interconnectedness (variables 1, 2, 3)
b: operating autonomy (variable 4, 5, 6)
c: capital expenditure autonomy (variables 7, 8, 9)

The interconnectedness variables were included in the study because divisional autonomy will be restricted by the extent to which divisions depend upon corporate headquarters and other divisions. Thus, positive associations are expected between the interconnectedness variables and the groups of variables representing operating and capital expenditure autonomy.

Hypothesis H_2:
The extent of divisional operating autonomy and capital expenditure autonomy are associated with the interconnectedness of divisions.

Since some divisional operating autonomy is necessary for the delegation of capital expenditure decisions, a positive association is expected between operating autonomy and capital expenditure autonomy.

Hypothesis H_3:
The extent of divisional capital expenditure autonomy is associated with the extent of divisional operating autonomy.

It was suggested earlier that accounting methods may be influenced by the extent of divisional autonomy. In particular, divisional autonomy may influence the use or non-use of performance measures which include an explicit adjustment for capital employed. Accordingly, positive associations are expected between PERFEVAL and each of the variables which reflect capital expenditure autonomy (NEWFIN, CAPEXP, and CAPBUD) and operating autonomy (BUDGET, PURCH, and SELLPR).

The interconnectedness of sections of the organization is also likely to influence accounting methods. A highly interconnected organization will require considerable central direction and will have little need for accounting methods designed to control autonomous divisions. Thus, positive associations are also expected between PERFEVAL and the variables which reflect interconnectedness, INTERDEP,

CENTFNC, and CASHRTN. The following hypothesis summarizes the expected associations involving PERFEVAL:

Hypothesis H_4:
The use of performance measures which include an explicit adjustment for capital employed is associated with the extent of divisional autonomy, as reflected by the interconnectedness, operating autonomy, and capital expenditure autonomy variables.

While it may be expected that the use of discounted cash flow techniques for the evaluation of divisional capital expenditures will be influenced by the extent of divisional autonomy, the direction of such influence is not clear. As a tentative hypothesis, it is suggested that there will be a positive association between INVAPP and PERFEVAL. Both accounting methods provide a means of controlling delegated capital expenditure decisions. It would seem to follow, therefore, that positive associations will be expected between INVAPP and the variables reflecting interconnectedness, operating autonomy, and capital expenditure autonomy.

Hypothesis H_5:
The use of discounted cash flow techniques to evaluate divisional capital expenditures is associated with the use of performance measures which include an explicit adjustment for capital employed and the extent of divisional autonomy reflected by the interconnectedness, operating autonomy, and capital expenditure autonomy variables.

It was argued earlier that the divisional performance measures which reflect capital employed (such as residual income and return on investment) may not be used because capital expenditure decisions are controlled in some other way, for instance, through *ex post* controls of capital expenditures. If this argument is accepted, a negative association would be expected between PERFEVAL and EXPOST.

Hypothesis H_6:
Ex post controls of divisional capital expenditures are used as alternatives to divisional performance measures which include an explicit adjustment for capital employed.

It must be emphasized that hypothesis H_6 is an alternative to hypothesis H_4—in other words, hypothesis H_6 could provide an explanation for PERFEVAL in the event that the associations between PERFEVAL and the divisional autonomy variables predicted by hypothesis H_4 are not observed. If hypothesis H_4 is rejected, the following additional hypotheses follow from hypothesis H_6:

Hypothesis H_{6a}:
Ex post controls of divisional capital expenditures will be used in conjunction with discounted cash flow analysis of divisional capital expenditures.

Hypothesis H_{6b}:
The use of ex post controls of divisional capital expenditures is associated with the extent of divisional autonomy as reflected by the interconnectedness, operating autonomy, and capital expenditure autonomy variables.

The associations predicted by the above hypotheses are summarized in Figure 1. Note that the last part of the figure (i.e., the line labelled EXPOST) cannot be interpreted in conjunction with other parts since it relies on the assumption that no associations are observed on the line labelled PERFEVAL.

Finally, the hypotheses set out above relate only to the associations which are expected between the variables included in the study. It is not suggested that these variables explain the diversity of accounting practices in divisionalized companies; many other variables would be needed for that purpose. In the statistical analysis which follows, we will be looking for associations which are statistically significant, in the sense that they are unlikely to occur by chance.

To summarize, positive associations are expected between the variables studied, with the exception that a negative association is expected between PERFEVAL and EXPOST if hypothesis H_4 is not supported. The general hypothesis is that there will be associations between the accounting variables and the divisional autonomy variables included in the study. The null hypothesis is that such associations will not be present.

Figure 1
EXPECTED ASSOCIATIONS

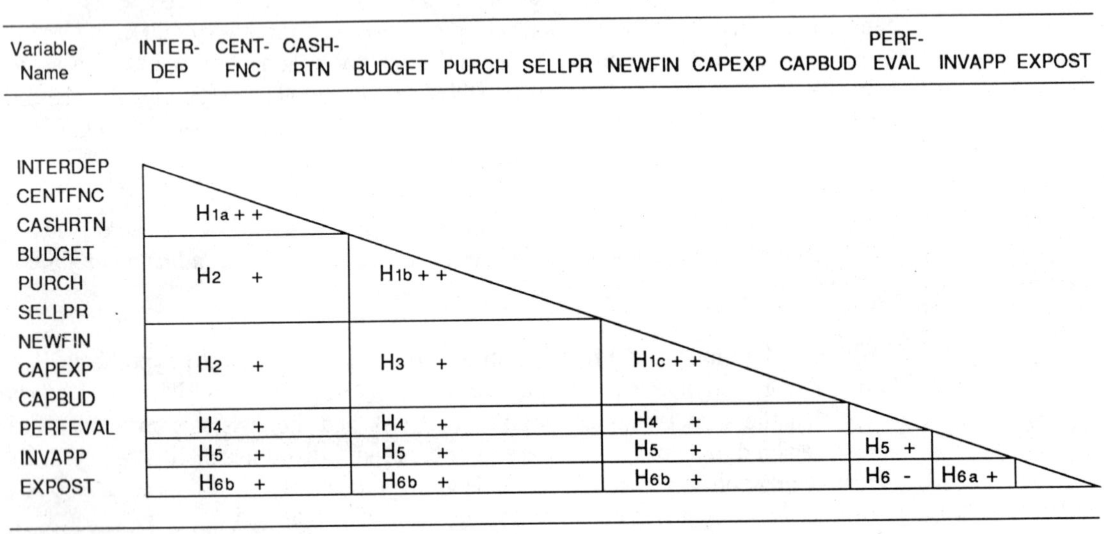

\+ Positive association
\+ + Strongly positive association
\- Negative association

Results

Because of the nature of the scales used to construct the 12 variables, parametric statistical techniques could not be used to analyze the data. Kendall's tau correlation coefficients were calculated for each pair of variables and further analyses were carried out to confirm the conclusions drawn.

Table 5 contains the Kendall's tau correlations for the U.S. and U.K. data. The most striking feature is the relatively few significant correlations. The variables within each of the first two groups, interconnectedness and operating autonomy, have significant correlations and there are some significant correlations between the vari-

Table 5

MATRICES OF KENDALL'S TAU CORRELATIONS

Variable Name	INTER-DEP	CENT-FNC	CASH-RTN	BUDGET	PURCH	SELLPR	NEWFIN	CAPEXP	CAPBUD	PERF-EVAL	INVAPP	EXPOST
U.S. Data												
INTERDEP	1.00											
CENTFNC	.52**	1.00										
CASHRTN	.55**	.52**	1.00									
BUDGET	.14*	.13*	.06	1.00								
PURCH	.15**	.25**	.23**	.16**	1.00							
SELLPR	.12*	.07	.18**	.18**	.20**	1.00						
NEWFIN	-.06	-.02	-.03	.12*	.04	.11	1.00					
CAPEXP	.02	.09	.07	.06	.01	.03	.01	1.00				
CAPBUD	.20**	.25**	.17*	.04	.10	.19**	-.07	-.09	1.00			
PERFEVAL	-.04	-.01	-.15*	-.01	.03	.10	-.10	.04	.22**	1.00		
INVAPP	-.18**	-.06	-.12*	-.06	-.10	-.03	.04	.07	-.04	-.07	1.00	
EXPOST	-.02	.04	-.01	-.05	.09	.01	-.04	.02	.08	.05	.24**	1.00
U.K. Data												
INTERDEP	1.00											
CENTFNC	.49**	1.00										
CASHRTN	.49**	.44**	1.00									
BUDGET	.06	.04	.08	1.00								
PURCH	.09	.18**	.10	.21**	1.00							
SELLPR	.08	.15**	.12*	.20**	.33**	1.00						
NEWFIN	.13*	.12*	.14*	.20**	.03	.10	1.00					
CAPEXP	.03	.03	.08	-.03	-.02	.04	-.01	1.00				
CAPBUD	.13*	.13*	.10	.05	.06	.03	.12	.12	1.00			
PERFEVAL	-.04	.05	.02	.04	.10	.07	-.08	-.08	.10	1.00		
INVAPP	-.13*	-.16**	-.13*	.05	.06	.06	-.04	.02	.03	.09	1.00	
EXPOST	.02	-.06	-.06	.02	-.01	-.01	.01	-.01	-.01	.15*	.16**	1.00

* Significant at the .05 level.
** Significant at the .01 level.

ables in those two groups, especially in the U.S. Otherwise, there are very few significant correlations.

Although NEWFIN in the U.K. and CAPBUD in the U.S. are positively associated with the variables representing interconnectedness and operating autonomy, the lack of significant correlations within the group of variables representing capital expenditure autonomy suggests that the three variables, NEWFIN, CAPEXP, and CAPBUD, may not capture an underlying factor. Thus, whereas the null hypothesis of no association can be rejected in favor of hypothesis H_1 in the case of interconnectedness and operating autonomy, it cannot be rejected in the case of capital expenditure autonomy.

The association between operating autonomy and interconnectedness predicted in hypothesis H_4 was found in the U.S. data, but not in the U.K. data (although there were some significant correlations in the U.K.). Since the third group of variables does not adequately reflect capital expenditure autonomy, the association between interconnectedness and capital expenditure autonomy cannot be tested. Nevertheless, the individual variables can be considered.

The significant correlations between CAPBUD and the interconnectedness variables indicate that highly interconnected organizations tend to centralize the preparation of capital budgets. The associations between NEWFIN and the interconnectedness variables are significant in the U.K., but not in the U.S. The lack of significance in the U.S. reflects a general tendency for U.S. companies to centralize the raising of new financing. In the U.K., however, there appears to be some decentralization in companies which have relatively independent divisions.

Hypothesis H_3 cannot be tested directly because the variables selected to reflect divisional capital expenditure autonomy do not appear to have captured an underlying factor. It is worth noting, however, that there are very few significant associations between the operating autonomy variables and NEWFIN, CAPEXP, and CAPBUD.

There are few significant correlations between the accounting variables and the divisional autonomy variables. Except for CASHRTN and CAPBUD in the U.S., there are no significant associations between the divisional autonomy variables and PERFEVAL. Thus, the null hypothesis cannot be rejected in favor of hypothesis H_4. A similar conclusion can be drawn concerning hypothesis H_5 although there are some significant correlations between the interconnectedness variables and INVAPP, both in the U.S. and the U.K. These significant correlations, however, do not have the predicted sign. There appears to be a tendency to use discounted cash flow techniques to evaluate divisional capital expenditure projects in the more highly interconnected companies. This suggests that such techniques are part of the centralized decision-making process, rather than a means of monitoring delegated decisions.

Since hypothesis H_4 was not supported, it was appropriate to consider hypothesis H_6. The expected negative correlation between PERFEVAL and EXPOST was not observed. The positive correlation in the U.K. data suggests a tendency for *ex post* capital expenditure controls to be used together with performance measures which reflect the capital asset base. The two accounting techniques do not appear to be alternatives as hypothesized. The significant positive correlation between INVAPP and EXPOST observed in both the U.S. and the U.K. indicates that *ex post* audits tend to be used when discounted cash flow techniques are used for the evaluation of divisional capital projects—as predicted by hypothesis H_{6a}.

Finally, hypothesis H_{6b} must be rejected since there are no significant correlations between EXPOST and the divisional autonomy variables.

Thus, the tau correlations provide little support for the general hypothesis of the study that there is an association between the accounting methods used in divisionalized companies and the autonomy of divisional managers. To confirm this conclusion, further analyses were carried out using the "Guttman-Lingoes (G-L) Nonmetric Program Series" [Lingoes, 1973].[2]

The G-L Conjoint Measurement III (CM-III) Program was used to rescale the data such that product moment correlation coefficients could be used. The resulting correlation matrices were not substantially different from the tau matrices. This similarity was confirmed by examining visual representations of the matrices, obtained using the G-L Smallest Space Analysis Program—MINISSA-1(M) [Guttman, 1968; Lingoes, 1965; Roskam and Lingoes, 1970].

The G-L Nonmetric Factor Analysis Program SSA-III [Lingoes and Guttman, 1967; Lingoes, 1966] was applied to both the Kendall's tau and the rescaled data as a further test of hypothesis H_1. This program extracted factors corresponding to interconnectedness and operating autonomy but was unable to locate any underlying factor corresponding to capital expenditure autonomy. This confirmed the conclusion concerning hypothesis H_1 reached using the Kendall's tau correlations. In general, the factor analysis and multidimensional scaling did not add to the insights obtained by examining the tau correlations. They did, however, provide confirmation of the interpretations discussed above.

Finally, tests were undertaken in an attempt to identify industry or size effects in the data. There were no significant correlations between the variables included in the study and the industry or size of the responding companies.

Conclusions

This study has failed to locate the expected associations between accounting methods used in divisionalized companies and the autonomy of divisional managers. There are no grounds to support rejection of the null hypothesis of no association. The expected relationships were observed within the groups of variables reflecting interconnectedness and operating autonomy, but the variables selected to represent capital expenditure autonomy failed to capture an underlying factor.

The associations between the accounting variables and variables within the interconnectedness and operating autonomy groups either were not significant or had the wrong sign. Thus, the study provides no support for the general hypothesis that differences in the extent of divisional autonomy contribute to the variety of accounting methods used to control divisionalized operations.

It was suggested earlier that the possibility of controlling capital expenditure decisions through *ex post* controls might explain some of the variety in divisional performance measures. The expected negative association between PERFEVAL and

EXPOST was not observed. In fact, there was a weak, but significant, positive association in the U.K. between the two variables. The only general comment that can be made about the accounting variables, PERFEVAL, INVAPP, and EXPOST, is that there is a slight tendency for all three accounting methods to be used together. The use of *ex post* controls does not, therefore, help to explain the variety of performance measures used in the divisionalized companies in this study.

Despite differences in the extent to which particular accounting methods are used in the U.S. and the U.K., especially in the case of discounted cash flow techniques and post-completion audits (see Tables 1, 2, and 3), the two tau correlation matrices in Table 5 look remarkably similar and the general conclusions of the statistical analyses of the two data sets are the same for both countries. This similarity in the statistical analyses of the two data sets provides a measure of confirmation for the statistical methods. Nevertheless, caution must be exercised in interpreting the results. The*ad hoc* nature of the scales used to quantify the 12 variables was discussed earlier.

A further problem may arise from the use of questionnaires. A mail questionnaire of the type used in this study will elicit responses which reflect formal control systems. Such formal control systems, however, are only one of the methods used to control complex organizations [Galbraith, 1977]. Informal systems which are embodied in the organization culture can be major components of the organizational control process [Ouchi, 1979]. The existence of informal control mechanisms may confound the relationship between accounting variables and variables used to reflect divisional autonomy [Scapens and Sale, 1981b]. Thus, the possibility of misspecification has to be acknowledged.

The post-questionnaire interviews suggested possible explanations for the failure to locate the expected associations. First, in most cases, all available accounting methods will be imperfect. There will not be a "correct" method. The choice of accounting methods, or combination of methods, will be influenced by anticipated costs and benefits of the information and these will be situation-specific [Demski and Feltham, 1976]. Second, the evolution of an accounting system is a dynamic process, and there are unlikely to be simple static relationships between accounting methods and organizational variables. Third, the personalities and backgrounds of key individuals within an organization can affect the choice of accounting methods. In a study of the role of controllers in large organizations, Sathe [1982] found only weak or no associations between controller involvement in management and organizational characteristics, but he found a strong association between controller involvement and the personal characteristics of corporate management.

These three factors could explain the failure of this exploratory study to find associations between accounting methods and divisional autonomy. Furthermore, they indicate that there may be no simple static relationships between accounting methods in divisionalized companies and organizational variables. There is a need for more research in this area. One possible approach would be to study the dynamics of management control processes in their organizational contexts through longitudinal studies of individual companies. The possibility of studying accounting practices in their organizational contexts is explored in Roberts and Scapens [forthcoming]. Such studies could then provide a basis for reformulating the hypotheses tested in this paper.

References

Amey, L. R., *The Efficiency of Business Enterprises* (Allen and Unwin, 1969).

———, "Tomkins on Residual Income," *Journal of Business Finance and Accounting* (Spring 1975), pp. 55–68.

Demski, J. S. and G. A. Feltham, *Cost Determination: A Conceptual Approach* (Iowa State University Press, 1976).

Emmanuel, C. R. and D. T. Otley, "The Usefulness of Residual Income," *Journal of Business Finance and Accounting* (Winter 1976), pp. 43–51.

Ezzamel, M. A. and K. Hilton, "Can Divisional Discretion be Measured," *Journal of Business Finance and Accounting* (Summer 1980), pp. 311–329.

Galbraith, J. R., *Organizational Design* (Addison-Wesley, 1977).

Guttman, L., "A General Nonmetric Technique for finding the Smallest Co-ordinate Space for a Configuration of Points," *Psychometrika* (December 1968), pp. 469–506.

Lingoes, J. C., "An IBM–7090 Program for Guttman-Lingoes Smallest Space Analysis—I," *Behavioral Science,* (April 1965), pp. 183–184.

———, "An IBM–7090 Program for Guttman-Lingoes Smallest Space Analysis—III," *Behavioral Science,* (January 1966), pp. 75–76.

———, *The Guttman-Lingoes Nonmetric Program Series* (Mathesis Press, 1973).

——— and L. Guttman, "Nonmetric Factor Analysis: A Rank Reducing Alternative to Linear Factor Analysis," *Multivariate Behavioral Research* (October 1976), pp. 485–505.

Mauriel, J. and R. H. Anthony, "Misevaluation of Investment Centre Performance," *Harvard Business Review* (March-April 1966), pp. 98–105.

Moser, C. A. and G. Kalton, *Survey Methods in Social Investigation,* 2nd Edition (Heinemann, 1971).

Otley, D. T., "The Contingency Theory of Management Accounting: Achievement and Prognosis," *Accounting, Organisations and Society* (Winter 1980), pp. 413–428.

Ouchi, W. G., "A Conceptual Framework for the Design of Organizational Control Mechanisms," *Management Science* (September 1979), pp. 833–848.

Reece, J. S. and W. R. Cool, "Measuring Investment Center Performance," *Harvard Business Review* (May-June 1978), pp. 28–46, 174–176.

Roberts, J. and R. W. Scapens, "Accounting Systems and Systems of Accountability—Understanding Accounting Practices in Their Organizational Contexts," *Accounting, Organisations and Society* (forthcoming).

Roskam, E. and J. C. Lingoes, "Minissa—1: A FORTRAN IV (G) Program for the Smallest Space Analysis of Square Symmetric Matrices," *Behavioral Science* (March 1970), pp. 204–205.

Sathe, V., *Controller Involvement in Management* (Prentice-Hall, 1982).

Sapens, R. W. and J. T. Sale, "The Control of Divisional Investment Projects: Some Evidence from the U.S. and U.K.," *Maanblad vor Accountancy en Bedrijfshuishoudkunde* (Spring 1981a), pp. 118–144.

——— and ———, "Performance Measurement and Formal Capital Expenditure Controls in Divisionalized Companies," *Journal of Business Finance and Accounting* (Autumn 1981b), pp. 389–419.

———, ——— and P. A. Tikkas, *Financial Control of Divisional Capital Investment* (The Institute of Cost and Management Accounting, 1982).

Shillinglaw, G., *Managerial Cost Accounting,* 4th Edition (Irwin, 1977).

Solomons, D., *Divisional Performance: Measurement and Control* (Irwin, 1965).

Tomkins, C. R., *Financial Planning in Divisionalized Companies* (Haymarket, 1973).

Notes

1. Copies of both the U.S. and U.K. questionnaires are available upon request from either author.
2. The results of the secondary analysis are available upon request from either of the authors.

IV MANAGERIAL ACCOUNTING: GLOBAL PRACTICES OF FOREIGN CURRENCY TRANSLATIONS

Translation of Foreign Currency Operations: SFAS No. 52
Richard E. Veasey and Suk H. Kim

SFAS No. 52: Expediency or Principle?
James A. Largay III

The Impact of Foreign Currency Translation on Reporting During the Phase-in of SFAS No. 52
James J. Benjamin, Steven D. Grossman, and Casper E. Wiggins

10. TRANSLATION OF FOREIGN CURRENCY OPERATIONS: SFAS NO. 52

RICHARD E. VEAZEY and SUK H. KIM

Richard E. Veazey is Associate Professor of Accounting at the F.E. Seidman College of Business and Administration, Grand Valley State College, Michigan. Suk H. Kim is Associate Professor of Finance and International Business at the College of Business and Administration, University of Detroit.

This article compares and contrasts the effect of SFAS No. 52 (current exchange rate method) with SFAS No. 8 (temporal method). It points out the simplicity of SFAS No. 52 because the current exchange rate is used during the translation process. A hypothetical example is presented to illustrate how the financial statements of a foreign subsidiary are restated into US dollars using the functional currency approach.

Financial statements are intended to present information about the performance, financial position, and cash flows of a company. To meet this purpose, the financial statements of separate entities within a business enterprise are consolidated and presented as though they were the financial statements of a single economic entity. Financial statements are frequently restated or translated from one currency into another to assist the users of financial statements, such as investors and creditors.

Although some international business operations have existed in foreign countries for centuries, there has been an unprecedented expansion of global economic activity since the end of World War II. There are many examples of the increasing importance of international transactions for the United States. Many US firms, such as IBM, Gillette and Pfizer, have earned more from international operations than from domestic operations. Multinational companies, such as Mobil Oil, IBM and Gulf Oil, do business with more than 50 countries around the world. US exports and imports have increased more than ten times in the last two decades. US direct investments abroad increased from \$32 billion in 1960 to \$213 billion in 1980, a sevenfold increase. International finance has also become increasingly important as it serves world trade and foreign investment. International earning assets for the Bank of America, for example, represent more than half its total earning assets. Citibank, N.A., maintains more than 250 overseas branches in over 100 countries.

The translation of foreign currency is important for many US companies and banks because they are involved in foreign currency transactions and/or foreign

Richard E. Veazey and Suk H. Kim, "Translation of Foreign Currency Operations: SFAS No. 52," *Columbia Journal of World Business* (Winter 1982): 17–22. Reprinted by permission.

operations that will produce different financial results. US firms that conduct business with a foreign entity must deal with a wide range of social, political, economic and legal differences between countries. In addition, a wide disparity exists between US Generally Accepted Accounting Principles (GAAP) and foreign GAAP regarding the measurement and recording of assets, liabilities, revenues, expenses, and gains and losses. As a result, the US accountant must reconcile foreign financial statements with US GAAP for the purposes of consolidation, combination, or equity accounting. Foreign currency translation became even more important in 1973 when the flexible exchange rate system was established. It abolished the old fixed exchange rate system that was established in 1944 based upon the Bretton Woods Agreement.[1]

The growing importance of foreign currency transactions and/or foreign operations has been recognized by the accounting profession since the Financial Accounting Standards Board (FASB) issued its Statement of Financial Accounting Standards No. 8 (SFAS No. 8), *Accounting for the Translation of Foreign Currency Transactions and Foreign Currency Financial Statements,* in October 1975.[2] SFAS No. 8 formally required US companies to translate their foreign currency financial statements into dollars by applying the appropriate exchange rate (historical rate, current rate or average rate) to the measurement basis of each account. This statement also required companies to show all foreign exchange gains or losses in their quarterly and annual reports, regardless of whether these gains or losses were realized or unrealized.

SFAS No. 8 was a product of considerable effort by the FASB to resolve the currency translation issue, which included an extensive exposure draft and discussion memorandum. However, from its inception in fall 1975, SFAS No. 8 was the subject of extensive debate. Most of the criticism of SFAS No. 8 centered around the recognition of foreign exchange gains or losses. Companies claimed that SFAS No. 8 grossly distorted their earnings because of the sharp fluctuations in foreign exchange rates. Early in 1976 the FASB acknowledged the criticism but concluded that it did not need to revise the statement. In May 1978, the FASB issued an invitation for public comment on FASB Statements 1–12. The majority of the comments received centered on SFAS No. 8. The respondents criticized the Statement for failing to reflect the underlying economic reality of foreign operations because of the abnormality of financial results and relationships, plus the volatility of reported earnings. Specifically, SFAS No. 8 required that inventories and fixed assets be translated at historical rates and debt at current rates. In addition, many respondents wanted some form of deferral or non-recognition of exchange adjustments resulting from the application of SFAS No. 8. In February 1979, a 22-member task force was established to advise the FASB on its recommendation of SFAS No. 8. A substantial portion of the FASB's time and effort was devoted to this project after February 1979. On August 28, 1980, the FASB issued an Exposure Draft of a proposed replacement for SFAS No. 8. The FASB held public hearings on its proposed draft on December 17, 18, 19 and 22, 1980; issued a revised Exposure Draft on June 30, 1981; and issued SFAS No. 52, *Foreign Currency Translation,*[3] on December 7, 1981. SFAS No. 52 supersedes SFAS No. 8 (which superseded SFAS No. 1); paragraphs 7, and 10–22 of Chapter 12 in ARB No. 43, and paragraph 18 of APB Opinion No. 6; and amended paragraph 5 of Chapter 12 in ARB No. 43; and paragraph 13 of APB Opinion No. 22. In addition SFAS No. 52 supersedes SFAS No. 20 and FASB Interpretation Nos. 15 and 17.

SFAS No. 52 requires use of the current exchange rate in translating foreign currency financial statements in US dollars. Such translation adjustments are placed directly in stockholders' equity rather than income. Thus, SFAS No. 52 is expected to greatly reduce fluctuations in many companies' reported earnings caused by gyrations in foreign exchange rates under SFAS No. 8.[4]

This paper is divided into two sections. The first section briefly outlines SFAS No. 52 and points out differences between SFAS No. 8 and SFAS No. 52. The second section examines major elements of the new statement and provides an example of translation of foreign currency operations.

Differences Between SFAS No. 8 and SFAS No. 52

According to SFAS No. 8, the objectives of translation were as follows: "For the purpose of preparing an enterprise's financial statements, the objective of translation is to measure and express (a) in dollars and (b) in conformity with US Generally Accepted Accounting Principles the assets, liabilities, revenue, or expenses that are measured or denominated in foreign currency."[5] The new objectives of translation, as stated in SFAS No. 52, are to "(a) Provide information that is generally compatible with the expected economic effects of a rate change on an enterprise's cash flows and equity. (b) Reflect in consolidated statements the financial results and relationships of the individual consolidated entities as measured in their functional currencies in conformity with US Generally Accepted Accounting Principles."[6]

The change in the objectives of translation is significant. The underlying assumption of SFAS No. 8 was that consolidated financial statements should reflect the transactions of the consolidated group as though all operations, including foreign operations, were extensions of the parent's domestic operations. This premise failed to recognize the fact that in many cases the operations of foreign subsidiaries existed in other environments and involved foreign currency cash flows in those other environments. Thus, the accounting results after translation did not portray the foreign currency cash flows.

SFAS No. 52 is intended to portray the foreign currency cash flows. Use of the functional currency approach and the current rate method enables companies to maintain compatibility in terms of income and cash flows before and after translation. Financial summary indicators such as profit margin, gross profit, and debt-to-equity ratio are almost the same after translation into the reporting currency as they are in the functional currency. In addition, the volatility of the company's reported earnings should be reduced under SFAS No. 52 because companies' foreign exchange gains or losses will be reported in a separate component of equity, not income. In order to achieve such new objectives of translation, some provisions of SFAS No. 8 were changed. Table 1 compares the major provisions of SFAS No. 8 with the same provisions of SFAS No. 52.[7]

Table 1
COMPARISON OF THE MAJOR PROVISIONS OF SFAS NO. 8 AND SFAS NO. 52

Provision	SFAS No. 8	SFAS No. 52
Translation method	Temporal method	Current exchange rate method
Functional currency	Not used	The currency of the primary economic environment in which an entity generates and expends cash
Foreign-exchange gains or losses from balance sheet translations	Included in current income	Placed directly in stockholders' equity on the balance sheet
Translation of operations in highly inflationary economies	Normally not serious under the temporal method	The financial statements of a foreign entity are remeasured as if the functional currency were the reporting currency
Gains or losses from foreign currency transactions	Included in current income	Included in current income
Realization of the separate component of equity	Not applicable	Upon sale or upon complete or substantial liquidation of the investment
Gains or losses from transactions intended to hedge a net investment	Included in current income	Placed directly in stockholders' equity on the balance sheet
Gains or losses from intercompany transactions	Included in current income	Accumulated as a separate component of stockholders' equity for all intercompany transactions that are of a long-term investment nature. Included in current income for other intercompany transactions

Major Elements of SFAS No. 52

Functional Currency

The functional currency of an entity as defined in SFAS No. 52 (paragraph 39) is "the currency of the primary economic environment in which the entity operates; normally, that is the currency of the environment in which an entity primarily generates and expends cash." For example, a French subsidiary with relatively self-contained and integrated operations in France would have the franc as its functional currency. Such translation adjustments do not affect cash flows and are not included in net income. Consequently, such translation adjustments are placed directly in stockholders' equity. However, if the French subsidiary has some transactions and open account balances denominated in deutschemarks from a German customer, those balances must be restated into francs and gains or losses must be included in the subsidiary's net income before the statements are translated into US dollars during the consolidation process.

The functional currency of an entity is not always identical with the currency of the country in which the foreign operation is located or the currency of the country in which the records are maintained. For example, for those foreign operations whose cash flows related to individual assets and liabilities directly affect the parent's US dollar cash flows on a current basis, the dollar is the functional currency and exchange gains or losses must be included in net income. Such a situation may occur when the foreign entity is merely an extension of the parent. In this case, the functional currency is the reporting currency of the parent company.

In some cases, it is difficult to determine the functional currency of a foreign operation. For example, an entity might have more than one distinct and separable operation, in which case each operation may be considered a separate entity. If those operations are conducted in different economic environments, they may have different functional currencies. If a foreign operation conducts significant amounts of business in two or more countries, the functional currency may not be clearly identifiable. In those instances, the functional currency depends on the economic facts and circumstances pertaining to a particular foreign operation. Those economic facts include the nature and extent of a foreign operation's cash flow, sales price, sales market, expense, financing, and intercompany transactions and arrangements.

Translation of Foreign Currency Financial Statements

Under SFAS No. 52, the current exchange rate method is used to translate foreign currency balance sheets from their functional currency into the reporting currency. The current exchange rate method is the easiest to apply because all assets and liabilities are translated at the current exchange rate (that is, the rates in effect at the balance sheet date). Only owners' equity is translated at the historical exchange rate. Unlike the controversial SFAS No. 8, SFAS No. 52 does not require companies to include translation adjustments in net income. Instead, these translation adjustments will be reported separately and accumulated in a separate component of equity (entitled "Equity Adjustment from Foreign Currency Translation") until the sale or the complete or substantially complete liquidation of the foreign net investment.[8]

Under SFAS No. 52, all income statement elements are translated in a manner that produces approximately the same result as using the exchange rate in effect on the dates on which these elements are recognized. However, SFAS No. 52 (paragraph 12) provides that "because translation at the exchange rates at the dates the numerous revenues, expenses, gains, and losses are recognized is generally impractical, an appropriately weighted average exchange rate for the period may be used to translate those elements."

In the following example, the Canadian subsidiary of a US multinational corporation with a Canadian dollar functional currency started business and acquired fixed assets on January 1, 1983 when the Canadian $/US$ exchange rate was 0.85. Table 2 applies the temporal method (SFAS No. 8) and the current exchange rate method (SFAS No. 52) to hypothetical financial statements which are affected by devaluation and revaluation of 11.8%, respectively. For devaluation, the exchange rate on December 31, 1983 was 0.75 and the weighted average exchange rate for the period was 0.80. For revaluation, the exchange rate on December 31, 1983 was 0.95 and the weighted average rate for the period was 0.90.

Since SFAS No. 52 requires companies to use a single rate in translating balance sheet items and to report translation adjustments in equity, fluctuations in reported earnings are reduced significantly under the new standard. Net income under the current exchange rate method is approximately the same as the expected level of earnings in Canadian dollars.

If the US dollar gained against the Canadian dollar by 11.8% during 1983, an $11 translation loss would be reported in the balance sheet as "Equity Adjustments from Foreign Currency Translation" under SFAS No. 52. On the other hand, under SFAS No. 8 a translation gain of $70 would be reported in the income statement. The $70 gain would be recognized because SFAS No. 8 requires fixed assets and inventory to be translated at historical rates and debts to be translated at current rates. In contrast, if the US dollar decreased in value against the Canadian dollar by 11.8%, under the current exchange rate method a translation gain of $11 would be placed directly in stockholders' equity on the balance sheet. Under the temporal method a translation loss of $58 would be recognized in the income statement.

Under SFAS No. 52, key operating and financial ratios, such as net income to revenue, gross profit, and long-term debt to equity, are maintained after translation from Canadian to US currency. However, these same ratios in the Canadian dollar under SFAS No. 52 are significantly different from those in the US dollar under SFAS No. 8.

There were numerous reports that SFAS No. 8 had caused many companies' reported earnings to fluctuate widely due to changes in foreign exchange rates. "In 1978 Exxon suffered foreign exchange losses of $316 million, which were larger than the profits of Chase Manhattan Corporation or US Steel or Goodyear Tire and Rubber Company."[9] "The experience of the Japanese electronics producer, Sony, which follows United States accounting rules because its shares are traded on the New York Stock Exchange, is illustrative. In 1979, Sony's consolidated second-quarter earnings were reduced by a $49.3 million foreign exchange loss; whereas, in 1978, the second-quarter net was restated to include a $19.3 million gain on currency conversion, a $68.6 million swing in pretax net income that might never be realized."[10] Many financial executives applauded the new rule because it is expected to significantly reduce such fluctuations in companies' earnings.

Highly Inflationary Economies

An issue perhaps unresolved to the satisfaction of financial executives is the question of how to deal with foreign subsidiaries in countries with runaway inflation. SFAS No. 52 (paragraph 11) states that "The financial statements of a foreign entity in a highly inflationary economy shall be remeasured as if the functional currency were

Table 2

TRANSLATION OF FOREIGN CURRENCY OPERATIONS

		After Devaluation of Can. $				After Revaluation Of Can. $			
		SFAS No. 8		SFAS No. 52		SFAS No. 8		SFAS No. 52	
Balance Sheet	**Canadian Dollars**	**Rates Used**	**US Dollars**	**Rates Used**	**US Dollars**	**Rates Used**	**US Dollars**	**Rates Used**	**US Dollars**
Cash and receivables	100	.75	75	.75	75	.95	95	.95	95
Inventory	300	.81*	243	.75	225	.91*	273	.95	285
Fixed assets, net	600	.85	510	.75	450	.85	510	.95	570
Total	1000		828		750		878		950
Current liabilities	180	.75	135	.75	135	.95	171	.95	171
Long-term debt	700	.75	525	.75	525	.95	665	.95	665
Common stock	100	.85	85	.85	85	.85	85	.85	85
Retained earnings	20		83		16		(43)		18
Equity adjustments from translation	—		—		(11)		—		11
Total	1000		828		750		878		950
Income Statement									
Revenue	130	.80	104	.80	104	.90	117	.90	117
Cost of goods sold	(60)	.83*	(50)	.80	(48)	.93*	(56)	.90	(54)
Depreciation	(20)	.85*	(17)	.80	(16)	.95*	(19)	.90	(18)
Other expenses	(10)	.80	(8)	.80	(8)	.90	(9)	.90	(9)
Exchange gain (loss)	—		70		—		(58)		—
Income before tax	40		99		32		(25)		36
Income tax	(20)	.80	(16)	.80	(16)	.90	(18)	.90	(18)
Net income (loss)	20		83		16		(43)		18
Ratios									
Net income to revenue	0.15		0.80		0.15		negative		0.15
Gross profit	0.54		0.52		0.54		0.52		0.54
Long-term debt to equity	5.83		3.125		5.83		15.83		5.83

*Historical rates for inventory, cost of goods sold, and depreciation of fixed assets.

the reporting currency." A highly inflationary economy is defined as one that has cumulative inflation of approximately 100% or more over a three-year period. The cumulative inflation for three years is a compounded rate; as a result, an annual inflation rate of about 26% produces a cumulative inflation of 100% over three years. According to *International Financial Statistics,*[11] a monthly publication by the International Monetary Fund, the following countries had cumulative inflation of more than 100% for the three-year period from 1978 to 1980: Argentina, Brazil, Chile, Ghana, Iceland, Israel, Jamaica, Nicaragua, Peru, Somalia, Turkey, Uruguay, and Zaire. The *International Financial Statistics* covers data only for member countries of the International Monetary Fund.

SFAS No. 52 does not specify which three years should be used to determine a highly inflationary economy. The new rule (paragraph 109) states "In some instances, the trend of inflation might be as important as the absolute rate. It is the Board's intention that the definition of a highly inflationary economy be applied with judgment." Thus, companies should not rely on an absolute rule to determine the three years used but should exercise sound judgment. As a practical matter, the three-year period may be the one that ends with the beginning of the current fiscal year.

SFAS No. 52 does not specify what index should be used to measure inflation. The FASB has issued an amendment to SFAS No. 33, *Financial Reporting and Changing Prices,*[12] to be consistent with the functional currency approach for foreign currency translation. The amendment is SFAS No. 70, *Financial Reporting and Changing Prices: Foreign Currency Translation,*[13] dated December 1982 (paragraph 16) and it states: "The index used to compute information in units of constant functional currency purchasing power shall be a broad-based measure of the change in the general purchasing power of that functional currency. If no reliable index is available for a particular functional currency, management shall estimate the change in the general purchasing power of that currency."

Foreign Currency Transaction

A foreign currency transaction is one whose terms are denominated in a currency other than the transacting entity's functional currency. Transaction gains or losses typically result from fluctuations in exchange rates between the transaction date and the settlement date. Examples include credit purchases or sales whose prices are denominated in foreign currencies, borrowed or loaned funds denominated in foreign currencies, and uncompleted forward exchange contracts.

Normally, the requirements for translation of foreign currency transactions in SFAS No. 52 are the same as those in SFAS No. 8. Outstanding obligations such as receivables or payables are recorded at the exchange rate in effect at the date of the transaction. They are subsequently translated at the exchange rate in effect at the date of the settlement. Because transaction gains or losses directly affect an entity's functional currency cash flows, they are reflected currently in net income.

Gains or losses on the following foreign currency transactions are not included in current income but are reported in the same manner as translation adjustments: (1) transaction gains or losses that are designated as an economic hedge of a net investment in a foreign entity; (2) transaction gains or losses that are designated as a hedge of a foreign currency commitment; and (3) intercompany transaction gains or losses that are of a long-term investment nature. A foreign currency transaction shall be considered a hedge if both of the following two conditions are met: (1) the foreign currency transaction is designated a hedge of a foreign currency commitment, and (2) the foreign currency commitment is firm. In essence, a hedge is the process of taking a position, and gains or losses result from taking such a position.

Intercompany Transactions

SFAS No. 52 differentiates between intercompany foreign currency transactions of a long term investment nature and other intercompany transactions. The intercompany transactions of a long-term investment nature are transactions and balances for which settlement is not planned or anticipated in the foreseeable future. Possible examples might include balances that take the form of an advance or a demand note payable, provided that payment is not planned or anticipated in the foreseeable future. Thus, exchange gains or losses from such transactions are to be reported in the same manner as translation adjustments when financial statements for those entities are consolidated, combined, or accounted for by the equity method. Other intercompany transactions are those of a trading nature. Transaction gains or losses attributable to other intercompany transactions affect the functional currency cash flows of the foreign operation because they are settled on a more current basis. Accordingly, increases or decreases in actual or expected functional currency cash flows from those transactions should be reported currently in net income.

Required Disclosure

SFAS No. 52 requires companies to disclose transaction gains or losses, as well as translation adjustments in the financial statements or notes thereto. The aggregate transaction adjustment, including gains or losses on forward contracts, must be disclosed. However, dealers in foreign exchange, primarily banks, are the exception. Although gains or losses from dealer transactions may fit the definition of transaction gains or losses, they may be disclosed as dealer gains or losses rather than transaction gains or losses.

An analysis of the changes that have occurred during the period must be disclosed in the separate component of equity for cumulative translation adjustments. At a minimum, the analysis must include: (a) beginning and ending balances of cumulative translation adjustments, (b) the aggregate translation adjustment for the period, (c) the amount of income tax expense for the period allocated to translation adjustments, and (d) the amounts transferred from the cumulative translation adjustments and included in net income for the period because of the sale or complete or substantially complete liquidation of the investment in a foreign entity.

Conclusion

SFAS No. 52 became effective for fiscal years beginning on or after December 15, 1982, although earlier application was encouraged. The FASB adopted the statement by a four-to-three vote. Mr. Kirk, Chairman of the FASB, stated, "The board's close vote on the final rule, which follows five years of debate on the thorny question of foreign currency translations, is 'reflective of strongly held views on the outside, too.' "[14] Many financial executives applaud the new rule, but they do not believe that it will resolve all the problems related to the translation of foreign currency financial statements into the reporting currency.

Nevertheless, SFAS No. 52 ended the Board's painstaking process of changing an accounting standard which did not reflect economic reality. Under SFAS No. 8, erratic exchange rates caused erratic earnings for two major reasons. First, receivables, payables, and other monetary items were translated at current exchange rates, while inventories and fixed assets hedging these monetary items were translated at historical exchange rates. Second, companies were required to reflect foreign-exchange gains or losses from balance sheet translations in the income statement. Since SFAS No. 52 has corrected these two problems, it is expected to significantly reduce fluctuations in earnings that existed under SFAS No. 8.

Notes

1. For details, see Suk H. Kim, *International Business Finance,* Robert F. Dame, Inc., Richmond, 1983. Chapters 1, 3, 8 and 10
2. Statement of Financial Accounting Standards No. 8, *Accounting for the Translation of Foreign Currency Transactions and Foreign Currency Financial Statements,* FASB, Stamford, Conn., 1975
3. Statement of Financial Accounting Standards No. 52, *Foreign Currency Translation,* FASB, 1981
4. See, for example, "FASB Replaces Standard on Foreign Currency Translation," *Journal of Accountancy,* January 1982, p. 9
5. SFAS No. 8, paragraph 6
6. SFAS No. 52, paragraph 4
7. Peat Marwick Mitchell & Co., *Foreign Currency Translation,* PMM & Co., New York, December 1981, p. 4
8. The retained earnings account is kept clean under SFAS No. 52. See, "FASB Statement No. 52: Keeping Retained Earnings 'Clean'," *Journal of Accountancy,* May 1982, p. 114
9. Arpan, Jeffrey S. and Lee H. Radebaugh, *International Accounting and Multinational Enterprises,* Warren, Gorham & Lamont, Boston, 1981, p. 88
10. Shapiro, Alan C., *Multinational Financial Management,* Allyn and Bacon, Boston, 1982, p. 115
11. *International Financial Statistics,* International Monetary Fund, Washington, D.C., February 1981
12. Statement of Financial Accounting Standards No. 33, *Financial Reporting and Changing Prices,* FASB, 1979
13. Statement of Financial Accounting Standards No. 70, *Financial Reporting and Changing Prices: Foreign Currency Translation,* FASB, 1982
14. Bettner, Jill, "Major Accounting-Rule Change Adopted Covering Foreign-Currency Translation," *The Wall Street Journal,* 8 December 1981, p. 8, cols. 2–3

11. SFAS NO. 52: EXPEDIENCY OR PRINCIPLE?

JAMES A. LARGAY III

James A. Largay III, Ph.D., CPA, is Arthur Andersen & Co. Alumni Professor of Accounting, Lehigh University.

Several colleagues made helpful suggestions on earlier drafts of this article; special thanks go to Professor Carl Beidleman, Lehigh University, and Professor Ferdinand K. Levy, Georgia Institute of Technology. The research in this paper was supported in part by an unrestricted grant from the Alcoa Foundation.

While many applauded the issuance of SFAS No. 52, others criticized its shortcomings. This article looks at SFAS No. 52 critically, taking stock of what is accomplished, and at what cost.

SFAS No. 52: A Critique

When SFAS No. 52, "Foreign Currency Translation" [1], was released on December 7, 1981, many breathed a sigh of relief. Some were relieved because the new Statement embodied the accounting rules they sought; others were simply glad that the uncertainty over the future of SFAS No. 8 [2] had ended. The controversy over foreign currency translation, however, will not likely end because the Board's approval of SFAS No. 52 by a bare 4-3 majority is symptomatic of continuing concern over the proper accounting for foreign operations. While these concerns will not fade away of their own accord, it is worth taking stock of what SFAS No. 52 accomplished, and at what cost.

The principal thrust of SFAS No. 52 relates to foreign currency *translation* as opposed to foreign currency *transactions,* including related hedging operations. The latter seem relatively noncontroversial and will be discussed only as they impact the translation problem. The next section of this article provides an overview of the SFAS No. 52 translation rules and is followed by sections on areas of accomplishment, problem areas, and a short conclusion.

Overview of SFAS No. 52's Translation Rules

Unlike its predecessor, SFAS No. 52 calls for reported financial information to be consistent with the underlying economic developments of interest to decisionmakers. It seeks to link the translation methodology to the nature of the economic exposure to exchange rate movements created by the foreign entity for its U.S. parent. The key is the factual determination of the entity's *functional currency,* "the currency of

James A. Largay III, "SFAS No. 52: Expediency or Principle?" *Journal of Accounting, Auditing, and Finance* 7.1 (Fall 1983): 44–53. Reprinted by permission.

the primary economic environment in which the entity operates and generates net cash flows" [1:¶5].

If an entity's functional currency is a *foreign currency* (as would normally be the case for foreign entities operating relatively independently of their U.S. parents), its accounts as measured in that currency are brought into conformity with U.S. GAAP and are translated into dollars by the *current rate method.* Other foreign entities whose operations are relatively dependent on their U.S. parents or that are located in countries experiencing cumulative inflation of 100 percent or more over the past three years use the U.S. dollar as their functional currency. Their accounts are brought into conformity with U.S. GAAP and are translated (technically "re-measured") into dollars by the *temporal* method embodied in SFAS No. 8. The detailed translation rules and treatment of translation adjustments under the two methods are summarized in Exhibit 1.

In sum, whereas SFAS No. 8 required that all companies use the same translation method and report the translation adjustment in earnings, SFAS No. 52 permits different translation methods for differing underlying economic circumstances. More-

Exhibit 1
SUMMARY OF TRANSLATION RULES UNDER SFAS NO. 52

Item	Current Rate Method (Functional Currency is Foreign Currency)	Temporal Method (Functional Currency is U.S. $)
Translation of assets	Current rate at balance sheet date	Current rate at balance sheet date for monetary items (cash, receivables, accounts payable, long-term debt, etc.) and items carried at current money prices (inventory carried at market, etc.); historical rates for other assets and liabilities
Translation of stockholders' equity	Historical rates	Historical rates
Translation of income statement accounts	Weighted average current rate for the period	Weighted average current rate for the period for most revenues and expenses; items representing amortization, expensing, or realization of assets and liabilities translated at historical rates are themselves translated at those historical rates
Treatment of translation adjustment	Entered directly in a special component of stockholders' equity	Included in current income statement

over, when the current rate method is used under SFAS No. 52, the translation adjustment bypasses the income statement altogether. The cumulative translation adjustment is recognized in income only when the foreign entity is ultimately sold or liquidated.

What SFAS No. 52 Accomplished

While most of SFAS No. 52's accomplishments relate to the neutralization of criticisms leveled at SFAS No. 8, some are worthwhile in their own right. The major accomplishments detected are discussed next.

Consistency With Decision-Oriented Financial Reporting

The FASB's Concepts Statement No. 1 [3], issued in 1978, concluded that *usefulness to decisionmakers* is the principal objective of financial reporting and that accounting information should help users to assess the amounts, timing, and uncertainty of prospective cash flows to be generated by the reporting enterprise. SFAS No. 52 clearly is intended to assist decisionmakers by providing information that is generally compatible with the expected economic effects of a change in exchange rates on an enterprise's cash flows and equity [1:¶4]. SFAS No. 8, however, was issued prior to Concepts Statement No. 1 and stressed the importance of measurement in dollars without change in accounting principles [2:¶6]; usefulness was either assumed or ignored.

Congruence of Accounting Exposure With Economic Exposure

Foreign entities face many of the same financial and business risks encountered by domestic entities. Since the foreign entity is located within foreign national boundaries, however, its exposure to "normal" risks is compounded from the perspective of its U.S. parent. While the presence of unstable or hostile foreign governments can lead to nonconsolidation of the foreign entity with the domestic parent, even in the best of circumstances realization of the foreign entity's net assets and earnings in U.S. dollars is affected by movements in the foreign exchange rate. It is this *exchange rate exposure* which compounds the risk to the U.S. parent.

For financial reporting purposes, the translation adjustment provides an estimate of the dollar equivalent of the foreign entity's exposure to movements in the exchange rate. This estimate is calculated by multiplying the change in the exchange rate during the period by the entity's *accounting exposure* to exchange rate movements—the accounts (and changes therein) which are to be translated at the current rate. Clearly both the amount and direction (gain or loss) of the translation adjustment are determined by (1) exogenous movements in foreign exchange rates and (2) the definition of accounting exposure promulgated by accounting standards-setters.

Under SFAS No. 8, accounting exposure generally consisted of net monetary assets (liabilities). Since long-term debt is considered a monetary liability, many foreign entities had net liability accounting exposure with SFAS No. 8. As the dollar weakened against many foreign currencies during the 1970s, translation *losses* resulted and were reflected in earnings. While these results will continue under SFAS No. 52 for those foreign entities having the U.S. dollar as their functional currency, they will no longer hold for foreign entities using the current rate method. First, because accounting exposure under the current rate method is defined as net assets (which normally is positive), a weakening dollar will produce a translation *gain.* Second, the translation adjustment, whether gain or loss, does not enter current earnings. Let us now examine how this important rule in SFAS No. 52 relates the U.S. parent's accounting exposure to its economic exposure to exchange rate movements derived from an analysis of the foreign entity's principal economic environment.

The Dollar as Functional Currency Consider first those foreign entities having the dollar as their functional currency. One such type of foreign entity will be very closely related to the parent as a component or extension of the parent's operations. Because dollars probably move to and from the parent and the foreign entity quite frequently, the parent's economic exposure may be adequately reflected in the foreign entity's monetary assets and liabilities. Through its effect on the dollar equivalents of these monetary assets and liabilities, an exchange rate movement may have a determinable impact on the parent's present and future cash flows and the translation adjustment should be reported in current earnings.

The other type of foreign entity having the dollar as its functional currency is located in a highly inflationary economy. In its June 1981 exposure draft, the FASB has proposed that a price level restatement of these foreign entities' accounts precede translation into dollars by the current rate method. While the Board made a pragmatic decision to revise the exposure draft and delete the price level restatement in favor of designating the dollar as the functional currency of those entities, it "believes that a currency that has largely lost its utility as a store of value cannot be a functional measuring unit" [1:¶107]. The rapid weakening of the foreign currency in a highly inflationary environment is quite consistent with the parent's economic exposure being reflected in the foreign entity's monetary assets and liabilities which make up its accounting exposure.

The Foreign Currency as Functional Currency In contrast, foreign entities with non-dollar functional currencies probably represent an entirely different form of economic exposure to their U.S. parents. Such entities will, by definition, be generating and expending cash flows primarily in the foreign economic environment. For example, goods are produced and sold in the foreign country and foreign debt is repaid with cash generated by operations in the foreign country. From the parent's perspective, its economic exposure is embedded in the viability of the foreign entity's operations, not in specific monetary assets and liabilities denominated in the foreign currency. Moreover, with a low volume of intercompany transactions, the parent's cash flows are affected only indirectly by exchange rate movements, if at all. Hence the exposed position under the current rate method (net assets), with reporting of translation adjustments directly in stockholders' equity, may faithfully reflect the parent's underlying economic exposure. In effect, SFAS No. 8 denied that this different type of economic exposure deserves different treatment in accounting reports.

This attempted linkage of accounting exposure to economic exposure via the functional currency determination is an important accomplishment. It injects flexibility into the reporting process so that circumstances in foreign operations deemed substantively different would be afforded different accounting treatments. Accordingly, SFAS No. 52 reflects a move away from the uniformity notion stressed in previous pronouncements such as SFAS Nos. 8 and 2 [4]. While uniform accounting for events characterized by similar economic circumstances is desirable, it actually weakens comparability by suppressing the differences that exist when economic circumstances are dissimilar.

Hedging and the Translation Adjustment

As previously mentioned, the current rate method under SFAS No. 52 treats the translation adjustment as a direct entry to stockholders' equity. This is another significant accomplishment for it recognizes that when the foreign entity is relatively self-contained in the host country (its functional currency is the foreign currency), translation adjustments have little economic significance to the U.S. parent. It also overcomes a criticism of SFAS No. 8 by removing this potentially distorting factor from net income and obviating the need to hedge the undesirable effects of movements in exchange rates on accounting exposure.

There is considerable evidence of corporate managements' reactions after the appearance of SFAS No. 8 in 1975.[1] Translation of long-term debt at the current rate and the related fixed assets at historical rates ignores the fact that the service potential of the assets provides an effective hedge against the debt. The translation adjustment on the debt entered net income while the offsetting effect from the hedging capability of the assets did not.

It is clear that incremental cash flows were devoted to managing exchange risk through increased hedging activities and refinancing of debt in other currencies. What is unclear, however, is whether such actions were undertaken primarily to ameliorate SFAS No. 8 translation adjustments without the corresponding economic benefits obtained by reducing foreign exchange risk. While this question cannot be answered definitively here, the possibility that various actions were taken to neutralize the financial statement effects of SFAS No. 8 certainly exists. Nevertheless, managements' concerns over any effect produced by SFAS No. 8 on stock prices appear unfounded. Studies by Dukes and Shank, Dillard, and Murdock found that security prices of multinational corporations were not significantly affected following the initial implementation of SFAS No. 8.[2]

The important point is that the incentive to hedge the income statement effect of translation adjustments occurring to entities with foreign functional currencies is no longer present. While such incentives continue to exist for entities having the U.S. dollar as their functional currency, the accounting exposure being hedged in those cases related directly to the underlying economic exposure. In the next section of the article, however, it is shown that SFAS No. 52 may produce its own incentives to enter into hedging for noneconomic reasons.

Problem Areas

In adopting SFAS No. 52, the four assenting Board members obviously believed that the benefits to be gained from its implementation exceeded the costs. That may be true in terms of out-of-pocket accounting costs. Nevertheless, SFAS No. 52 raises other troubling issues which are costly in terms of the inherent consistency of financial accounting and the interpretability of some of the information provided. I begin with a brief discussion of the extensive dissents by the three Board members who voted against SFAS No. 52.

Departures From Established Accounting Principles

The dissenters generally favored retention of SFAS No. 8 with modifications. Two aspects of SFAS No. 52 seen by the dissenters as being inconsistent with some long-established principles in financial accounting are particularly noteworthy and warrant special discussion. A more complete treatment of their views appears in pages 15–23 of SFAS No. 52.

(1) Adoption of the functional currency approach to translation introduces multiple perspectives and multiple units of measure into consolidated results long characterized by a single perspective and unit of measure, that of the U.S. parent. Paragraphs 140–152 of SFAS No. 8 rejected the notion of "dependent" and "independent" foreign operations crucial to the functional currency determination in SFAS No. 52.

(2) By calling for direct entries to stockholders' equity for translation adjustments, SFAS No. 52 is seen as backing off from the "clean surplus" principle developed over the years in financial accounting. The dissenters believe that failure to recognize translation adjustments in income as gains or losses conflicts with the FASB's Concepts Statement No. 3 conclusion that:

> *Gains and losses result from enterprises' peripheral or incidental transactions and from other events and circumstances stemming from the environment that may be largely beyond the control of individual enterprises and their managements [5:¶69].*
>
> *Still other gains or losses result from holding assets or liabilities while their values change . . . and from changes in foreign exchange rates [5:¶70].*

The Board dealt with both alleged inconsistencies in SFAS No. 52. As to the first, the Board concluded that "for an enterprise operating in multiple currency environments, a true 'single unit of measure' does not, as a factual matter, exist" [1:¶85] and "that for many foreign entities, adhering to a 'single unit of measure' was artificial and illusory" [1:¶88]. As to the second, the Board concluded:

> *Translation adjustments do not exist in terms of functional currency cash flows. Translation adjustments are solely a result of the translation process and have no direct effect on reporting currency cash flows. Exchange rate*

changes have an indirect effect on the net investment that may be realized upon sale or liquidation, but that effect is related to the net investment and not to the operations of the investee. Prior to sale or liquidation, that effect is so uncertain and remote as to require that translation adjustments arising currently should not be reported as part of operating results [1:¶111].

My own view is that the concept of consolidated statements is not compromised by including subsidiaries which, due to their different economic circumstances, are afforded different accounting treatments. This seems analogous to consolidating affiliated companies having substantial operating leases and capital leases. Members of the same generic class of transactions—leases—do not have the same accounting because of substantive differences. Nor am I troubled by the "multiple currency" notion although I shall indicate some misgivings about the current rate method later in the article. Even the clean surplus issue raised by the dissenters, while valid in theory, does not quite fit the foreign currency translation case. The translation adjustment is the mechanical result of an arithmetic process, forced upon us by double-entry accounting. Its economic significance is questionable, especially for nondollar functional currency entities. Perhaps it can best be viewed as a capital transaction. Note that the treatment under the current rate method is similar to GAAP for long-term investments in marketable equity securities—lower-of-cost-or-market adjustments are accumulated directly in a special component of stockholders' equity.

Analysis of Translated Financial Statements

The advent of SFAS No. 52 will have significant effects on the attempts of both external users and internal management to evaluate the financial position and performance of foreign entities. Two principal areas of concern are discussed next.

Financial Statement Relationships and Ratio Analysis Security analysts have told me that they would like to be able to evaluate foreign operations just as they evaluate domestic operations; that is, they are interested in what the foreign currency financial statements show. Unfortunately, the financial results and relationships measured in dollars under SFAS No. 8 often differed from the same results and relationships expressed in the foreign currency because of the different translation rates used to translate various accounts. This problem is largely solved for foreign functional currency entities under SFAS No. 52. For these entities, all assets and liabilities are translated at a single current rate and all income statement items are translated at a single weighted average rate. In effect, all foreign currency financial statement results and relationships are preserved in dollars by multiplying them by a constant. Consequently, they are not comparable with previous data based on SFAS No. 8.

At least one problem remains, however. Consider a financial ratio such as the return on assets (ROA), which incorporates both income statement and balance sheet information. If the exchange rate is rising over a period of years, the foreign currency is strengthening against the dollar thereby making the foreign entity more attractive to the U.S. parent. Yet if the foreign entity's operations are relatively constant, ROA based on dollar measurements actually *decreases,* a signal at variance with underlying economic developments. This phenomenon occurs because operating income (the numerator) is translated at a weighted average rate lower than the ending current rate used to translate total assets (the denominator). Similarly, if the dollar is strengthening against the foreign currency, ROA based on dollar measurements will rise, leading to the possibly erroneous conclusion that the foreign entity is a good candidate for additional investment.

Meaning of Certain Translated Asset Balances In my view, a serious shortcoming of SFAS No. 52 is created by the requirement to translate the nonmonetary assets of foreign functional currency entities at the current exchange rate. The resulting translated balances are *not* translated current values, except by coincidence. Such assets are measured in the foreign functional currency at foreign historical cost. Translation of these amounts at the current exchange rate leads neither to a historical dollar measure of historical cost nor to a current dollar measure of current value. In fact, the interpretation of translated foreign assets such as land, buildings, equipment, and LIFO inventories is unclear when the current rate method is used. Management and other financial statement users must wrestle with the question: If these translated asset balances are neither entirely cost nor entirely value measurements, what is their meaning?

Hedging and Financing Strategies

As previously indicated, the incentive to neutralize the income statement effect of the translation adjustment accruing to net assets no longer exists for foreign functional currency entities. Yet it must also be recognized that the current rate method does not remove this translation adjustment. It shifts the adjustment from the income statement to the balance sheet where it is now highlighted with disclosure of an analysis of the "equity adjustment from foreign currency translation" account in stockholders' equity. Moreover, a foreign entity's debt denominated in currencies other than its functional currency produces its own translation adjustments which are included in the dollar-based consolidated income statement. For these reasons, it seems possible that costly hedging or refinancing activities may be undertaken to neutralize these translation adjustments. To the extent these strategies are designed to reduce only accounting exposure and not economic risk, SFAS No. 52 may be subjected to some of the same criticisms leveled at SFAS No. 8.

Conclusion

SFAS No. 52 offers a new solution to a very complex fundamental problem. Fluctuating exchange rates are the result of many factors, and they contribute to the inherent difficulty of attempting to devise a reporting scheme which adequately reflects the economics of foreign operations.

It is not surprising that SFAS No. 52 embraces different objectives and a different translation method than its predecessor, SFAS No. 8. What is surprising, however, is that the translation objectives adopted in each statement were specifically rejected in the other statement after careful and extended analysis. While I hope that this switch represents nothing more than the conscientious correction of an error by the Board, it surely raises questions about standards-setting in this area. Perhaps the best that can be said is that we won't have SFAS No. 8 to kick around anymore.

References

1. Statement of Financial Accounting Standards No. 52, "Foreign Currency Translation" (Stamford, Conn.: FASB, 1981).
2. Statement of Financial Accounting Standards No. 8, "Accounting for the Translation of Foreign Currency Transactions and Foreign Currency Financial Statements" (Stamford, Conn.: FASB, 1975).
3. Statement of Financial Accounting Concepts No. 1, "Objectives of Financial Reporting by Business Enterprises" (Stamford, Conn.: FASB, 1978).
4. Statement of Financial Accounting Standards No. 2, "Accounting for Research and Development Costs" (Stamford, Conn.: FASB, 1974).
5. Statement of Financial Accounting Concepts No. 3, "Elements of Financial Statements of Business Enterprises" (Stamford, Conn.: FASB, 1980).

Notes

1. For an overview of the studies providing this evidence, see Paul A. Griffin, "What Harm Has FASB 8 Actually Done?" *Harvard Business Review,* July/Aug. 1979, pp. 8, 12, 14, 18. For more detail, see (1) the study commissioned by the FASB: Thomas G. Evans, William R. Folks, Jr. and Michael Jilling, *The Impact of Statement of Financial Accounting Standards No. 8 on the Foreign Exchange Risk Management Practices of American Multi-nationals: An Economic Impact Study* (Stamford, Conn.: FASB, 1978), and (2) the study commissioned by the Financial Executives Research Foundation: John K. Shank, Jesse F. Dillard and Richard Murdock, *Assessing the Economic Impact of FASB 8* (New York: Financial Executives Research Foundation, 1979), especially Chs. 4, 5.
2. Roland E. Dukes, *An Empirical Investigation of the Effects of Statement of Financial Accounting Standards No. 8 on Security Return Behavior* (Stamford, Conn.: FASB, 1978); Shank, Dillard & Murdock, note 1 *supra,* especially Chs. 6, 7.

12. THE IMPACT OF FOREIGN CURRENCY TRANSLATION ON REPORTING DURING THE PHASE-IN OF SFAS NO. 52

JAMES J. BENJAMIN, STEVIN D. GROSSMAN, AND CASPER E. WIGGINS

James J. Benjamin, DBA, CPA, is the Arthur Andersen professor of accounting at Texas A & M University. Steven D. Grossman, Ph.D., is an associate professor of accounting at Texas A & M University. Casper E. Wiggins, DBA, is an assistant professor of accounting at Texas A & M University.

This article examines the impact of the adoption of FASB Statement No. 52 on foreign currency reporting for multinational companies during the optional three-year adoption period (1981–1983). The results of the study suggest that early adoption of SFAS No. 52 for many companies was motivated by a favorable impact on income and earnings per share but that the relative rankings of the companies before and after SFAS No. 52 were not significantly affected.

Foreign currency translation has been one of the most frequently discussed accounting issues. The Financial Accounting Standards Board (FASB) attempted to resolve this problem in 1975 with the issuance of Statement of Financial Accounting Standards (SFAS) No. 8, *"Accounting for the Translation of Foreign Currency Transactions and Foreign Currency Financial Statements"* [1]. This pronouncement required that monetary items and items carried at current money prices be translated at the current rate, that nonmonetary items be translated at the historic rate, and that the exchange gains and losses produced by the translation process be reflected in earnings. Instead of resolving the foreign currency translation issue, however, the pronouncement resulted in additional and more intense debate. Changes in foreign currency exchange rates caused significant fluctuations in companies' earnings, especially interim earnings, and the accounting rules were widely criticized as a poor mirror of corporate economic performance.

Due to the adverse reaction to SFAS No. 8, the FASB issued SFAS No. 52, "Foreign Currency Translation," in December 1981 [2]. Under the new rules, the translation adjustments of many foreign entities are made directly to stockholders' equity on the balance sheet instead of being included in income. Generally, this approach will reduce the variable impact on net income for which SFAS No. 8 was frequently criticized. Proponents of this approach also maintain that the revised rules

James J. Benjamin, Steven D. Grossman, and Casper E. Wiggins, "The Impact of Foreign Currency Translation on Reporting during the Phase-in of SFAS No. 52," in *Journal of Accounting, Auditing, and Finance* 1.3 (Summer 1986): 177–84.

will enable many companies to eliminate risk management practices that were designed to reduce the impact of fluctuating exchange rates on reported earnings. The new rules, which were instituted by only a 4–3 vote of the FASB, were not mandatory until 1983. However, companies were allowed to begin applying the new rules for their 1981 and 1982 annual reports. Companies had the additional option, whether they elected early adoption or not, to apply the new rules retroactively or only in current and future years.

This study examines the impact of the adoption of SFAS No. 52 on foreign currency reporting for multinational companies during the three-year phase-in period (1981–1983). Specifically, the study analyzes the annual reports of 400 Fortune 1,000 companies for each year of the adoption period; the impact of adopting SFAS No. 52 on each company's reported earnings per share, stockholders' equity, and net income is computed. In addition, the impact of the new rules upon the rankings by net income to total assets and by earnings per share of the sampled companies is determined. The ranking results for each of the three years are then compared.

Research Methodology

The sample was restricted to companies that had December 31 year-ends because the earliest adoption was for companies having December 31, 1981, year-ends. The sample of 400 companies was selected to provide a reasonable cross section of the standard industry classifications represented in the Fortune 1,000 list and encompassed thirty-five two-digit SIC codes.

From the sample of 400 companies, approximately 200 companies representing a wide variety of major manufacturing and nonmanufacturing industries changed to the current rate method when they adopted the SFAS No. 52 provisions during the 1981–1983 period. Of the group adopting the provisions during the study period, ninety-five companies first applied the new rules in 1981, sixty companies made initial adoption in 1982, and 38 companies first applied the new rules in 1983. Approximately 85 percent of the sample companies were classified as manufacturers.

The financial impact of the new rules was analyzed in two phases. The first phase assessed the effect of SFAS No. 52 upon three key financial measures: (1) earnings per share (EPS), (2) income from continuing operations, and (3) stockholders' equity. The second phase investigated the impact of the new rules upon rankings of adopting companies with respect to two rate of return measures: (1) earnings per share and (2) rate of return on assets. This analysis was performed for all companies adopting in each year of the three-year adoption period.

Effect on Financial Measures

The analysis of the impact of SFAS No. 52 on key financial measures was gauged by developing three financial ratios for each company:

1. Impact on EPS was measured by the ratio of the net change in primary EPS from adopting SFAS No. 52 to primary EPS using SFAS No. 8 [$(EPS_{52} - EPS_8)/EPS_8$].

2. Impact on stockholders' equity (SE) was measured by the ratio of the cumulative adjustment in stockholders' equity to total stockholders' equity under SFAS No. 8. $[(SE_{52} - SE_8)/SE_8]$.
3. Impact on net income (NI) was measured by the ratio of the change in net income from continuing operations from adopting SFAS No. 52 to net income from continuing operations under SFAS No. 8 $[NI_{52} - NI_8)/NI_8]$.

All ratios were expressed as percentages.

For example, the three ratios for Eli Lilly and Company are computed as follows:

$$(EPS_{52} - EPS_8)/EPS_8 = \$.17/\$4.76 = 3.6\%$$
$$(SE_{52} - SE_8)/SE_8 = (\$32{,}700{,}000)/\$1{,}920{,}960{,}000 = (1.7\%)$$
$$(NI_{52} - NI_8)/NI_8 = \$13{,}000{,}000/\$1{,}752{,}314{,}000 = 3.6\%$$

The first ratio measures the impact on earnings per share from adopting SFAS No. 52. This ratio provides an indication of both the significance and the direction of the impact of the new rules on the corporation's earnings for the year of adoption. We hypothesized that those companies for which adoption would have a negative impact on income would avoid the optional early implementation of the rules.

The second ratio relates the impact of adoption on stockholders' equity. This ratio provides a measure of the magnitude of the adjustment relative to the equity of the company.

The final ratio expresses the impact on net income from adopting SFAS No. 52. This ratio provides a measure of the significance of making the adjustments to stockholders' equity (as provided for in SFAS No. 52) rather than as a direct effect on income as had been required under SFAS No. 8.

Preparing the Data for Analysis

Although SFAS No. 52 requires disclosure of the impact of the new rules upon net income and EPS in the year of adoption, our analysis revealed that many companies failed to make these disclosures. This apparent lack of disclosure may not be due to neglect, however, because accounting and auditing standards do not require the disclosure of such items if they are not material in amount.

Consequently, surrogate measures were developed for these net income and EPS impacts for companies in which these data were not available. First, the current translation adjustment as reported in stockholders' equity was used as an approximation of the impact of the new rules upon net income. Second, the ratio of adjusted net income (without the effect of SFAS No. 52) to reported net income (with the effect of SFAS No. 52) was multiplied by reported EPS to approximate EPS without the new rules. The EPS impact was then calculated as the difference between reported EPS and the surrogate measure of EPS without application of SFAS No. 52. Thus, the impact upon net income and EPS of the new rules, when expressed as a percentage, would be identical for those companies in which surrogate measures are employed. These surrogate measures were utilized as needed in both phases of analysis. Comparison of the performance rankings for 1981 and 1982 adoptees with and without inclusion of companies for which surrogate measures were used indicates that any bias produced by use of the surrogate measures was negligible.

Rankings of Adopting Companies

The second phase of analysis addressed the impact of SFAS No. 52 upon performance rankings of adopting companies in each year. The purpose of this analysis was to determine if the application of the new rules significantly impacted the reported results of the entities that opted for voluntary application of SFAS No. 52. Two performance measures, earnings per share and rate of return on assets, were utilized to evaluate the effect upon relative performance. The Spearman Rank Correlation test was employed to compare rankings of the adopting companies by each measure under SFAS No. 52 and SFAS No. 8. The Spearman correlation coefficient (rho) that is generated provides a measure of the degree of statistical association between two ordered sets of data. Rho values may range from zero (no association) to 100 (perfect association). The effect of the new rules upon EPS and net income, which is required disclosure for adopting companies, was used to adjust reported SFAS No. 52 net income and EPS to the balances that would have been reported had SFAS No. 8 been in force.

Results

Tables 1 and 2 present the results of the first phase of analysis. This analysis investigated the impact of adoption of SFAS No. 52 upon three key financial ratios. Table 1 presents the mean and median effects of the new rules upon the three financial ratios, while Table 2 provides a distribution of the percentage impacts on the financial ratios for all of the companies included in the sample.

Table 1 reveals that the mean change in earnings per share was 7.8 percent in 1981, 6.0 percent in 1982, and −1.4 percent in 1983. In sixty-eight of the ninety-five companies in 1981, in forty-five of the sixty companies in 1982, and in nineteen of the thirty-eight companies in 1983, the mean change was between 0 and 20 percent. (See Table 2.) A limited number of companies, however, had large percentage changes. Therefore, the analysis in Table 1 was restricted to the middle 80 percent of the companies to eliminate the bias created by these outliers. The percentage change for the manufacturing sector is larger than for the nonmanufacturing sector for 1981; however, this relationship reverses in 1982 when the EPS impact is 5 percent for the manufacturing sector and 7 percent for the nonmanufacturing sector. The median change was only about 6 percent during the first two years and 0.5 percent in 1983. It was expected that the impact on income would tend to be positive for 1981 and 1982 because the adoption of the new rules was optional during that time. Similarly, it was not surprising that the effect on earnings moved to slightly negative for 1983 when the rules became mandatory.

The impact on stockholders' equity of adopting SFAS No. 52 is negative in 1981 and 1982 and positive in 1983, with most of the change being between −5 and +5

Table 1

SUMMARY PERCENTAGE IMPACT OF SFAS NO. 52 ON SELECTED FINANCIAL RATIOS*

	Year of Initial Application		
	1981	**1982**	**1983**
Number of Companies	95	60	38
Financial Ratios:			
Change in EPS:			
Sample Mean	7.8%	6.0%	−1.4%
Sample Median	6.0	5.9	0.5
Sample Mean:			
Manufacturing	9.0	5.0	−2.0
Nonmanufacturing	4.0	7.0	2.0
Cumulative Adjustment to Stockholders' Equity:			
Sample Mean	−1.5	−1.0	1.5
Sample Median	−1.0	−1.0	−0.5
Sample Mean:			
Manufacturing	−2.0	−1.0	2.0
Nonmanufacturing	−1.0	−1.0	−2.0
Change in Net Income:			
Sample Mean	9.0	5.0	−1.5
Sample Median	6.0	5.8	0.5
Sample Mean:			
Manufacturing	10.0	5.0	−2.0
Nonmanufacturing	4.0	7.0	2.0

*The sample mean results exclude the 10 percent largest and the 10 percent smallest changes in each category.

percent. (See Table 2.) These results give evidence to the expected small magnitude of the cumulative translation adjustment in relation to total stockholders' equity for most adopting companies.

For the companies that voluntarily adopted the new rules in 1981 and 1982, the impact on net income was 9 percent and 5 percent for the sample. Again, this result is consistent with the expectation that companies that would have a significant negative impact on income under the old rules would choose the voluntary application of the new provisions provided by SFAS No. 52. Further, the impact was larger in 1981 in the manufacturing sector than in the nonmanufacturing sector. Most of the impact for all three years was between −5 and 20 percent.

Table 2

DISTRIBUTION OF PERCENTAGE IMPACT OF SFAS NO. 52 ON SELECTED FINANCIAL RATIOS

	Number of Companies								
	Change in Earnings Per Share			Cumulative Adjustment to Stockholders' Equity			Change in Net Income		
Financial Impact	**1981**	**1982**	**1983**	**1981**	**1982**	**1983**	**1981**	**1982**	**1983**
Less than −100%	3	4	1	0	0	0	2	4	1
− 50% to −99.9%	0	0	2	0	0	1	0	0	2
− 30% to −49.9%	2	0	1	0	0	0	2	0	1
− 20% to −29.9%	1	1	1	0	0	1	1	1	1
− 10% to −19.9%	1	2	2	0	0	2	0	2	2
− 5% to − 9.9%	0	0	3	10	6	2	0	0	3
− .1% to − 4.9%	1	2	7	56	48	9	1	4	7
0% to 4.9%	36	20	16	28	6	14	35	18	16
5% to 9.9%	14	12	1	1	0	2	14	13	1
10% to 19.9%	18	13	2	0	0	2	18	12	2
20% to 29.9%	9	1	1	0	0	0	10	2	1
30% to 49.9%	6	1	0	0	0	1	7	1	0
50% to 99.9%	2	3	0	0	0	1	2	2	0
Over 100%	2	1	1	0	0	3	3	1	1
Total Companies:	95	60	38	95	60	38	95	60	38

Table 3

EFFECT OF SFAS NO. 52 ON PERFORMANCE RANKINGS

		Spearman Rank Correlation Coefficient	
	Number of Companies	**Rate of Return on Assets**	**Earnings Per Share**
Companies adopting in 1981	95	.999*	.988*
Companies adopting in 1982	60	.999*	.981*
Companies adopting in 1983	38	.999*	.983*

*Significant at .001 level.

The results of the second phase of analysis, which assessed the impact of adoption of SFAS No. 52 upon relative performance rankings, are presented in Table 3. The adopting companies for each year were ranked on rate of return on assets and earnings per share both including the effect of the adoption and excluding the effect. The rho values are all significant at the .001 level and are all in excess of 98 percent. A rho value of 100 percent represents perfect association; therefore, the rho values of 98–99 percent found in this study indicate that, statistically, the adoption of SFAS No. 52 had a negligible effect upon the performance rankings of these adopting companies. Although SFAS No. 8 caused considerable controversy, the resulting impact of the adoption of SFAS No. 52 on the relative performance rankings of those companies that voluntarily applied the new rules was not significant. Of course, because the impact of the rules is affected by a number of variables (including the relative fluctuation of exchange rates), an analysis of a different time period might yield different results.

Conclusions

Many members of the business community have claimed that the FASB's rules are costly, complicated, difficult to carry out, and confusing to investors. SFAS No. 52 has been criticized for making a straightforward exercise tortuously complicated. In fact, prior to the adoption of SFAS No. 52, the business community tried to pressure the Financial Accounting Foundation to require that at least five votes be required to adopt an FASB Statement. (As noted earlier, SFAS No. 52 was adopted on a 4–3 vote.)

Companies might adopt FASB Statements earlier than required for a number of reasons. The adoption of the new accounting principle might have a favorable effect on reported income and earnings per share or it may have a negligible effect on these financial variables. In the latter case, especially, a company might adopt an SFAS early in order to demonstrate its support for the FASB, despite the fact that the business community is not entirely satisfied with the FASB's actions. In the case of SFAS No. 52, early adoption during the phase-in period seems to have been largely motivated by a favorable impact on income and earnings per share.

Those companies that adopted the new rules voluntarily in 1981 and 1982 reported larger positive effects on earnings per share and on net income than those that adopted them in 1983. As might be expected, the early adoption decision appears to have been influenced to a large extent by the potential effect on the financial statements.

References

1. Financial Accounting Standards Board, Statement of Financial Accounting Standards No. 8, *Accounting for the Translation of Foreign Currency Transactions and Foreign Currency Financial Statements* (Stamford, Conn.: FASB, 1975).
2. Financial Accounting Standards Board, Statement of Financial Accounting Standards No. 52, *Foreign Currency Translation* (Stamford, Conn.: FASB, 1981).

ANNOTATED BIBLIOGRAPHY

ANNOTATED BIBLIOGRAPHY

Note: The annotated bibliography is organized into five major topics to allow a more focused literature search.

I. The Environment of International Accounting

Amernic, Joel H., Rabindra Kanungo, and Nissim Aranya. "Professional & Work Values of Accountants: A Cross-Cultural Study." *The International Journal of Accounting, Education, and Research* 18.2 (Spring 1983): 177–92.

This paper is intended to help develop an understanding of cross-cultural differences and similarities in the professional and work values of accountants.

Barrett, Edgar M. "Annual Report Disclosure: Are American Reports Superior?" *Journal of International Business Studies* 6.2 (Fall 1975): 15–24.

This paper describes and discusses the extent and the quality of corporate financial disclosure among the largest publicly held corporations in the United States, the U.K., Japan, France, W. Germany, the Netherlands, and Sweden over the period 1963 to 1972. The overall extent and quality of American annual report disclosure may well be no better than that of British firms. In some areas, American annual report disclosure appears to be inferior to that of firms in several foreign countries.

Bazley, M., P. Brown, and H. Izan. "An Analysis of Lease Disclosures by Australian Companies." *ABACUS* 1.21 (March 1985): 44–62.

This study seeks an answer to the question: What factors influenced Australian lessees in their decision whether or not to disclose lease commitments in their annual reports? Based on tests, the authors conclude that some of the factors influencing the frequency of voluntary disclosure were industry, firm size, identity of the lessee's audit firm.

Brault, R., N. Chlala, and L. Menard. "Accounting for Leases: Why Canadian Standards Don't Measure Up." *CA Magazine* 118 (December 1985):42–51.

This article describes the related Canadian and U.S. accounting standards (accounting for leases), and suggests a few ambiguities existing in some of the accounting treatments recommended by the CICA handbook. To highlight these observations, the authors have discussed three particular problem areas: (1) a lease involving land and buildings; (2) a sale-leaseback transaction; and (3) a renewal, extension, or change in the provisions of an existing lease. In conclusion, the authors call for a remedy to the situation.

DaCosta, R. C., James Fisher, and W. M. Lawson. "Linkages in the International Business Community: Accounting Evidence." *Journal of International Business Studies* 11.2 (Fall 1980): 92–102.

This paper investigates two hypotheses about the international linkage between accounting practices and the information needs of the financial community. On the evidence presented, no case can be made that international convergences have occurred between users' needs and accounting practices.

Enthoven, Adolph J. H. "International Management Accounting: Its Scope and Standards." *The International Journal of Accounting, Education, and Research* 17.2 (Spring 1982): 59–74.

The paper addresses some of the issues involved in unifying international management accounting so that it can effectively serve international operational structures and flows. The article delineates a series of elements that need attention in designing an international accounting "conceptual framework."

Frank, W. G. "An Empirical Analysis of International Accounting Principles." *Journal of Accounting Research* 17.1 (Autumn 1979): 3593–605.

The objective of this study is to examine the extent to which different patterns of accounting concepts and practices exist in thirty-eight noncommunist countries, and to relate these differences to the economic and social environment prevalent in those countries. The hypothesis that a country's cultural and economic environment influences its accounting principles and reporting practices is supported by this study.

Golub, Steven J. "A Global Perspective to Financial Reporting." *The International Journal of Accounting, Education, and Research* 18.1 (Fall 1982): 37–44.

The geographical dispersion of MNEs raise many reporting questions—especially the choice of selecting a single set of accounting standards to be used uniformly throughout the world. A substantial effort is needed to create an increasing amount of dialogue concerning financial accounting and reporting issues that presently affect MNEs.

Gray, S. J. "The Impact of International Accounting Differences from a Security-Analysis Perspective: Some European Evidence!" *Journal of Accounting Research* 18.1 (Spring 1980): 64–76.

This paper specifically explores the question of impact and the extent to which the measurement of company profits is correlated with national characteristics. These characteristics can be expected to reflect the different influence of factors such as managerial philosophy, the structure and development of capital markets, legal requirements, professional accounting standards, and tax law, which constitute a nation's accounting policy-making system. Some implications arising from the findings of the study are discussed.

Horngren, C. T. "Uses and Limitations of a Conceptual Framework." *Journal of Accountancy* (April 1981): 86, 88, 90, 92.

The author gives his views on the FASB's conceptual framework project. He believes that a framework will help in the standard-setting process, but he cautions that, due to the complexity of accounting policymaking, a framework alone is not enough.

IFAC: International Auditing Guideline No. 21, International Auditing Guideline No. 22 (127). *Accountancy* 97 (January 1986): 125–27.

The guidelines cover (1) Date of the Auditor's Report, (2) Events After Balance Sheet Date, and (3) Discovery of Facts After the Financial Statements Have Been Issued.

Kanaga, W. S. "International Accounting: The Challenge and the Changes." *Journal of Accountancy* 150 (November 1980): 55–60.

The recent surge in foreign investments in the United States and the expansion of U.S. companies abroad have resulted in the increased visibility of U.S. accountants on the international accounting scene. The author discusses some of the problems of international practice and explains why he is optimistic that the profession will eventually achieve harmonization of international accounting and auditing standards.

Ogan, P. "Turkish Accountancy: An Assessment of Its Effectiveness and Recommendations for Improvements." *The International Journal of Accounting, Education, and Research* 14.1 (Fall 1978): 133–32.

This article concentrates on the degree of effectiveness of the gathering and reporting of accounting information in Turkey. Comparisons of Turkish accountancy with those of similarly developed nations are made where appropriate in order to highlight similarities or to draw attention to the unique Turkish situation.

Pomerany, Felix. "International Auditing Standards." *International Journal of Accounting, Education, and Research* 11.1 (Fall 1975): 1–14.

This article attempts to develop a perspective of recent developments in international auditing. The author begins by examining the history of auditing. Next, there is a discussion of the standards that exist in various countries in the areas of independence, audit procedures relating to inventory, accounts receivable, and reporting standards. Finally, a case study is discussed which concentrates on Coopers' and Lybrand's experience in developing an international practice. The author concludes that the prospect of a standardized international audit approach would appear to be inevitable and that this is the time to endorse it.

Qureshi, M. A. "Pragmatic and Academic Bases of International Accounting." *Management International Review* 19.2 (1979): 61–67.

The author discusses three basic questions in his article. A definition of international accounting includes the concepts of: (1) parent-foreign subsidiary accounting; (2) comparative accounting; and (9) universal accounting. The article also answers the questions why and how one should study international accounting. He concludes that the study of international accounting should not be confined to any single body, but should be widely distributed over the citizens of the world.

Rundfelt, R. "Views from Abroad: Europe." *Journal of Accounting, Auditing, and Finance* 9.1 (Fall 1985): 81–84.

This article discusses the question: Can Europe contribute to the harmonization of accounting standards? The fear of "the American dominance" is also discussed.

Saunders, L. "The Dutch Shell Game [Netherland Antilles]." *Forbes* 134 (December 3, 1984): 184–88.

Big firms use financial shell companies in countries with more favorable tax treaties to lower their tax on intracompany financial transactions. This article describes the "shell game" as it is played in the Netherland Antilles.

Scott, G. M., and Ward, B. H. "The Internal Audit—A Tool for Management Control." *Financial Executive* 46.3 (March 1978): 32–37.

Complexity and flux in the organizational structure create both challenge and opportunity for the modern corporation and its audit staff. The authors contend that in order to meet these challenges, successful management must plan for coordinated audit review activity. The scope of such reviews must include not only operational performance, but also managerial and strategic decision-making activities.

Stoner, G. "Forward Dealing—How Can the Auditor Keep Pace?" *Accountancy* 96 (April 1985): 72–75.

This article indicates that the effect of a variable exchange rate on reported earnings, when there is no real exposure to currency movements, and the timing of income recognition when gains are made from deals with known results, are related accounting problems with major implications for the accountant and auditor.

Violet, William J. "A Philosophical Perspective on the Development of International Accounting Standards." *The International Journal of Accounting, Education, and Research* 19.1 (Fall 1983): 1–14.

The author submits that if international accounting standards are to be established successfully, the establishment process must be accomplished within the perspective of accounting as a rational system, that is, a system based on universally accepted postulates.

Weele, V. R. "Catching China Fever: A Management Accountant's Perspective." *Management Accounting* 67 (October 1985): 19–25.

In the People's Republic of China, Western business principles such as profit, ROI, and budgeting have been virtually unknown until recently. Now with government reforms taking shape, Chinese business people are eagerly learning new methods from visitors the government has invited to share their knowledge. The author recounts his experiences while teaching management accounting to upper– and middle–management personnel from industry and government.

II. International Standards and Organizations

Bavishi, V., and H. E. Wyman. "Foreign Operations Disclosures by U.S.-Based Multinational Corporations: Are They Adequate?" *International Journal of Accounting, Education, and Research* 16.1 (Fall 1980): 153–68.

This article reviews reporting of international operations by U.S. corporations—it provides useful information for those interested in financial reporting of international operations. The authors explain what is required by the FASB, describe the nature of the data examined, analyze the data for adequacy, suggest improvements based on the analysis, and finally contrast the FASB requirements with information desired by the UNCTC, OECD, and IASC.

Chang, Lucia S., Kenneth S. Most, and Carlos W. Brain. "The Utility of Annual Reports: An International Study." *Journal of International Business Studies* 14.1 (Spring/Summer 1983): 63–84.

This article reports on a research project aimed at testing the following hypothesis: Financial statements published as a part of corporate annual reporting are useful for investment decisions. The research was also designed to find out if users of corporate annual reports constitute a homogeneous group.

Chetkovich, M. N. "The International Federation of Accountants: Its Organization and Goals." *International Journal of Accounting, Education, and Research* 15.1 (Fall 1979): 13–20.

This article suggests that there is a recognition of the need for better communication and closer cooperation among accountants on a worldwide basis for greater harmonization of accounting standards. The author discusses a new development in the field of international accounting: the creation of the IVAC.

Choi, Frederick D. S. "A Cluster Approach to Accounting Harmonization." *Management Accounting* 63 (August 1981): 27–31.

A regional approach to accounting harmonization is necessary because it offers a feasible way to bridge the gap between international accounting standards and those of developing nations.

Coopers & Lybrand Newsletter. "International Financial Reporting and Auditing" 21.7, 8 (July/August 1979). Special International Report.

Easy-to-follow monograph on international financial reporting and auditing to aid multinational companies doing business overseas. Tax laws in various countries are briefly summarized.

Enthoven, Adolf J. H. "International Management Accounting—A Challenge for Accountants." *Management Accounting* 62 (September 1980): 25–32.

This article discusses the need for an international management accounting institute to coordinate research and development of standards and techniques. In appraising the impact and changing role of management accounting in the international area, the author discusses two interrelated aspects—one of a technical nature and one of an organizational/structural nature.

Fitzgerald, R., and E. Kelley. "International Disclosure Standards—The United Nations' Position." *Journal of Accounting, Auditing, and Finance* 3.1 (Fall 1979): 5–20.

The U.N. is taking a serious interest in international standards of accounting and reporting. This article discusses the various aspects of the report. Some of the topics covered are disclosure, consolidation, and materiality.

Gray, Sidney J., Jack C. Shaw, and Brendan McSweeney. "Accounting Standards and Multinational Corporations." *Journal of International Business Studies* 12.1 (Spring/Summer 1981): 121–36.

This paper attempts to identify and evaluate emerging issues and trends relating to accounting standards and multinational corporations. The analysis has centered on three fundamental questions: Should there be standards for MNCs? What should be required by the standards? Who should set the standards? Some tentative conclusions follow.

Hampton, Robert. "A World of Differences in Accounting and Reporting." *Management Accounting* 62 (September 1980): 14–18.

The work of the international accountant can be far more complicated than that of his domestic counterpart because no two countries follow the same standards of accounting and financial reporting.

"International Taxation." *CPA Journal* 52.2 (February 1983): 63–67.

Describes the regulations for reporting FIRPTA.

Mueller, G. G., and Walker, L. M. "The Coming of Age of Transnational Financial Reporting." *The Journal of Accountancy* 142 (July 1976): 67–74.

To make transnational financial reporting meaningful to the different national audiences-of-interest requires more than the translation of languages and currencies. Transnational financial reporting relates to the financial activities of multinational enterprises—predominantly the utilization of long-term money capital from whatever source is economically available, without respect to its nationality. The authors discuss three approaches of dealing with transnational accounting. They conclude that with the aid of the International Accounting Standards Committee, internationally accepted accounting standards will be achieved in the future.

Mueller, G. G. "St. Louis to Munich: The Odyssey of the International Congress of Accountants." *International Journal of Accounting, Education, and Research* 15.1 (Fall 1979): 1–12.

The author describes the creation of the IFAC and summarizes a few of the effects it has produced. One of the findings shows that there are many instances in which international data access and comparative analysis have led to more reliable accounting research results.

Schieneman, Gary S. "International Issues and Perspectives." *Journal of Accounting, Auditing, and Finance* 3.1 (Fall 1979): 21–30.

The author argues that the "lingufa franca" concept and more harmonization of international account standards would overcome problems faced by international investments and multinationals. The article examines this proposition and discusses some reasons why more uniformity in international accounting has not been achieved at the present time. It then looks at the possible future developments in this area.

Schweikart, James A. "We Must End Consolidation of Foreign Subsidiaries." *Management Accounting* 63 (August 1981): 15–25.

The author calls for an end to consolidating foreign financial data. He believes that the information from consolidation only destroys the value of information with which it is combined. To preserve the value of information about foreign subsidiaries, careful segment reporting needs to be instituted using unchanged foreign accounting information.

III. Managerial Accounting

Abdallah, Wagdy M., and Donald E. Keller. "Measuring the Multinational's Performance." *Management Accounting* 67.4 (October 1985): 26–30.

This article addresses the objectives to be considered in the management accounting evaluation process.

Banker, Pravin. "You're the Best Judge of Foreign Risks." *Harvard Business Review* 1.2 (March-April 1983): 157–65.

A guide to the best techniques for managing your international exposure without having to rely on outside experts.

Barrett, E. M. "The Extent of Disclosure in Annual Reports of Large Companies in Seven Countries." *International Journal of Accounting, Education, and Research* 12.2 (Spring 1977): 1–25.

The author studies and attempts to measure the relative importance and the extent of disclosure, of selected types of information. The study deals with more than one annual report and more than one country. A thorough study of comparative national accounting practices is also included. The conclusions indicate that there is a great deal of variability across the sample firms in amount and quality of data.

Bavishi, Vinod. "Capital Budgeting Practices at Multinationals." *Management Accounting* 63.2 (August 1981): 32–35.

This article discusses the theory of capital budgeting for multinational corporations and answers the question: Do the current capital budgeting practices of U.S.-based multinational corporations coincide with the theory?

Choi, Frederick D. S. "Primary-Secondary Reporting: A Cross-Cultural Analysis." *International Journal of Accounting, Education, and Research* 16.1 (Fall 1980): 83–104.

Foreign readers of financial statements are accustomed to analyzing and interpreting reports in the context of their own national set of accounting and reporting norms. The author examines a proposal that recommends that multiple sets of statements, primary and secondary, be prepared for a firm with audiences of interest in more than one country. The author concludes that contrary to the proposal's intent, primary-secondary reporting has the potential to mislead rather than improve the communication of financial information to foreign audiences of interest. To overcome this shortcoming he has suggested some remedies.

Choi, Frederick D. S., et al. "Analyzing Foreign Financial Statements: The Use and Misuse of International Ratio Analysis." *Journal of International Business Studies* 14.1 (Spring/Summer 1983): 113–32.

In order to investigate possible misinterpretation by the U.S. investment community, the unadjusted financial statements of eighteen Japanese and Korean sample firms were subjected to a rigorous financial ratio analysis. The objective was to compare their accounting-base liquidity, leverage, efficiency, and profitability ratios with a sample of matched U.S. firms. An attempt is made to restate the unadjusted Japanese and Korean financial statements to U.S. GAAP in hopes of discerning the degree to which differences in ratios might be explained by differences in accounting principles.

Daley, L., J. Jiambalvo, G. L. Sundem, and Y. Kondo. "Attitudes Toward Financial Control Systems in the U.S. and Japan." *Journal of International Business Studies* 16.3 (Fall 1985): 91–110.

Recently researchers have begun to investigate issues of differences in the use of managerial accounting tools across differing national environments. This study uses a survey of attitudes toward various aspects of budgeting and control systems to gain insight into the existence of differences for a large sample of Japanese and U.S. controllers and line managers.

Dufey, G., and I. H. Giddy. "International Financial Planning: The Use of Market-Based Forecasts." *California Management Review* 21 (Fall 1978): 69–81.

International corporations, facing greater risks than domestic ones, also have wider opportunities and, therefore, require a planning system specifically adapted to international market uncertainties. This article introduces the reader to financial planning in corporations with international operations and identifies the forecasts necessary in the process. The author provides a guide to the analysis, interpretation, and use of the market's forecasts of future interest rates and exchange rates in financial planning and performance evaluation.

Moustafa, Mohamed E. "Pricing Strategy for Export Activity in Developing Nations." *Journal of International Business Studies* 9.2 (Spring/Summer 1978): 95–102.

The purpose of this article is to examine the type of accounting data deemed useful in planning and implementing a pricing strategy for export activity in manufactured products from developing nations. The author suggests that the use of direct-costing methods combined with the increment-cost approach will help establish a floor price leading to profit maximization.

Nair, R. D. "Empirical Guidelines for Comparing International Accounting Data." *Journal of International Business Studies* 13.3 (Winter 1982): 85–98.

The primary purpose of this paper is to provide empirical guidelines for determining when cross-national comparisons of financial accounting data are appropriate. Groups of countries that have similar accounting practices are identified by comparisons between accounting data of the countries within each group.

Srinivasan, C. A., and M. M. Schoenfeld. "Some Problems and Prospects in Design and Development of Corporatewide Information Systems." *Management International Review* 18.2 (1978): 15–20.

The authors begin by identifying the characteristics of an adequate information system. Their examination of problems in developing an enterprise-wide information system is restricted to (1) identifying information needs of potential users, (2) designing a coherent operational system, and (3) evaluating the performance of the system. Points one and two pertain to the problems of systems planning, design, integration, and data management; point three deals with the problems of information/data from external sources, their acquisition and transfer.

Sudi, Ephriam F. "The Role of Comparative Productivity Accounting in Export Decisions." *Journal of International Business Studies* 15.1 (Spring/Summer 1984): 105–18.

This paper explores analytically the importance of comparative productivity accounting and productivity-based analysis in export decisions at the firm level under diverse market conditions. Comparative productivity analysis can make an important contribution toward improving the quality of export decisions.

Van Breda, M. F. "Accounting Rates of Return Under Inflation." *Sloan Management Review* 22.4 (Summer 1981): 15–27.

Few enterprises who use accounting-based ratios take into consideration the effects of inflation, varying growth rates, and different accounting rules on these ratios. This article shows managers how they might establish appropriate hurdle rates for their organizations. The author also includes a graph that illustrates how managers might translate a market-based cost-of-capital ratio into an accounting-based hurdle rate. The conclusion of the article is that it is not enough to differentiate various enterprises in the corporation on the basis of risk or growth individually, but that all these factors and inflation must be taken into account collectively.

IV. Foreign Currency Translations

Clay, M. "Exchange Rates: Cause of Problems or Just an Excuse?" *Accountancy* 96 (May 1985): 122–24.

The article discusses three ways by which exchange rates effect companies with regard to importing, exporting, and investing.

Feskoe, Gaffney. "Reducing Currency Risks in a Volatile Foreign Exchange Market." *Management Accounting* 62 (September 1980): 19–24.

As it now stands, mismatch exposure stemming from FAS No. 8 is creating a dilemma for the typical multinational enterprise. Although it is impossible to overcome the uncertainty of the exchange markets, it is possible to plan strategies for dealing with uncertainty. The article discusses some of these strategies.

Gernon, Helen. "The Effect of Translation on Multinational Corporations' Internal Performance Evaluation." *Journal of International Business Studies* 14.1 (Spring/Summer 1983): 103–12.

This paper presents the results of a study of the effect FASB No. 8 had on the internal performance evaluation practices of MNCs. The treatment of foreign exchange gains and losses relative to internal performance evaluation is disclosed. The paper includes explanations offered by the IDEs about how and why translation affects internal evaluation of foreign subsidiaries and their managers. Recommendations for performance evaluation strategies are developed by integrating the results of the data analysis with a review of the current literature, including FASB No. 52.

Shen, Paul. "Cash Flow Budgeting for the Importer." *Management Accounting* 62.3 (September 1980): 33–35.

The basic premise of this article is that a balance must be maintained between foreign exchange risk and cash flow.

Timms, Mike. "Coordinating the Overseas Audit." *Accountancy* (March 1985): 131–32.

The author discusses a step-by-step approach to an overseas audit. He suggests that only careful planning can avert, or at least minimize, those last-minute problems that often threaten to disrupt the completion of consolidated statements.

Tsui, Winston W. "Inflation Accounting and Foreign Currency Translation." *Management Accounting* 61 (September 1979): 23.

With inflation running rampant, many MNCs must confront the issue of which inflation rate to use for consolidating purposes when auditing a foreign subsidiary's financial statements—the domestic inflation rate or the foreign inflation rate. The translate-restate/restate-translate method may be the answer.

V. International Taxation and Transfer Pricing

Barrett, E. M. "Case of the Tangled Transfer Price." *Harvard Business Review* 55.3 (May-June 1977): 20–22, 26, 28, 32, 36, 176–78.

This article is a case study of a European subsidiary of Universal Data Corporation. UDC-Europe indulges in what one executive calls "creative transfer pricing." Computer hardware arrives in Brussels from Spain, Ireland, and the United States with three different price tags for identical machines! The case probes a common problem that has ramifications not only for net income, but also for matters like morale and managers' incentive bonuses.

Burns, Jane O. "Transfer Pricing Decisions in U.S. Multinational Corporations." *Journal of International Business Studies* 11 (Fall 1980): 32–39.

This article provides information about the effect fourteen variables have on transfer pricing decisions in sixty-two MNCs. One of the conclusions is that U.S. and foreign income taxes apparently have more influence on intracompany export pricing decisions for some MNCs.

Fowler, D. J. "Transfer Prices and Profit Maximization in Multinational Enterprise Operations." *Journal of International Business Studies* 9.3 (Winter 1979): 9–26.

One of the principle methods that MNEs use to influence profitability is by adjusting the price of goods shipped between affiliated companies in the network. Variables such as the level of ownership in the subsidiary, the dividend payout ratios, the effective marginal tax rates in both the parent and the subsidiary countries, and the tariff on the goods transferred, all interact in such a way that different levels of transfer price are optimal for different industries.

"International Taxation." *The CPA Journal* 56.1 (January 1986): 61–65.

The IRS issues final regulations regarding information returns required of certain foreign-owned corporations. The purpose of the regulation is to identify intercompany transactions of U.S. subsidiaries and of foreign subsidiaries engaged in trade or business in the U.S with their foreign affiliates.

Lieberman, Edward H. "Whether and to What Extent a Foreign Tax is Creditable Under Final Regulations." *Journal of Taxation* 60.2 (February 1984): 98–102.

This article discusses whether and to what extent a foreign tax is creditable under final regulations under Section 901. The adoption of Final Regulation 901 may spell an end to the turmoil in this area that started with oil-price increases. The author examines the final rules and notes differences from the temporary ones, which can still apply if elected.

Misawa, Mitsuru. "SMR Forum: A Japanese Perspective:—Is Worldwide Unitary Taxation Fair?" *Sloan Management Review* 26.2 (Winter 1985): 51–55.

Unitary taxation has been adopted by California and twelve other states. The validity of this method is open to question. In the paper the author summarizes the problems that unitary taxation has created for Japanese corporations. An alternative "water's-edge" approach is suggested, which would exclude income outside the United States from taxation by a state.

Plasschaert, S. R. F. "The Multiple Motivations for Transfer Pricing Modulations in Multinational Enterprises and Governmental Counter-Measures: An Attempt at Clarification." *Management International Review* 21.1 (1981): 49–63.

This article draws attention to the multiple reasons why MNEs may be tempted to modulate to their benefit, the volumes and the "prices" of payment flows between affiliated units of the MNE. The author discusses four areas that have attracted attention: (1) corporate profit taxes, (2) customer duties, (3) exchange risks, and (4) profit and capital repatriation. He also has some general comments on transfer pricing and its impact. In conclusion, he admits that the issue of TP is a complex one since it involves numerous technicalities and also raises some conceptual problems. Finally, he suggests some possible solutions.

Schwartz, B. N. "Partial Income Tax Allocation and Deferred Taxation: An International Accounting Issue." *Management International Review* 20.4 (1980): 74–82.

The author defines partial income tax allocation and illustrates how it is used. He also describes the major aspects of the recent rulings by two authoritative bodies (ASC of the ICA of England & Wales and the IASC) and discusses some of the implementation problems that firms may encounter in applying the requirements.

Wu, F. H., and D. Sharp. "An Empirical Study of Transfer Pricing Practice." *International Journal of Accounting, Education, and Research* 14.2 (Spring 1979): 71–99.

The authors contend that transfer pricing theories may be grouped into three major classifications. The article discusses which of these three TP theories is more accepted in the economic world. The authors have taken an empirical and statistical approach to studying transfer pricing.

Yunker, Penelope J. "A Survey Study of Subsidiary Autonomy, Performance Evaluation, and Transfer Pricing in Multinational Corporations." *Columbia Journal of World Business* 18.3 (Fall 1983): 51–64.

This study reports the results of a survey that investigates the relationship between performance evaluation and transfer pricing policies of MNCs. The evidence produced by this survey generally supports the working hypotheses that corporate policy in various areas is systematically related to corporate characteristics and environment, and that the accommodations between the various areas of corporate policy are to be interpreted as associational relationships with simultaneously determined endogenous variables.